APR '98

Gangs, Groups, and Crime

Gangs, Groups, and Crime

Perceptions and Responses
of Community Organizations

DISCARD

Chester G. Oehme III

CAROLINA ACADEMIC PRESS

Durham, North Carolina

Library of Congress Cataloging-in-Publication Data

Oehme, Chester G., 1962–
   Gangs, groups, and crime: perceptions and responses of
community organizations / Chester G. Oehme III.
         p.   cm.
   Includes bibliographical references and index.
   ISBN 0-89089-872-3
   1. Gangs—North Carolina. 2. Juvenile delinquency—
North Carolina. 3. Juvenile delinquency—North Carolina—
Prevention.
   I. Title.
   HV6439.U7N86   1997
   364.1'06'609757—DC21   97-2318
                                             CIP

Printed in the United States of America

CAROLINA ACADEMIC PRESS
700 Kent Street
Durham, North Carolina 27701
Telephone (919) 489-7486
Fax (919) 493-5668
www.cap-press.com

for my mother and father

Contents

Preface

This research addresses the collective youth crime problem in North Carolina, a state that has received very little attention in previous research on youth gangs and youth groups. The primary methodological challenge involved acquiring sufficient information and data so that the characteristics of the problem could be explored. Three general research goals were established: first, identify respondents who could best address the problem of collective youth crime at some specific level—informational, operational, or administrative; second, acquire information from a variety of professionals in order to mitigate the effects of bias, as well as increase the validity and reliability of perceptions; and third, geographically cover as much of North Carolina as possible. In order to achieve these research goals, a survey instrument was developed from two previous national-level youth gang projects and forwarded to a nonrandom sample of 410 respondents, all of whom work in criminal justice and educational organizations across the State. The 62.7 percent response rate included professionals from local law enforcement agencies (police and sheriff's departments), youth services organizations (probation and corrections), and educational services.

Respondents were asked to address four broad areas: the perceived scope and nature of the problem, their organizations' response to the problem, the effectiveness of prevention and intervention strategies, and the perceived causes of the problem. There was a strong perception that the youth gang and group problem had become more serious and widespread in recent years, largely due to the prevalence of drug-related activities and the presence of nonindigenous collectives. Suppression techniques dominated the response to the problem, but social intervention, opportunities provision, and neighborhood mobilization strategies were also utilized by some organizations. There was an unusually strong perception among respondents that their organizations' prevention and intervention strategies were effective at addressing youth gang and group problems. However, the effectiveness ratings were strongly associated with the implementation of organizational features (e.g. policies, procedures), rather than the characteristics of the problem. The central theme throughout this study involved comparing and contrasting the characteristics of youth gangs and groups, their activities, and the organizational responses to the problem. It was not only important to identify the locations that were experiencing perceived or actual collective youth crime problems, but also to discern the form in which the problems manifest. Youth gangs, which may have crossed a "tipping point" in the evolutionary stages of a group, operate under different group processes and may be differentially amenable to certain prevention and intervention strategies.

Acknowledgments

The North Carolina Governor's Crime Commission and the North Carolina Attorney General's Office deserve a significant amount of recognition for the successful completion of this research endeavor. Because of their financial support and keen interest in the problem of collective youth crime across the State, this study came to fruition. In particular, the North Carolina Justice Academy—which is responsible for law enforcement training standards and evaluation with the North Carolina Department of Justice—was the singular agency that was instrumental in ensuring specific research requirements and requests were fully supported.

I wish to thank the entire staff of the North Carolina Justice Academy for the outstanding support and encouragement they provided during every phase of this project. There were a number of key staff members who deserve special recognition for their contributions: Ms. Martha Stanford (Director) and Mr. Ed Boelte (Assistant Director) for supporting the original research proposal and for guiding the necessary documentation through the appropriate channels within the Attorney General's Office; Ms. Tere Chipman (former Research Coordinator) for her enthusiastic support and superb commitment to this project since the first day I walked into her office; Mr. Cliff Herring for his assistance in ensuring all system support requirements, both hardware and software, were fulfilled; and Mr. Don Stacy and Ms. Jan Chauncey, whose information resource expertise greatly aided in finding the copious, as well as obscure, documents, reports, and references that were requested over the years.

I would especially like to express my deepest gratitude to Dr. Jen-Siang Lin of the Department of Economics, Methodist College, for his generous support in tutoring me on the finer points of statistical analysis and interpretation, and for assisting in the programming of SAS statistical software. Dr. Lin's exemplary support and professionalism undoubtedly contributed to the successful completion of this research. Thanks must also be given to the following individuals and organizations: Professor George Knox of the National Gang Crime Research Center, Chicago State University; Professor Irving Spergel of the School of Social Service Administration, University of Chicago; Professors Malcolm Klein and Cheryl Maxson of the Social Science Research Center, University of Southern California; the Office of Juvenile Justice and Delinquency Prevention, U.S. Department of Justice; and the National Youth Gang Information Center, which has since become part of another organization within the U.S. Department of Justice. These individuals and organizations provided valuable advice, guidance, and informative research studies on various topics related to youth gangs and juvenile delinquency.

Special recognition must also be given to Professor David Farrington of the Institute of Criminology, Cambridge University, for his meticulous and critical editing of numerous drafts that were provided to him over the past couple years. Professor Farrington's guidance and recommendations undoubtedly helped improve the overall quality of the study. Most importantly, without the endless support, encouragement, and humor of my closest friends—Mr. Paul Wade, Mr. Scot Gere, and Ms. Anne-Lise Ammeux—this research would have been substantially more difficult and demanding. I am most indebted to my parents, the two people who taught me that the greatest rewards in life come from those things that are most difficult to achieve.

Important Note. This project was substantially funded by the North Carolina Governor's Crime Commission under research grant number 170-194-D3-J025. The North Carolina Justice Academy, which monitored and administered the grant, permitted the necessary access to its research facility, database systems and networks, and information resources. The findings, points of view, and opinions are those of the author and do not necessarily reflect the position of the granting organization nor the North Carolina Department of Justice.

List of Tables and Figures

Gangs, Groups, and Crime

1

Introduction

A. Contemporary Issues

Youth gangs have existed in the United States for almost 100 years (Vigil, 1988; Moore, 1978), but have only been the subject of extensive research since the 1930s. Even though the gang phenomenon has been documented and studied by social scientists for decades, our knowledge can hardly keep up with the dynamic and changing nature of gangs. Refined, expanded, and integrated theories have emerged to help guide our research and improve both prevention and intervention strategies, but nothing appears to effectively and conclusively reduce or mediate gang-related delinquent or criminal activities. The scope, nature, and severity of youth gang crime around the country continues to elicit many opinions, but most will probably agree on two points: that the level of violence and criminality of gangs has reached alarming levels in many cities and there is a great need for more systematic and multilevel research (Spergel, 1990).

This study attempts to address this last point by examining some of the basic issues that have concerned youth gang researchers in recent years. However, the context of this study is somewhat narrow, in that its primary focus is on the youth gang and youth group situation in the state of North Carolina. In a sense, then, the findings could be viewed more as a case study for a particular area, though many of the findings may also be consistent with those discovered by other researchers around the country. Klein (1995) identified four basic issues or concerns that are particularly important in the study of youth gangs, all of which, coincidentally, have a great deal of relevance in the present study. These concerns include: definitions, the issue of youth gang proliferation, the connection between gangs and drugs, and the central organizational concepts that differentiate gangs from other groups. The last concern is particularly important because throughout my study the differences between youth gangs and youth groups — e.g. the variations in definitions, activities, and responses to the problem — are compared at almost every stage of the research. Perhaps nongang youth groups are close to what Klein describes as the "tipping

3

point" of becoming gangs, when a group of youths begins to orient itself around collective criminal activities, develops some identity that sets it apart from other groups, and accepts intergroup rivalry. Knowing where youth groups, as well as youth gangs, are present has some obvious intervention and prevention implications. These issues are discussed in greater detail as the chapters unfold and the data are presented. The remainder of the discussion in this section briefly addresses the four major concerns and highlights how these concerns drove the methodological framework for this study.

Definitions

The first topic of concern in this study involves getting to the bottom of how organizations define the youth gang phenomenon, and how the concepts and characteristics chosen vary by organizational orientation and across jurisdictions. Theorists, researchers, and, in the case of this study, government and community officials, all have different reasons, methods, and purposes for defining problems associated with youth gangs. Theorists may be looking for concepts and terms that can be logically integrated into a postulatory framework; researchers seek a standardized definition to steer them towards a common phenomenon that would facilitate the comparison of findings; and officials need standardized definitions for consistency in recordkeeping (Ball and Curry, 1995). The second point is of particular interest here: obtaining some idea of how organizations define youth gangs *and* nongang youth groups should better provide the opportunity to analytically compare and contrast the different concepts and properties that go into defining these two phenomena. It may then be possible to clarify the meaning of youth gangs and youth groups and to establish a conceptual framework for analyzing the actual or perceived problem—e.g. its prevalence, scope, and nature—in North Carolina.

However, this process entails some difficulty, since there are two well-established facts that complicate the whole definitional process: most juvenile delinquency is committed in small, informal groups that do not constitute true gangs (Short and Strodtbeck, 1965; Miller, 1982; Reiss and Farrington, 1991); and secondly, at the present time there are no national-level agencies nor organizations within the state of North Carolina "which take a continuing responsibility for the collection of information based on explicit and uniformly-applied data collection categories which would permit comparability from city to city and between different periods of time" (Miller, 1975, p.3). Reliable gang data at the local level in the State is extremely sparse, with the exception of a few large metropolitan areas where gang problems are considered established, such as in Raleigh and Charlotte. Even where the data are collected locally, the data are most often based on intelligence information and not verifiable statistics. Furthermore, the definitions of what constitute a gang, gang member, and gang-related incident appear to vary substantially by professional orientation, but less so between organizations in the same jurisdictions. Factors such as local values and traditions, public pressures, academic influences, and the statutory language all influence how community organizations and law enforcement agencies define gangs and ultimately determine the scope and nature of the local problem. These factors and issues may lead to theoretical and methodological problems in "distinguishing norms from behaviors, subcultures from gangs, gangs from delinquent groups, different ethnic patterns, variability in gang problems in different cities, and gang patterns within the same city over time." (Spergel 1990, p. 9). This research, to some extent, attempted to address some of these concerns.

To further complicate the definitional problem, there has been a general evolution in defining contemporary gangs and gang activity over the years, with a conspicuous shift from liberal, social reform assumptions prevalent in the 1950s and 1960s to a definition that reflects a more conservative philosophy, where the emphasis is on the violent and criminal nature of gangs (Klein and Maxson, 1989). A key element that has typically distinguished gangs from other delinquent groups is criminal propensity, and it just so happens that the criminal propensities of gangs have escalated in scope and form in recent years (see discussions in Miller, 1982; Klein and Maxson, 1989; Gardner, 1993; Klein, 1995). As a result, definitions derived in many diverse areas—research, theory, and practice— have similarly been forced to evolve and to include crime and delinquency as intrinsic properties of gangs. Horowitz (1990, p. 45) notes that "by defining the gang primarily in terms of illegal activities, we may shift attention away from the complex and problematic relationship between legal and illegal actions." However, even though understanding the sociological dynamics of gang behavior and what influence the community has in their formation and perpetuation is important, gangs are first and foremost perceived as an immediate threat to civil order, endemically and intrinsically associated with crime and violence. If gangs did not commit delinquent or criminal acts at the rate they do, they would undoubtedly not create such a great concern to our criminal justice system or intervention agencies, nor would gangs be examined by academics with the same level of interest. One only needs to compare the number of gang offense studies with more sociologically oriented studies to see this point.

The *criminal* criterion as a salient property in definitions is particularly important in distinguishing gangs from groups in this study, and it may also signal the tacit acceptance of the law enforcement perspective of the problem (Ball and Curry, 1995). Nevertheless, basing the scope and severity of the gang problem on police recorded incidents — where this method exists — or their perceptions may provide the most reliable indication of seriousness, since recorded statistics and intelligence information typically focus on criminal activity (Spergel, 1990; Spergel at al., 1990). When focusing on criminal activity to determine the scope of the problem, it should be no surprise that police figures may be somewhat conservative when compared to figures provided by academics, reporters, community organizations, school officials, and other government agencies (Spergel, 1991a). The latter groups, which most likely use a less restrictive definition of gangs to include activity not necessarily serious or illegal, may view the gang problem from quite a different perspective. This last issue, which will receive greater attention in the forthcoming chapters, was a significant concern when the sample universe for the study was determined. There was a need to select a balanced sample for reliability purposes, but also the need to minimize the likelihood that respondents would exaggerate the problem.

Because gang definitions serve as the foundation for a community's response to the problem and influence the allocation of available resources, it is important to establish some consensus on key definitional properties so that the scope and nature of gang activities across the State can be more objectively determined (see Spergel, 1990; Covey et al., 1992). With an increase in more violent and criminal gang activity, contemporary prevention and intervention approaches have also shifted emphasis away from individual and group-level intervention programming towards suppression approaches that involve law enforcement and criminal justice agencies. The prevention and intervention strategy emphasis partly depends on whether the gang problem is perceived as established or emerging, each of which requires different time and resource commitments (Spergel, 1990, 1991a; see also Spergel et al., 1990). Herein lies the crux of the problem: without establishing a definitional framework that can be used to analyze the problem with a standard of consistency, there will be no opportunity to even suggest how widespread and serious the problem is — e.g. whether the problem is developing or well-established, involving youth gangs or youth groups — nor will there be an opportunity to suggest the appropriate responses to ameliorate it.

Gang Proliferation

The second topic of concern — one that has more to do than any other factor with the growing public and official interest in youth gangs — is that youth gangs have proliferated from a few cities to several hundred in recent years (Klein, 1995; see in particular Maxson, 1993; Maxson and

Klein, 1993). North Carolina is no exception to this assertion. Just how serious and prevalent is the "gang problem" in North Carolina? This is a most difficult question to answer because State-level data on youth gangs over time is poor due to a lack of comparable and historical data on gang membership. The available intelligence provided by local law enforcement organizations and the rough estimates by other State government agencies, as fluid as they may be, indicate that gangs may be present in modest numbers in a variety of social and cultural contexts, and are committing serious criminal acts with regularity (see for example Miller, 1982; Spergel, 1991a; and Needle and Stapleton, 1983). The general perception that gangs have become more ubiquitous and violent in North Carolina has encouraged my systematic examination of the scope and nature of the crime problem across the State.

Since there has not previously been any systematic research that specifically addresses the gang issue in North Carolina, what evidence or trend exists that may indicate a growing problem? Miller's (1982) landmark study, *Crime by Youth Gangs and Groups in the United States*, was the first detailed data collection effort and assessment of "collective youth crime" at the national level. Even though Miller's study was conducted during the 1970s, he discovered the presence of youth gangs in 13 percent of all cities with populations greater than 10,000 and in almost 30 percent of all cities with populations of 100,000 or more. Miller also made a number of significant findings: according to law enforcement agencies gangs existed in 17 of the 26 cities surveyed that had populations greater than 10,000; gang crime was more lethal, costly, and widespread than at any other point in history; and there was an unprecedented proliferation of predatory activities by groups other than gangs. Curry (1994), in his preliminary findings, discovered that 88.2 percent of the largest U.S. cities reported youth gang problems, and for cities with populations over 25,000, 59 percent reported gang crime problems. Between the period of Spergel et al.'s (1990) 1987 survey and Curry's (1994) present research, there has been a 23.8 percent increase in the number of cities reporting gang problems. Curry's (1994) survey was the first tabulation of national gang statistics that relied specifically on police records, and by his estimates, the number of gangs and gang members had increased substantially since the 1987 study. Finally, Klein (1995) indicates that there has been a serious gang proliferation problem since 1960, with a 74 percent increase in cities reporting gang problems between 1960 and 1970, 83 percent increase between 1970 and 1980, and a remarkable 345 percent increase between 1980 and 1992. With respect to North Carolina, Klein's research indicated that in 1980 there was only one city that reported gang problems, but by 1992 there were 13. So by extrapolating this pattern up to 1994—when the initial data collection was conducted for the present research—it seems highly probable that more cities in North Carolina will report gang problems compared to 1992.

The trend in research findings (Miller, 1982; Reiner, 1992; Spergel, 1990; Klein, 1995), as well as reports by the media, clearly indicates that the 1980s and 1990s have been the boom years for gang growth around the country, including North Carolina. There has also been a growing concern that gangs have become much more serious and sophisticated in recent years. This general assessment is in sharp contrast to views from the preceding years, when youth gangs were not considered a major object of concern nor a major crime problem (see Miller, 1982; Spergel, 1990, 1991a; Spergel and Curry, 1990a; Needle and Stapleton, 1983). Yet there is also evidence that youth gang problems in general terms wax and wane, where serious problems emerge and recede (or vice-versa) from decade to decade (Spergel and Curry, 1990). According to recent studies (Spergel et al., 1990; Spergel and Curry, 1990; see also Spergel, 1995), the terms *emerging*, *chronic*, and *re-emerging* have evolved to define the changing and variable scope and nature of the gang problem in many cities.

However, there is very little reliable information at this time and few systematic methods that would enable either an initial determination or periodic reassessment of the nature of the collective youth crime problem in North Carolina cities and municipalities. This study attempts to address this deficiency. By initiating the collection of data on youth gangs and groups in the State, it becomes possible to determine the perceived or actual nature of the problem. Using the initial findings in this study as a starting point, there would be an opportunity to follow the trends over the years, to determine if the problem has become worse or even improved, and what factors may have contributed to these fluctuations. If some periodic and systematic data collection process is not instituted, officials and researchers will be left to speculate on these trends, and will most likely be unable to grasp fully why gangs have emerged or receded in some cities or remained chronic in others. As Conly (1993) further stresses, there may be a strong connection between gangs and the communities in which they evolve, in that gangs possibly represent a symptom of more serious community problems.

Even though the measurement of gangs and gang-related crimes in North Carolina proved quite difficult—due to the lack of formal (official) and standardized data collection procedures—there was extensive intelligence information to suggest that youth gangs, as well as youth groups, had become a major law enforcement and criminal justice system concern in many large urban centers, smaller municipalities, and correctional environments. Fueling this concern was the increasing involvement of gangs in serious criminal activity—particularly aggravated assaults and larceny—and their actual or perceived involvement in organized drug trafficking. This last point, the connection between youth gangs and drugs, is the third topic of concern in this study.

Gangs and Drugs

There has been a growing debate as to the extent youth gangs and youth groups are active in drug-related criminal activities. The debate is not whether the prevalence rates for individual drug use and dealing is higher for youth who join collectives, since this appears to be well-established in the literature (Fagan et al., 1986; Hagedorn, 1988; Skolnick et al., 1988; Fagan, 1989, 1990; Reiner, 1992; Moore, 1993), but whether youth collectives, especially gangs, are in any way involved in organized drug-trafficking activities. There is very little evidence in previous research that indicates a strong connection between gangs and drug trafficking, but this fact does not necessarily make the debate moot.

On one side of the debate are the individuals who believe that gangs are particularly well-suited to operate an organized drug trafficking enterprise, and on the other side there are individuals who believe there are only cliques or individual members who are actively involved in drug transactions, but this activity is conducted outside the context of the collective. Implicit in this debate is whether youth gangs and groups have the organizational capabilities, cohesiveness, and structure necessary to carry out the sophisticated activities typically associated with drug trafficking operations. Is there any room for compromise in this debate? Should the debate be about an either/or proposition? According to Spergel (1995), the distinction between "drug gangs" and "street gangs" may have been extended too far, in that drug-dealing members of street gangs, subgroups, cliques of different gangs, and some drug dealing organizations have developed traditional communal characteristics, making the distinction less discernible. This last assertion makes it very difficult to determine if gang-related violence is in any way associated with drug trafficking activities. Intuitively the answer should be yes, but research in recent years (Fagan, 1989, 1990; Klein et al., 1991; Bobrowski, 1988; Inciardi, 1990; Institute of Law and Justice, 1994) has generally concluded that the relationship is not very clear. The motive for gang violence has very little to do with drug trafficking activities.

The most relevant issue, as it pertained to this study, was to determine if there were perceived connections between youth gangs or groups and the general drug trafficking problem in local jurisdictions. Even in areas where there appears to be a drug-related problem, it was beyond the scope of this project to determine whether the collectives in a particular community could be classified as "drug gangs" or "street gangs", even though these may be important distinctions (see Klein, 1995). However, efforts were made to identify and broadly classify the activities of these collectives. The research findings may demonstrate a plausible connection between youth collectives and the general drug trafficking problem, but until more convincing evidence becomes available, the conclusions must remain tentative. If the presence of youth collectives, drug-related problems, and criminal adult organizations are concomitant, there may exist a more direct and consequential relationship that warrants a closer investigation.

Gang and Group Characteristics

The final topic of concern, and one that is central to the analyses throughout this study, involves comparing and contrasting the characteristics of youth gangs and youth groups, their activities, and the organizational responses to the nature of the problem. Research through the years has established the well-known pattern that juvenile delinquent acts and crime often occur within dyadic, triadic, and larger group formations (Short and Strodtbeck, 1965; Short, 1968; Cohen, 1969; Erickson and Jensen, 1977; Zimring, 1981; Reiss and Farrington, 1991) and that most juvenile delinquency is conducted by youth groups, not gangs (Klein and Crawford, 1967; Miller, 1975, 1982). The distinction between youth gangs and other law-violating youth groups, however, must be made because gangs typically have a more variable and complex structure than delinquent groups: the more complex gang structure and its group processes facilitate more serious forms of criminal activity (Thornberry et al., 1993, 1994). Furthermore, crime committed by youth gangs is also generally a more serious and widespread problem (Maxson et al., 1985; Curry and Spergel, 1988; Spergel, 1990). Needle and Stapleton (1983) found that violent behavior was one of the key criteria for distinguishing youth gangs from groups and that the seriousness of gang activity was best measured "by the dimension of their antisocial behavior, by the numbers and types of crimes committed by gang members, and by the severity of these crimes" (p. 13).

It is possible that youth gangs and groups represent two quite distinct phenomena, each requiring different intervention and prevention approaches to mitigate the seriousness of activities (Curry and Spergel, 1988). With this argument in mind, there exists not only a necessity to identify the cities and municipalities that were experiencing perceived or actual collective youth crime problems, but also to discern the form in which the problems manifest. Youth gangs, which may have crossed some line or "tipping point" in the evolutionary stages of a group, operate under very different group processes than other criminal or delinquent youth groups. Youth gangs and groups may therefore be differentially amenable to certain intervention strategies. By analyzing the characteristics of the problem, how organizations responded to the nature of the problem, and if the responses were perceived as effective or not, there may be an opportunity later to improve the delivery of community and organizational prevention and intervention approaches.

B. Purpose and Significance of the Present Study

The impetus for this exploratory study on youth gangs and groups in North Carolina comes from a number of sources and reports citing collective youth criminal activity as a growing problem throughout the State. A recent report by the North Carolina Governor's Crime Commission (1992) found that illicit drug use and trafficking have become substantial problems in many jurisdictions, and that much of this activity can be attributed to non-traditional organized groups, such as outlaw motorcycle gangs, drug posses, and youth gangs.[1] These organizations, according to the report, "are responsible for most crimes and the escalation of violence, much of which is wanton. They involve increasing numbers of neighborhood youth [and] they perpetuate and complicate the problems surrounding illicit drug crimes due to their highly organized and effective methods of operation" (p. 21).

The more serious groups—namely the biker gangs and the Jamaican, Dominican, and Guyanese drug posses—are most responsible for the proliferation of crack cocaine and heroin, since these organizations have established hierarchies and infrastructures that facilitate the transshipment of illegal substances (N.C. Governor's Crime Commission, 1992). The report does not adequately present any convincing evidence of youth gang involvement in drug activity, nor, for that matter, the extent of the youth gang problem in other than general terms. Without citing supporting re-

---

1. For the purpose of the present study, a youth gang is composed of individuals who are twenty-four years old and younger; most studies indicate an average age range from the early teens to mid-twenties (e.g. 13 to 24). Because of restrictive legal definitions, it is also necessary to distinguish juvenile gangs from youth gangs. A juvenile, according to North Carolina's Juvenile Code, is any person who has not reached his or her 16th birthday and a delinquent juvenile (for criminal purposes) is a person between 6 and 16 years of age who has committed a criminal offense under State law or under ordinance of local government [N.C. General Statutes § 7A-517 (12,20)]. Thus a juvenile gang would be composed of youths under the age of 16.

search, it is difficult to ascertain the reliability of the report's assessment on youth gang activity in the State; therefore a more systematic research project was necessary to test the validity of the crime commission's general findings. Press reports throughout North Carolina—particularly the research triangle metropolitan region of Raleigh - Durham- Chapel Hill (Brooks and Bailey, 1992; Healy, 1993; O'Brien, 1993a, 1993b; Heimberger, 1993; and Eisley and Seymore, 1993)—report that youth gangs may be quite active throughout the State and particularly in highly populated regions. Even though these media reports typically depended on the cooperation of and information provided by law enforcement and criminal justice officials, reporter assessments must be viewed with a great deal of caution and scrutiny.

To date, there have not been any systematic evaluations, assessments, nor analyses of the youth gang or youth group problem in the State, neither in local jurisdictions nor across the wider region. Official statistics from the most recent annual Federal Bureau of Investigation (FBI) Uniform Crime Report (U.S. Department of Justice, 1992), the North Carolina Uniform Crime Report (N.C. Department of Justice, 1992), and special crime statistics provided by the North Carolina State Bureau of Investigation, all indicate a relatively high overall general youth crime rate when compared to other states (statistically ranked 16th). The Annual Report of the Administrative Office of the Courts (Administrative Office of the Courts, 1993) indicates that there were 22,425 total crimes charged to juvenile (youths under 16 years of age) offenders in the State, of which thirty percent (7,757) were felony charges.

North Carolina's five most populated counties—Mecklenburg, Wake, Guilford, Cumberland, and Forsyth—accounted for almost fifty (48) percent of all Part 1 (Index) Offenses[2] charged to individuals up to and including the age of 24. Most striking is that youths 15 years and younger accounted for ten percent of all Part 1 (Index) Offenses, while youths up to the age of 20 accounted for 36 percent (Table 1.1). Looking at crime in general, the FBI Uniform Crime Report (U.S. Department of Justice, 1992) found that the largest metropolitan area in the State (Charlotte) ranks as the 18th most violent city in the United States, followed by Winston-Salem, Durham, Raleigh, and Greensboro (ranked 30th, 82nd, 106th, and 108th respectively). These statistics tell us nothing about the crime that may be attributed specifically to youth gangs, but they do provide a context that warrants investigation.

Since there are no official data or studies of collective youth crime in North

---

2. The North Carolina State Bureau of Investigation defines these crimes as murder, manslaughter, forcible rape, robbery, aggravated assault, burglary, larceny, motor vehicle theft, and arson.

Table 1.1
Total Arrests for Part 1 (Index) Crimes: 1992
North Carolina's Five Largest Counties

County	15 & under	16	17	18	19	total (<20)	all ages	% (<20)
				Age				
Mecklenburg	1087	351	385	367	325	2515	9630	26
Wake	337	216	214	297	228	1292	4901	26
Guilford	1029	444	428	456	391	2748	7321	38
Cumberland	681	163	181	145	136	1306	3364	39
Forsyth	67	246	300	241	247	1101	4623	24
TOTALS	3201	1420	1508	1506	1327	8962	29839	30
	(36%)	(16%)	(17%)	(17%)	(15%)	(100%)		

(source: N.C. State Bureau of Investigation)

Carolina, there is very little knowledge, beyond speculation, of the actual or perceived scope, nature, and prevalence of the problem. Is there a perceived youth gang or youth group problem? Is the perceived activity serious in nature? Based upon the available statistics on the youth crime problem in general, what is the perception that gangs may be involved in many of these incidents? It has been suggested that, possibly in pursuit of profits, youth gangs have begun to migrate from larger metropolitan areas to conduct illicit business (Maxson and Klein, 1993; Maxson, 1993). To what extent is this evident in North Carolina? Are the gangs in smaller communities influenced by metropolitan gangs from larger cities within and outside the State?

A number of other salient issues needs to be addressed regarding youth gang and youth group criminal activities. For instance, how sophisticated are the perceived illegal activities of the participants? Are the organizations structured in any way? Two studies (Hardman, 1969; Rosembaum and Grant, 1983) assert that large gangs in metropolitan areas command a great deal of influence on the structure, organization, and activity of smaller gangs in nearby communities. Hagedorn (1988), on the other hand, found little evidence in his research of structural ties or similarities between suburban and metropolitan gangs. Because these questions and others have never been sufficiently addressed in previous research in North Carolina, a great deal of guesswork currently exists in prevention programming at the State and local levels.

As a result of this void in research, very little is known about perceived or actual youth gang and group criminal patterns in particular metropolitan and suburban communities, and the structural determinants that aid in the formation and perpetuation of these collectives. According to Zevitz (1993), there is no *a priori* reason for assuming that factors that facilitate youth gang delinquency in large cities also explain suburban and rural crime patterns. "Community size, [therefore] may prove to be one of the most important structural determinants of youth group delinquency long sought by researchers" (p. 50). Needle and Stapleton's (1983) survey of police handling of youth gangs and Miller's (1982) national youth group survey concluded that a vast majority of youth group crime occurred in smaller sized communities (less than 100,000) throughout the United States. Unfortunately, these studies yield little data on the nature, structure, and organization of small-city and rural criminal youth collectives.

There have only been a few attempts to measure youth gang crime in small cities, with interviews of youth gang members the primary procedure for gathering data on the nature of the activity (Hardman, 1969; Moore, 1978, 1985; Zevitz, 1993). There have not been any studies that attempted to measure the perceptions of small city or rural collective youth crime problems and their characteristics from the youth practitioner's perspective: namely law enforcement organizations (police and sheriff's departments), probation officers (court counselors), correctional administrators, and educators. Nor has there been any attempt to measure the perceived effectiveness of prevention and intervention programs. Though it has been hypothesized that nonmetropolitan youth gangs and groups lack a distinct delinquent subculture, there is reason to believe that these collectives are nevertheless capable of sustaining serious forms of delinquency (Zevitz, 1993).

Whether the focus is on the large city, small town, or rural community, research has consistently indicated that there is a clearly discernible group dimension to most youth crime. By gaining knowledge of the perceived scope, nature, and characteristics of the collective youth crime problem in the State from the practitioner's perspective, and examining the organizational response to the problem, there is an excellent opportunity to compile valuable data that will undoubtedly benefit and potentially affect crime prevention and intervention policy directions in the State. From a general research perspective, the findings not only supplement the considerable body of research on youth gang delinquency, they also provide more detailed insight into the perceptual differences between youth gangs and youth groups (e.g. defining characteristics and activities), an important area that has only received scant attention in the research on collective youth crime.

C. General Study Design

This research project was conducted with the cooperation and support of the North Carolina Governor's Crime Commission (Office of Juvenile Delinquency and Prevention), the North Carolina Office of the Attorney General, and the North Carolina Justice Academy. Driving this project was the need to develop and provide innovative, effective, and informative training for criminal justice professionals and youth practitioners throughout the State. The long-term and broad goal involves increasing the general awareness—particularly within the State's criminal justice system—of the perceived prevalence, scope, and nature of youth gang and group criminal activity. The key emphasis is on the *perceptions* of the problem, since the lack of available and verifiable statistical data on youth gangs and other groups preclude making any judgments as to the *actual* scope of the problem. But it is also important to note that the perceived and actual scope of the problem may possibly be the same; it is just that there were no avaı ble methods or resources to determine the magnitude of any variation that may exist.

Three short-term measurable objectives were also articulated: 1) Identify the cities and communities that were experiencing a perceived or actual youth gang or group problem in order to ascertain the perceived scope and seriousness of the activity; 2) Determine if there were significant differences in how organizations responded to the specific nature of the perceived problem (e.g. youth gang versus youth group) and whether the responses were perceived as effective in reducing the scope and nature of particular activities; and 3) Make the data available to State and local law enforcement officials, as well as practitioners in other fields, in order to expand their general awareness of the perceived or actual problem.

In order to gather the data necessary to meet both long-term and short-term project objectives, the present research utilized a survey instrument derived from two well-known and highly reputable national youth gang projects. Both research projects have produced data that have revealed new insights in our understanding of youth gangs. Spergel et al. (1990) developed one of the most comprehensive questionnaires in order to gather data from a variety of practitioners in the National Youth Gang Intervention and Suppression Research and Development Project and Needle and Stapleton (1983) developed a questionnaire to determine specifically how police departments handle youth gangs within their communities and to ascertain promising strategies for coping with the crime problem. The survey instrument (see Appendix) that was eventually designed for this project consisted of a ten page, 55 question open and closed-ended questionnaire that elicited data unique to the exploratory nature of this research.

Questioning public officials about their perception of the problem (e.g. scope and nature of activities, characteristics, and definitional criteria), as well as their organization's response, was deemed the most effective and efficient research method for gathering the necessary data across a large geographic region; moreover, public officials who were closest to the problem were also considered to be the most reliable sources of data and, as it was later discovered, very supportive of this research endeavor.

The design objectives of this research were similar in scope to those of the aforementioned national studies. The present research similarly focussed on organizational responses and the perceptions of respondents from the particular organizations. And as mentioned above, the survey also elicited information on definitional characteristics and the distinctions that may exist between youth gangs and youth groups; the nature, scope, and variations of the criminal activities; and departmental and organizational goals, objectives, and policies in regard to collective youth crime. However, there were distinct differences between the perspectives of the national studies and the present research. Spergel et al.'s study was "concerned with [the] analysis of the gang problem and the organizational response to it in two types of cities: *chronic* gang problem cities, which often had a long history of gang problems, and *emerging* gang problem cities, often smaller cities that recognized and began to deal with the gang problems since 1980" (1990, p. xv). Furthermore, the criteria used to determine city and site (e.g. correctional facilities) samples were the presence and recognition that a *gang* problem existed; the existence of prevention and intervention programs for at least one year; articulated program goals that involved a multidimensional response; and the ability to determine the program impact. Thus, the non-random sample universe (45 cities and six sites) in Spergel et al.'s (1990) study was chosen based on the strict criteria mentioned above. The present study also selected city samples non-randomly, but the only criterion was that the populations were at least 5,000.

Another major difference involved the respondent categories. In addition to the law enforcement, corrections, probation, and school officials used in the present research, Spergel et al. included prosecutors, judges, academics, security staff for schools, youth service and grassroots organizations, youth and family treatment agencies, and comprehensive crisis intervention programs for community organizations. Reasons for not including more agencies in the present research were due to resource constraints and the need to maintain a manageable sample universe. Thus, the national study was able to gather a wider variety of data on the gang problem and analyze the diversity of responses based on professional orientation. Again, it is important to note that Spergel et al.'s study targeted cities that not only had a recognized youth gang problem, but also had established prevention programs. Because the present study was exploratory in nature, the paramount interest was first to identify cities where there was a perception that youth gang and/or group (non-gang) problems existed, and then examine the perceived characteristics of the problem, the organizational response, and the perceived effectiveness of any existing prevention strategies.

Needle and Stapleton (1983) utilized a random sample of 60 cities' police departments from around the country with the goal of measuring the level of the organizational response to youth gangs. Both national studies focused on cities with sizable populations: 50 percent of the cities sampled in the Needle and Stapleton study had populations in excess of 250,000, with the other 50 percent ranging from 100,000 to 249,999; Spergel et al.'s sample had only seven cities with populations below 100,000, 23 percent between 100,000 and 500,000, and five cities with populations exceeding one million. The most recent national level youth gang assessment (Curry, 1994; Curry et al., 1993, 1994) extended Spergel et al.'s original research project. Curry's (1994) survey research focused on law enforcement information about gang-related crime and included data on all U.S. cities with populations between 150,000 and 200,000 and a random sample of 284 municipalities with populations between 25,000 and 200,000.

Contrasting these studies with the present research, the largest city sampled (Charlotte) had a population of 396,000, but the vast majority had populations below 50,000 (91 out of 100 cities). Focusing on metropolitan areas or smaller municipalities, however, precludes any assessment of youth gang and group activities in less populated, rural areas. Therefore, county officials (e.g. sheriffs' departments, county school superintendents) and organizations delineated by judicial districts (e.g. court counselors) were also identified for sampling in this project. The perspective from which the data were gathered and analyzed—even though substantially different from the national studies—is still quite important, since the general premise—that there were very high correlations between the number of gangs and gang members and the population size of cities—was still relevant.

In summarizing the similarities and differences between the three national studies (Needle and Stapleton, 1983; Spergel et al., 1990; Curry, 1994) and the present research, one must first note the differences in the samples. As recent researchers (Zevitz and Takata, 1992; Zevitz, 1993) on small-city youth gangs have discovered, much of the gang research over the past decades has focused on major metropolitan areas, and the research that examined gangs in nonmetropolitan areas has often interpreted the results within the framework of large-city gang research. The present research is the largest project to date in North Carolina that examined the collective youth crime problem, and one of a very few nationally that examined youth gangs and groups from a predominantly small-city and rural perspective, albeit with five cities that had populations greater than 100,000.

A similar study was conducted by the Texas Attorney General's Office (Morales, 1992), but very few cities in the sample fell below a population of 50,000, and seven cities exceeded 250,000. More importantly, many cities in the Texas study had a history of youth gang problems, particularly the largest ones, so there may have been certain expectations prior to conducting the research. Other state-wide gang studies, utilizing either semi-structured interviews or surveys, have generally focused on law enforcement perceptions to assess the scope of the problem (Governor's Organized Crime Prevention Commission, 1991; Virginia State Crime Commission, 1991) or a combination of law enforcement and school officials (Arizona Criminal Justice Commission, 1991). Few studies, however, have widened the sample base to include the perceptions of youth probation and corrections officials.

The major contribution this research project makes to the larger body of literature on collective youth crime involves not only the focus on smaller cities and rural areas, but that the perceptions elicited from youth practitioners in a variety of fields—even with the variations in operational definitions—provide the first step towards gaining some understanding of the actual or perceived problem within North Carolina. There were a number of similarities between the studies that were previously discussed and the present research. Each study attempted to obtain data utilizing very similar research methods and procedures (survey instruments); all had the goal of ascertaining information on gang characteristics—e.g. definitions, size, demographics, location, level and type of activity—based on official perceptions; all elicited information on the organizational response to the problem and the perceived effectiveness of approaches; and each study focused on a particular state. The significance of all these studies, including the present research, is that they provide data and information on a problem that appears to vary considerably by geography.

D. Method of Organization

This study is divided into eight chapters, each of which provides a unique analysis and discussion of the youth gang and group crime problem in North Carolina. Chapter 2, *Methods and Procedures*, discusses and specifies the survey sample size, its relevant and unique characteristics, and how it was selected. The chapter further describes how the data were collected, provides information on the survey instrument that was eventually designed and utilized, and addresses the validity and reliability problems inherent in the methods, procedures, and the sample; lastly, the chapter describes, in general terms, the statistical analyses performed on the data.

Chapter 3, *Definitions of Law-Violating Youth Groups*, begins the critical analysis of youth gangs and groups by ascertaining the differences and variation in respondents' perceptions of what constitutes a gang and group, gang and group member, and gang and group-related incident. This chapter thus lays the conceptual framework for the most important discussion in Chapter 4, *Prevalence and Location of Law-Violating Youth Groups*. In this chapter, an analysis of the size and scope of the problem is discussed, in addition to presenting data on the prevalence and seriousness of criminal activities attributed to both gangs and groups. Chapter 5, *Youth Gang and Group Characteristics*, examines the similarities and variations of racial and demographic characteristics, organizational parameters, level of criminality and associated crime patterns, and the influence of adults and drugs on group activities.

Chapter 6, *Perceived Causes of Collective Youth Crime*, focuses on the substantial body of theoretical research on the causes and conditions that contribute to collective youth crime problems. This discussion provides the theoretical foundation for the analysis of what respondents in the present research perceived to be as the primary causes. Chapter 7, *Prevention and Intervention Strategies*, examines the level and pattern of the organizational response to collective youth crime and the prevention and intervention strategies employed by organizations. This chapter also identifies potentially effective prevention and intervention approaches, the relevant organizations in which they have been employed, and the cities where these organizations are located. The final discussion, Chapter 8, *Summary and Recommendations*, summarizes the most important findings of this study, placing the findings within the context of the theoretical and empirical research on youth gangs and groups. The chapter also presents a number of ideas and recommendations for future research endeavors on youth gangs and groups in North Carolina.

2

Methods and Procedures

A. Introduction

One of the most common dilemmas in collecting reliable information on youth gangs, whether the research methods involve surveys, field research, or official data is "how or who defines gang membership and how to control for gang member researcher and organizational response bias" (Spergel, 1995, p.15). These two dilemmas have likely had the most significant impact on contemporary gang research, and were particular concerns when the research methods and data analyses techniques were developed for the present study. Though there are differing strengths and weaknesses with any method used in the research process, all methods may be effected by the problems of conceptualizing and defining key aspects of the phenomenon. Both quantitative data, such as statistical information collected from official sources, and qualitative data derived from field interviews and various ethnographic techniques, have inherent reliability and validity problems. These issues, as they pertain to the present research, will be discussed in due course. By highlighting some of the methodological strengths and weaknesses of different research methods, it should become more apparent why the survey method was chosen. It is always a strategic decision to utilize specific research methodologies and sources, depending upon the goal of the research, and important to understand the inherent validity and reliability issues involved.

One of the most common methods and readily available sources of information on youth gangs and groups comes from surveying local governmental authorities. The reliance on official data sources — especially where gangs and gang activity are defined by criminal justice organizations — raises a number of issues. Criminal justice records, particularly from law enforcement agencies, may confound individual and gang activity if stringent definitional guidelines and incident criteria are not consistently followed; in other words, some individually motivated criminal activity, such as drug dealing, may be classified and labeled as gang-related, especially if the activity occurs in known gang territory (Moore, 1993;

Ford and Chavez, 1992). Hagedorn (1990) asserts that two other problems also arise when relying on official statistics and data gathered by surveying law enforcement and public officials: first, the survey data may be imprecise and distorted; and second, because gangs are defined primarily as a law enforcement concern, they are analyzed in those terms. More succinctly, Hagedorn concludes:

> The reporting of a gang problem varies with the needs for city officials to promote a respectable image of their city, for police officials to make a case for hiring more officers, for community agencies to lobby for funds for "outreach" [intervention programs], and for other reasons. Given all of the above conditions, information on gangs from surveys of public officials must be treated with extreme caution (1990, p. 247).

The problem is not that the criteria law enforcement agencies use to define gangs and gang-related incidents are inappropriate—albeit definitions are often more specific, conservative, and involve elements of criminality—but the inconsistency in which they are applied across jurisdictions. This definitional inconsistency—which is also a common problem among social scientists and researchers—makes the comparison of incident rates very difficult (see Maxson and Klein, 1990).

Despite some of these inherent weaknesses with survey data collected from public agencies and organizations, data gathered utilizing other popular qualitative methods—particularly those that involve participant-observation (e.g. street ethnography), and interviewing gang members identified by community agencies (e.g. youth services, probation, and parole)—can be equally problematic. Participant-observation, a method that requires building a rapport with those observed, often leads to the over-identification by the researcher with the gang member, which in turn may reduce the researcher's objectivity (Spergel, 1995). A number of researchers (see Horowitz, 1983; Hagedorn, 1988; Vigil, 1988; Fagan, 1989; Taylor, 1990) were successful in acquiring valuable insight into the important cultural context of gangs and their communities using sociological and anthropological techniques. However, a major concern and limitation with interviewing gang members, particularly if they were identified by community agencies and criminal justice organizations (e.g. youth services, corrections, and law enforcement) involves sample bias. Information gathered may be distorted since the samples may only be representative of gang members who have come to the attention of authorities, presumably because of criminal or delinquent activity. Furthermore, using agencies as intermediaries to identify gang members for sample research is inherently subject to selective and interpretive bias, since these organizations may also have ulterior motives, such as program justification and resource allocation (Hagedorn, 1990).

Spergel (1995) concluded that the ethnographic approach, in general, may not provide the necessary information to initiate community actions to control, ameliorate, or prevent gang involvement and unlawful behavior. In other words, the data derived from research that utilizes many of the popular sociological and anthropological field methods, as interesting as the findings may be, may have very little weight in affecting the design and implementation of intervention programs and policies. Since "[t]he focus is usually not systematically on the interests and reactions of the police, school, agency, neighborhood resident, or even family members to gang phenomenon" (p.15)—all important components in understanding the gang problem—there may be no indication as to what extent the community response contributes to the problem, or whether the response contributes to the problem's development at various phases (Spergel, 1995). Thus, if research objectives include providing a reasonable and systematic assessment of a crime problem, determining the actual or perceived effectiveness of prevention and intervention efforts, and providing recommendations for action, then other methods and sources, such as survey data and official statistics, may be most appropriate.

B. Method and Scope

This study of law-violating youth groups provides the first attempt at acquiring general knowledge on collective youth crime in North Carolina. Presently, there is a veritable dearth of information on this pressing topic. The perceived scope of the problem, types of crimes committed, numbers, locations, and the effectiveness of contemporary intervention strategies are but a few areas where reliable data are limited or nonexistent. The lack of data on North Carolina is due to the fact that most research on youth gangs and groups has been relatively narrow, focusing on the cities where gangs are most problematic (e.g. Spergel, 1986; Hagedorn, 1988; Jankowski, 1991; Klein et al., 1991; Zevitz, 1993). Furthermore, research trends have followed a familiar pattern, focusing on particular ethnic and racial characteristics of gangs in problem cities (Moore, 1978; Vigil, 1988), particular gangs in different cities (Horowitz, 1983) and variations in criminal activities in the same city (Maxson et al., 1985; Klein et al., 1991). Research has all but neglected what appears to be a growing problem in the State. The present study attempts to fill part of the void that presently exists.

Miller (1982) asserts that in addressing a serious social problem such as collective youth crime, there are three major questions that require attention: 1) What is the scope and nature of the phenomenon? 2) Can it be explained? and 3) What can be done to eliminate, reduce, or mitigate the problem? Because of the survey research methods employed in the present study, the first question can be answered to some extent, albeit based on the perception of respondents rather than on any quantifiable or official data sources. The other two questions, where explanations have been elusive to many individuals and organizations involved in youth crime prevention, also receive considerable attention. The reader must be cautioned to view the discussion of findings throughout this study within the context of the individual perceptions of respondents, which may or may not be officially reported information nor necessarily the position of the organization to which the respondent belongs. Even though the study is descriptive and exploratory in nature, it does provide a critical first step towards acquiring information on the perceived nature, scope, and prevalence of law-violating youth groups, organizational responses to the problem (goals and activities), the perceived effectiveness of contemporary intervention and prevention strategies, and the perceived causes of the problem. The study is also significant in that it provides a springboard from which more detailed and focused research (e.g. prevention and intervention program evaluations, ethnographic studies) on collective youth crime in North Carolina can be initiated.

The primary methodological challenge of the present study, as it was also addressed by Miller (1982, p. 8) in his landmark research, was to construct "a reasonably accurate and comprehensive picture of collective youth crime out of materials that were for the most part scattered, incomplete, and hard to obtain." Unfortunately, verifiable and corroborative data were not readily available nor accessible—there were no crime statistics, such as those found in Uniform Crime Reports, on collective youth crime; there were no official reports from North Carolina agencies and organizations that deal with youth gang and group delinquency; and there were no databases from which to more objectively assess the extent of the problem across the State. Hence, the validity, objectivity, and reliability of some data may be questionable and this must be considered the primary limitation of the research findings. Only recently has progress been made in developing reliable statistics on youth gang crime in certain jurisdictions across the United States (Curry, 1994; Curry et al., 1994). However, in North Carolina, with its many small and medium sized cities and towns, the criminal justice community at both the local and State levels has not yet developed any systematic method for collecting the necessary data that could be readily used for reporting and measuring changes in the problem across the State.

In light of the methodological constraints, the central goal of this study was to gather as much information as possible from youth practitioners—those who had the greatest likelihood of coming into contact with youth gangs and groups and their members—throughout North Carolina. Three criteria were established to meet this central goal: first, it was important to identify organizations that could best assess the problem of collective youth crime at some specific level—informational, operational, or administrative; secondly, operationalizing the principle of triangulation was necessary in order to gather information from a variety of professional perspectives, not only to account for professional, personal, and sample bias, but also to gain unique insights; and thirdly, a wide geographic coverage of the State, including both cities and counties, was critical to determine, in broad terms, the perceived seriousness and prevalence of the problem across the region (see Miller, 1982; Spergel et al., 1990; Spergel and Curry, 1990a, 1990b; Spergel et al., 1994b). The study was successful in meeting all of these criteria.

The methodological triangulation used in this study involved what Jupp (1989) described as within-method and cross-method procedures. Within-method involved the use of differing strategies within the same broad research method—in this case the use of a survey instrument and interviews that included both closed-ended structured questions to generate key statistical data and open-ended questions to generate useful qualitative information. Cross-method procedures involved using dissimilar methodologies to examine the phenomenon of law-violating youth groups. The study actively used and cross-referenced official crime statistics (UCR reports) provided by the North Carolina State Bureau of Investigation and other relevant, though limited, reports and studies provided by the North Carolina Administrative Office of the Courts, North Carolina Department of Justice, Governor's Crime Commission, and the U.S. Department of Justice (Federal Bureau of Investigation, Office of Juvenile Justice and Delinquency Prevention, Bureau of Justice Statistics, and the National Institute of Justice). Triangulation balanced the weaknesses and strengths of the differing approaches used for gathering and analyzing the data in this study.

1. Data Collection and Procedures

A survey instrument was developed from two previous national-level youth gang studies (Spergel et al., 1990; Needle and Stapleton, 1983) and forwarded to a nonrandom sample of 410 respondents whose organizations and agencies covered 90 cities with populations ranging from 5,000 to 396,000; all 100 counties in the State; and 18 youth detention and correctional facilities. Respondents were classified into the following categories: 1) *Law Enforcement*, which includes both city police agencies and county sheriff's departments; 2)*Youth Services*,[1] consisting of juvenile court counselor of-

---

1. This category encompasses the responsibilities of the N.C. Youth Services Command (N.C. Division of Prisons) and the Division of Youth Services (N.C. Department of Human Resources). The former is responsible for youthful offenders under the age of 21

fices which are assigned to the 38 judicial districts located throughout the State, and youth corrections which constitutes all regional detention facilities, training schools, evaluation centers, and correctional facilities; and 3) *Education*, which encompasses the offices of superintendents within the 100 county school systems and the largest city school systems, and principals from selected high schools in the largest metropolitan areas. The nonrandom sample universe of jurisdictions for the study differs from Spergel et al.'s (1990) national youth gang survey in that there were no specific criteria (e.g. recognized gang problem, organized responses) for selecting the sample. The present study did, however, eliminate potential respondents from the many small towns with populations below 5,000 people. This action was done primarily to maintain a manageable sample, but it also proved to be fortuitous since there were only four cities out of 17 whose respondents reported youth gang problems and four cities out of 18 whose respondents reported other law-violating youth group problems within the smallest population category of 5,000-10,000 inhabitants. Thus, it appears likely that respondents from cities with populations below 5,000 would have reported collective youth crime problems at even lower rates.

A number of necessary actions were taken to ensure that a sufficient number of surveys were received to perform the study's analysis. Follow-up letters, telephone enquiries, and network electronic mail messages were sent periodically over the three months immediately following the initial survey response deadline. These actions significantly improved the response rate during this period. However, a secondary mailing of 150 surveys was also initiated and completed two months after the initial deadline, in addition to the many individual mailing requests for surveys due to loss, misplacement, or nonreceipt. Subsequent to the content analysis of surveys, interviews were conducted with selected respondents in order to clarify or expand on information provided in surveys, or in many cases to collect more specific information. Furthermore, for reliability purposes, all respondents who self-reported youth gang or group problems were interviewed specifically to determine whether the characteristics of their problems conformed to the consensual definition that was established for youth gang. A similar reliability check was made in regard to the criteria used

---

who have been tried and sentenced as adults but are committed to the N.C. Division of Prisons under segregated conditions according to age. The latter is responsible for institutionalizing anyone under the age of 16 who is adjudicated as delinquent by a N.C. District Court. This category also includes the Juvenile Services Division, which is found within the N.C. Administrative Office of the Courts and is responsible for juvenile (under the age of 16) intake, probation, and aftercare; these professional are known as Juvenile Court Counselors.

to designate an incident as gang-related. The high concurrence scores of some respondents, particularly those from law enforcement, for both the consensual youth gang definition and the incident criteria increase confidence in their estimates of the number of gangs and gang members within their communities, and the proportion and types of index offenses attributed to members (see forthcoming chapter).

The survey instrument (Appendix A) elicited a substantial amount of both quantitative and qualitative information with regard to the perceived or actual activities and characteristics of youth collectives throughout North Carolina. The survey questions encompassed four broad topical areas, each of which provided the opportunity to examine different features, characteristics, and the organizational responses to the problem. The goal of the first major section of the survey instrument (Section II) was to ascertain whether the selected respondents had youth gang or group problems within their respective jurisdictions, some of the general characteristics of the problem, and if the activities of the youth collectives originated outside their communities. This information became substantially important — particularly if the respondents self-reported gang or group problems — since it placed the responses to the remaining questions in context. In all cases where gangs and groups were self-reported in the same locality, the respondent went on to discuss the problem as it pertained to youth gangs, so there was little confusion.

The next section (Section III) elicited the most pertinent and detailed information regarding the characteristics of the problem. In this section, respondents were asked to define their problem, provide information on activities, identify distinguishing characteristics of the problem, provide estimates on membership and the proportion of index offenses attributable to gangs or groups, and to specify socio-demographic features. The questions elicited important information that could have an impact on the prevention and intervention strategies employed by organizations and the wider community. In the broadest perspective, the information provided some insight into the characteristics and features of the problem across many jurisdictions in the State.

The remaining sections (Sections IV through VIII) focused on key organizational and community-level interests, such as the organizational goals and objectives for dealing with youth gang and group problems and whether special policies and coordination practices had been established or implemented. Questions in these sections also asked respondents to identify and evaluate their own organizations' programs and policies, as well as the coordination efforts of the community. One important question requested respondents to rank what they perceived to be the five most important causes of the youth gang or group problem within their communities. The causal rankings and the ratings of organizational and community effectiveness may provide critical information that could affect which prevention and intervention strategies and programs should be adopted in the future, or if present programs should be modified in any way. The responses to all the questions in the survey instrument were critically important in terms of descriptiveness, but it was the statistical correlations of multiple responses (variables) that provided the most meaningful information with regard to how the many variables interact and influence one another.

Because respondents provided a wide diversity of views and a relatively large amount of data pertaining to the activities and characteristics of the problem, there was a significant effect on the manner in which the data could be efficiently and accurately analyzed. Since the survey instrument included both open and closed-ended questions, a coding system had to be developed in order to classify the data in such a way that it could be analyzed using the necessary statistical methods and procedures. Responses to each question in the survey were assigned numerical codes that could be used for aggregate analyses, such as comparing and contrasting the responses from the different respondent categories, summarizing information within the same respondent categories, for examining the data derived from a particular query, and for correlating responses or variables from several questions. SAS statistical software programs (e.g. PROC REG, PROC FACTOR, PROC COR, and PROC TTEST) were utilized for the more complex procedures, while simple programs, such as PROC FREQ, were used for extracting descriptive data.

It was a relatively simple task to code the responses to closed-ended questions—e.g. those that required a yes or no response or figure estimate —but the open-ended responses required a much more elaborate approach. The data from open-ended questions required the careful classification and numerical coding of key terms, concepts, and descriptions that could later be analyzed using various SAS procedures. One example involved the coding of definitions—e.g. youth gang and gang-related incident. The research literature has established the general definitional parameters of what constitutes a youth gang and what activities or characteristics are necessary to differentiate a gang-related incident from one that is not. Using previous research findings as a guideline, key words and concepts could be identified in the definitions provided by respondents, coded accordingly, and analyzed statistically to determine the response pattern based on the professional orientation of respondents. The coding method was the only practical way in which responses from a modest sized sample universe could be analyzed, given the time and resource constraints and the fact that only one researcher was involved in the entire coding and analytical process.

Table 2.1
Organizational Response Rates

Organizational Category	Received (Sent)	% Received	Received (Sent)	% Received
1. Law Enforcement	121 (178)	67.9%		
Police			59 (78)	75.6%
Sheriff			62 (100)	62.0%
2. Youth Services	43 (56)	76.7%		
Court Counselors			32 (38)	84.2%
Corrections			11 (18)	61.1%
3. Education	86 (176)	48.8%		
County School Systems			57 (100)	57.0%
City School Systems			10 (29)	34.5%
Selected High Schools			19 (47)	40.4%
4. Unknown Category and/or location	7			
TOTALS:	257 (410)	62.7%		

Percentage of Sample Universe

1. Law Enforcement	47.6%
2. Education	33.8%
3. Youth Services	16.5%
4. Unknown	2.1%
Totals:	100.0%

2. Respondent Overview

Table 2.1 illustrates the total number of respondents and the return percentages for each respective category and subcategory. The highest response rate came from Youth Services (76.6%), followed by Law Enforcement (67.9%) and Education (48.8%). Criminal justice organizations —composed of organizations and agencies found in the Law Enforcement and Youth Services categories—comprised 64.1% of the entire sample universe of the study. The overall sample response rate of 62.7% included 257 respondents. This response rate is respectable, but is much more significant when considering that 58 cities and 95 counties were geographically represented by the respondents. In other words, at least one survey was received from organizations that had jurisdiction within particular cities (city police agencies and/or city school system officials) and at least one survey was received from county officials (sheriff's departments and/or county school system officials). Furthermore, the high response rate (84.2%)

from court counselor offices, which have jurisdiction in districts that range from one to seven counties, also assured a wide and overlapping geographic coverage of the State. There were seven surveys returned anonymously, of which two had neither the organizational identification nor location listed.

Listed in Table 2.2 are the cities, counties, judicial districts, and correctional sites that were represented by respondents. The cities and counties were categorized according to population size, with the total number within each particular population range identified as *n* ; the percentage figure represents the proportion of all North Carolina cities and counties within the respective population ranges that had respondents who participated in the survey. Annotated in parentheses are the number of respondents from each city and county location. As mentioned earlier, respondents from cities were either city police agency or city school system officials, or both; likewise, county respondents were either sheriff's department or county school system officials, or both. Court counselor offices, which are divided into judicial districts representing one or more counties, are annotated separately.

For all the cities and counties represented by respondents in the sample, multiple respondents could be found in 36 (36.0%) counties—in other words, respondents from both the sheriff's department and county school system returned their surveys; the pattern for cities was slightly lower, with multiple respondents found in only 12 (20.6%) cities. In two of the largest cities, Charlotte and Fayetteville, there were three and four respondents, respectively. For these two cities, the city police agency and city school system representatives responded, as well as representatives from selected high schools where surveys were directly forwarded. The number of respondents from each of the court counselor agencies is annotated (1=respondent, 0=no respondent) according to the State's 38 judicial district offices, and the number of respondents and the names of each youth correctional facility are listed accordingly.

Table 2.2
Cities and Counties Represented by Respondents

Cities   Totals: N=58

Population Group

5,000 to 10,000   n=20 %=48.7

Belmont (1)	Moorehead City (1)	Southern Pines (1)
Brevard (1)	Mt. Airy (2)	Washington (1)
Clinton (2)	Mt. Holly (1)	Waynesville (1)
Conover (1)	Newton (1)	Williamston (1)
Edentown (1)	Oxford (1)	
Forest City (1)	Pinehurst (1)	
Hendersonville (1)	Rockingham (1)	
Kings Mountain (1)	Smithfield (1)	

10,001 to 20,000   n=18 %=69.2
  Albermarle (3)   Graham (2)   Mathews (1)
  Ashboro (2)   Henderson (1)   Monroe (1)
  Boone (1)   Kennersville (1)   Morganton (1)
  Carrboro (1)   Lenoir (2)   Roanoke Rapids (1)
  Elizabeth City (1)   Lexington (1)   Shelby (2)
  Garner (1)   Lumberton (1)   Thomasville (2)

20,001 to 30,000   n=6 %=100
  Concord (1)   Kannapolis (1)
  Havelock (1)   Kinston (1)
  Hickory (1)   Salisbury (1)

30,001 to 40,000   n=3 %=75.0
  Burlington (1)   Chapel Hill (1)   Wilson (1)

40,001 to 50,000   n=2 %=50.0
  Cary (1)   Goldsboro (1)

50,001 to 100,000   n=4 %=100
  Gastonia (1)   Wilmington (1)
  High Point (1)   Fayetteville (4)

> 100,000   n=5 %=100
  Charlotte (3)   Raleigh (1)
  Durham (2)   Winston-Salem (1)
  Greensboro (2)

Counties   Totals: N=95   % Return = 95.0

<10,000   n=7 %=87.5
  Allegheny (1)   Gates (1)   Hyde (1)   Tyrell (1)
  Clay (1)   Graham (1)   Jones (1)

10,001 to 20,000   n=11 %=84.6
  Avery (2)   Mitchell (1)   Polk (1)   Washington (1)
  Chowan (1)   Pamlico (1)   Swain (1)   Yancey (1)
  Madison (1)   Perquimans (1)   Warren (1)

20,001 to 30,000   n=17 %=94.4
  Alexander (2)   Caswell (1)   Hoke (2)   Northampton (1)
  Anson (1)   Cherokee (1)   Jackson (1)   Transylvania (1)
  Ashe (1)   Dare (1)   Macon (1)
  Bertie (1)   Davie (1)   Martin (1)
  Bladen (2)   Hertford (2)   Montgomery (2)

30,001 to 40,000   n=12 %=100
  Chatham (2)   Granville (1)   Person (1)   Vance (1)
  Duplin (2)   McDowell (2)   Scotland (1)   Watauga (1)
  Franklin (1)   Pasquotank (1)   Stokes (1)   Yadkin (2)

40,001 to 50,000   n=6 %=100
  Beaufort (1)   Haywood (2)   Richmond (2)
  Columbus (2)   Lee (2)   Sampson (2)

50,001 to 60,000   **n=10 %=100**

Brunswick (3)	Halifax (1)	Moore (1)	Wilkes (2)
Carteret (1)	Lenoir (1)	Rutherford (1)	
Edgecombe (2)	Lincoln (1)	Stanly (1)	

60,001 to 70,000   **n=4 %=100**

Harnet (2)	Henderson (1)	Surry (1)	Wilson (2)

70,001 to 80,000   **n=3 %=100**

Burke (2)	Caldwell (2)	Nash (1)

80,001 to 90,000   **n=5 %=100**

Cleveland (1)	Johnston (2)	Union (2)
Craven (1)	Rockingham (2)	

90,001 to 100,000   **n=3 %=100**

Cabarrus (1)	Iredell (2)	Orange (2)

100,001 to 150,000   **n=10 %=100**

Alamance (1)	New Hanover (1)	Randolph (2)	Wayne (1)
Catawba (2)	Onslow (2)	Robeson (1)	
Davidson (1)	Pitt (1)	Rowan (1)	

150,001 to 200,000   **n=3 %=100**

Buncombe (3)	Durham (1)	Gaston (1)

> 200,000   **n=5 %=100**

Cumberland (2)	Guilford (3)	Wake (3)
Forsyth (2)	Mecklenburg (2)	

Judicial Districts (Court Counselors)   Totals: N=32

1 (0)	8 (0)	16A (1)	21 (1)	29 (1)
2 (1)	9 (1)	16B (1)	22 (1)	30 (1)
3A (0)	10 (1)	17A (1)	23 (1)	
3B (1)	11 (1)	17B (1)	24 (1)	
4 (1)	12 (0)	18 (1)	25 (1)	
5 (0)	13 (1)	19A (1)	26 (1)	
6A (1)	14 (0)	19B (1)	27A (1)	
6B (1)	15A (1)	19C (1)	27B (1)	
7 (0)	15B (1)	20 (1)	28 (1)	

Corrections   Totals: N=11

Facility

Blanch Youth Center (1)	Juvenile Evaluation Center (1)
Sandhills Youth Center (1)	Juvenile Services Center (1)
Cameron Morrison Youth Center (1)	Dobbs School (1)
Stonewall Jackson School (1)	Western Correctional Center (1)
C.A. Dillon School (1)	

Cumberland County Reg. Juv. Detention Center (1)
Wake Regional Juvenile Detention Center (1)

A modest number of respondents did not respond to the survey, despite the continuous efforts to contact these individuals. The School category had the highest nonresponse rate at 51.2 percent, followed by Corrections, Sheriff and Police Departments, and Juvenile Services. The nonresponse rate may have had an effect on the overall assessment of the problem, but there is no way to be sure as to the actual extent. Most of these potential respondents—72.0 percent of the city respondents (police departments, city school systems) and 70.0 percent of the county respondents (sheriff departments, county school systems)—were from the three smallest population categories, 30,000 or less for cities and 70,000 or less for counties. The respondents who were in these population tracks and did respond to the survey reported youth gang and group problems at relatively modest rates (20 to 30 percent). Therefore, it may be reasonable to argue that had a larger proportion of responses been received, it is quite possible that these "nonrespondents" could have reported youth gang and group problems at similar, or even higher rates.

It is also necessary to point out that the majority of nonrespondents from the School category predominantly came from cities and counties within the two smallest population tracks (20,000 and 40,000 and less, respectively). Incidentally, school respondents from these population tracks reported gang and group problems at rates that ranged from only six to eight percent, depending on whether the respondent was a city or county official. In contrast, the law enforcement respondents from these same population tracks self-reported gang and group problems at much higher rates, approximately 25 percent. The nonresponse from school officials may therefore be of little consequence or at least not as problematic, but the same cannot be said for the nonresponse rates from the law enforcement officials. The higher reporting rates of gang and group problems by the latter category of respondents may support the argument that, had more responses been received from officials within the law enforcement category, there would most likely have been a higher self-report rate of gang and group problems across the State. However, this argument is purely conjectural in the absence of supporting information.

The nonresponse rate from the Corrections category, which happened to be the second highest (38.9 percent), also needs to be discussed. Of the seven facilities where there were no responses, six were relatively small detention/evaluation centers (25 to 129 youth, 18 years of age and younger) rated as minimum (or Delinquent) security institutions, and one was a modest size (460 person, 18 years of age and younger) youth correctional facility with a medium security rating. Incidentally, most of the respondents reporting neither gang nor group problems came from small institutions (training schools or detention facilities) with similar security ratings (minimum) and whose youth varied in age ranges; but all of the respondents (N=5) from the larger institutions (130 and more youth, various age ranges), with ratings from minimum to maximum security, self-reported both youth gang and other group problems. Therefore, based on institution size and security classification patterns, a strong possibility exists that the one large institution (Western Correctional Center), whose respondent failed to return the survey, also had or currently has some type of collective youth crime problem. Lastly, the nonresponse rate of juvenile court counselors located across the State's many judicial districts was very low (15.8 percent) and demonstrated no pattern in regard to district populations, making it difficult to determine the effect of nonresponse, if any.

3. Data Reliability and Validity Considerations

A primary consideration that guided data collection methods (survey, interviews, and official reports) concerned the feasibility of obtaining reliable information on the three basic questions that would assist in evaluating and designating localities as experiencing either youth gang or youth group problems (Miller, 1982): 1) Are there any collectives that conform to the definitional criteria of law-violating youth group (see e.g. Miller's definition in the following chapter) and can any of these groups be further classified as youth gangs? 2) Are the collectives, both youth gangs and groups, identified by reliable and knowledgeable individuals? and 3) Do these collectives pose crime problems?

In addressing the first two questions, the analysis presented in the next chapter will indicate that there was a modest degree of consensus among respondents on many of the key definitional components that distinguish youth gangs from youth groups, in particular the organizational characteristics and the greater use of symbols by youth gangs. The key issue was whether the *problem* classification, presumably made by knowledgeable individuals who had attained a significant level of experience dealing with youth or youth issues, was necessarily reliable. There are probably very few organizations, professional or private, that have substantially more experience interfacing with youth than the organizations from which respondents were selected. However, the problem with multi-site and multi-organizational research, especially where the organizations are dispersed over a large geographic area such as North Carolina, involves interdepartmental differences in regard to how organizations collect and maintain relevant data pertaining to youth gangs and groups (see Maxson, 1995). The issue of data reliability becomes even more complex when respondents from organizations with multidisciplinary responsibilities and missions are relied upon to provide insights on the characteristics and activities of a very complex social phenomenon. In this particular project, there was wide variation in the professional backgrounds of respondents, not only between organizations with different professional orientations (e.g. police versus corrections), but also within the same respondent category. Not only did the professional backgrounds of respondents have an effect on their perceptions of the problem, but their level of experience, personal biases, and prejudices could also have contributed significantly to the way they responded to certain questions in the survey. Moreover, respondent organizations — whether they were schools, police departments, or correctional institutions — most likely employed different policies (e.g. data recording and reporting practices) and programs to address gang or group problems, all of which affected the ability to make truly accurate assessments. Without visiting each site and evaluating the respective organizational procedures and practices as they pertain to gang and group activities, it is difficult to determine the extent to which the different practices could have influenced the findings made in this study.

The third question from above was problematic for a number of reasons. There were no statistical studies, official reports, nor estimates that measured the seriousness of crime committed by youth collectives in North Carolina. High-profile youth gang convictions reported in the press (McClain, 1994) often link gang and group members to index crimes, particularly drug-trafficking and aggravated assault, but few organizations, including law enforcement, annotated incidents as youth gang or group-related for official purposes. Nevertheless, the criminal justice organizations sampled in this study — namely law enforcement — may have provided the most reliable estimates on the percentage of index crimes attributed to youth gangs and groups, as well as member population estimates. As the data will demonstrate in the forthcoming chapter, the respondents from police agencies and sheriff's department attained the highest consensus scores in terms of what concepts they used to define youth gangs and gang-related incidents. So collectively, these respondents likely applied the most consistent definitional standards across the State. It is also important to note that respondents from law enforcement organizations typically provided some of the most detailed — quite often the only — information and estimates of law-violating youth group involvement in the Part 1 (Index) Crimes listed in the North Carolina Uniform Crime Report. However, only a modest number of organizations (including law enforcement) maintained extensive records on collective youth crime and activities, and the information compiled was most often sporadically collected (see also Needle and Stapleton, 1983). Interestingly, the State Bureau of Investigation does have an information system for collecting and reporting crime by youth gangs and other criminal groups, but it is not widely utilized by field agencies. A large number of police and sheriff's departments did keep intelligence information on known gangs and gang members, as well as gang-related incidents, yet the information was not collected nor maintained for official reporting purposes, and was generally difficult to access. Where incidents were recorded, they were most often the most serious index offenses (e.g. homicide, aggravated assault, larceny, robbery), while data on less serious offenses were rarely collected or maintained in agency records. Nevertheless, the perceptions and assessments provided by law enforcement respondents were considered essential in this study. An emphasis and reliance on law enforcement respondents was also found in both Miller's (1982) and Spergel et al.'s (1990) research, but particularly in Needle and Stapleton's (1983) study, since the entire sample of their study consisted of city police organizations. Curry et al's (1994) recent survey of 79 metropolitan police departments further demonstrates the importance placed on law enforcement record-keeping when it comes to determining the seriousness and magnitude of gang criminal activity.

Information provided by juvenile court counselors was also considered important, since these individuals have unique responsibilities as juvenile probation officers and intake counselors, directing cases through the juvenile justice system from preliminary hearings to aftercare. Their intimate knowledge of particular offenders' social and criminal backgrounds provided an insight unavailable to officials and organizations in the other categories. School officials, especially county school system representatives, also provided unique information on perceived collective youth crime problems in schools, particularly for nongang groups since they constituted the large majority of the disciplinary problems formally documented. This fact may indicate that gangs and other youth groups are more active outside schools and do not, at the present time, pose a serious threat to faculty and students. This is quite a contrast to Miller's (1982) finding that gangs constituted a very serious or moderately serious threat in local schools. Lastly, information from youth and juvenile correctional authorities provided a unique insight into law-violating youth group problems in the correctional setting, with gang problems existing in only a small number of facilities. Though studies have discovered that most youth gangs found within correctional facilities have few ties to gangs within the community, the implications are nevertheless important for identifying and controlling these individuals while they are incarcerated. Furthermore, the influence of paroled gang members on other youths in the community should not be underestimated.

Actions were taken to ensure that surveys were answered by the individuals most qualified to provide information about the problem of collective youth crime; where possible, the survey was directed by name to the respective respondents. If a particular respondent was not available for whatever reason, requests were made to forward the survey to another individual within the organization who was most qualified to provide the necessary information. For law enforcement, senior juvenile division detectives (e.g. sergeants and lieutenants) specifically assigned to investigate youth crime or manage division operations most often answered the survey. However, in a small number of cases, other division captains and lieutenants (e.g. patrol, criminal investigations, and administration/records) and even police chiefs and sheriffs were responsible for survey information. Even though the information provided by officers more operationally involved in youth crime investigations and operations was generally more detailed and informative, the information provided by chiefs and other division supervisors was also considered informative.

In youth correctional facilities and evaluation centers, the institute director, superintendent, or their senior assistants provided the requested information. The only exception was a correctional sergeant supervisor at one facility housing a moderately sized youth inmate population. At the judicial district level (court counselor offices), surveys were typically completed by senior supervisors and in many cases by the chief court counselor. The officials who addressed the problem of collective youth crime in the school systems (city, county, and selected schools) in contrast to the other organizations in the study, came from a much wider variety of positions. For example, there were many surveys from directors and assistant directors of student services, coordinators for alternative leaving programs and recreational enrichment programs, directors of safe school programs, special counselors, security personnel, and in many cases superintendents and principals. The smaller the school district, the greater the likelihood that an individual holding an upper-level position of responsibility provided the information. The variety of respondents in the school sample most likely had a greater effect on the general analysis of responses when compared to the more uniform characteristics of the respondents from the other categories. Whether the information provided by the respondents sampled in the survey could be considered truly representative of the actual problem is the topic of the following discussion on research bias and nonsampling error.

4. Research Bias and Nonsampling Error Considerations

This section discusses the potential biases in the sampling outcome and the possible effect these biases may have had on the findings in this study. The most pertinent issues for this discussion include the biases inherent in purposive sampling, such as the extent to which the information provided by respondents is "representative" of the true scope and nature of the collective youth crime problem; biases that may arise when an individual respondent within an organization provides the survey data and that information is considered the accepted position of the larger organization; the professional biases of the respective respondents; researcher coding and tabulation errors; and the potential bias of nonresponse (see Hansen et al., 1954).

Because a large-scale random sample survey that canvassed the entire state of North Carolina was impractical, costly, and time-consuming, a more focused nonrandom, purposive survey was necessary to attain the research goals of this study. The purposive sampling method was the best strategy for obtaining reasonably reliable information on the collective youth crime problem from respondents who were deemed to have particular knowledge or experience in dealing with criminal and deviant youth. Though purposive sampling may be inherently biased—since the sample universe for this study included respondents primarily from the criminal justice community—the respondents, who were geographically dispersed, provided a source of information that would likely not have been available had a larger and predominantly noncriminal justice sample been used. Simply stated, organizations that do not maintain disciplinary records, criminal intelligence information, offense data, or the like, are most likely unable to make reasonably reliable assessments of the problem. However, in purposive sampling, the methods used to obtain the results are largely based on assumptions and judgments that cannot be measured in totally objective terms. In adopting a very conservative position, the results and findings in this study can be considered "representative" of the collective youth crime problem in North Carolina only after considering two key issues: first, the data, which are based predominantly on the perceptions of individuals familiar with the problem, must be demonstrably reliable; and two, the effect of nonresponse must be negligible. These two issues are specifically addressed in the forthcoming chapters.

A point that is particularly relevant and related to the above discussion is the extent to which one respondent's views within a given organization actually reflect that organization's positions and views of the problem. In other words, does the information provided by a detective in a police agency's juvenile investigative division, or an assistant superintendent of a county school system, reflect personal views or are his views based on official information collected or maintained by his organization? Moreover, would the information provided in the survey questionnaire have differed substantially if another individual within the same organization had completed the survey? It was not possible to unravel this potential bias, other than requesting that each survey be completed by a specific individual or by someone within a department who could best provide the necessary information. Even at this point, the survey responses were still prone to individual experiences, knowledge, and background —all of which were uncontrollable by the researcher. There may have been response errors that were either accidental or intentional, or responses that were improper or inaccurate, based on the qualifications and positions of the respective respondents. It is not unrealistic to presume that some respondents may have solicited inputs from colleagues, or perhaps even coordinated with supervisors the appropriate responses to certain questions. Generally, those individuals who completed the survey were in senior supervisory or management positions, and were most likely acting under the authority of their positions within their organizations and departments. The only exception may have been the few respondents who requested anonymity.

Professional and organizational bias was another major concern. In their research, Spergel et al. (1990) found a diversity of views based on the professional orientation of respondents, though the diversity between respondents was less pronounced across locations. Nevertheless, the professional orientation most likely had some effect on how respondents perceived, defined, and responded to the problem. All respondents have a particular perspective from which they define the scope and nature of the problem. Criminal justice organizations typically view the problem from a crime control and enforcement perspective, whereas community organizations, grassroots groups, and social agencies often view youth gang and group activities from a community and social problem perspective. And even within the criminal justice perspective, the perceived or actual severity of the problem may be based on certain activities, which, consequentially, may be considered more or less severe depending on such factors as city size, the general crime problem, the extent of the gang and group activities, and the gang and group member populations. What may be considered serious activity in one town may be viewed only as a nuisance in another. It was therefore necessary to develop a standardized definition of key operational terms—youth gangs and gang-related incidents—in order to measure the perceived scope and nature of the problem with some degree of consistency and standardization.

Researcher coding and tabulation errors were also a source of potential bias. The coding procedures discussed earlier were carefully designed to reduce researcher subjectivity, but because of the diversity of responses, it was still necessary to interpret many responses and properly code them. An important reliability check was performed on the coded data for all respondents, whether they self-reported youth gang or group problems, reported neither as problems, or were uncertain. Ten percent of the surveys (N=26) were randomly chosen and recoded to determine if there were any discrepancies. The correspondence between the original and subsequent coding was a very high 93.0 percent for all variables, which at least provides a high level of confidence in the consistency of coding procedures. During the telephonic interview phase of the research, care was taken to ensure the questions were consistently posed to respondents to preclude the bias that could have occurred by asking the same question differently.

The final concern involved nonresponse bias. To what extent did nonresponse affect the findings of the study? Are the respondents adequately representative of the combined total of both respondents and nonrespondents? These are very important issues that must be addressed in order to determine the reliability and validity of the findings. Complete sample coverage was never achieved, despite the repeated survey mailings and the follow-up procedures that were instituted. The nonresponse rate for each of the organizational respondent categories, as well as the potential implications, receive greater attention in the chapter on the prevalence and location of law-violating youth groups. But to recapitulate briefly, most of the nonrespondents were from localities in the three smallest population categories (30,000 and less for cities; 70,000 and less for counties) in the sample universe. Incidentally, respondents—particularly those from the law enforcement category—from these same population categories reported youth gang and group problems at relatively modest rates. It is possible (but unlikely) that, had the nonrespondents answered the survey, they could have reported problems at similar, or even higher, rates. In the worse case scenario, there may have been a modest underreporting of youth gang and group problems across the localities in the three smallest population categories for cities and counties. With respect to the prevalence of the collective youth crime problem across the State, respondents from the three lowest population groups, regardless of their professional orientation, may have been the least representative of the sample universe, since the modest nonresponse rates make it difficult to ascertain the "true" dimension of the problem in the less populated areas. Again, a forthcoming chapter expounds on this issue with greater clarity, offering extrapolated figures that provide insight on the potential size of the problem, as well as a more thorough discussion of the nonresponse rates (and their effect) of particular organizations in the sample.

5. Terms and Concepts

This study endeavored to follow the conceptual framework of Miller (1982) by using *law-violating youth group* as its major unit of analysis. This was done for a number of reasons. A primary concern was to avoid the use of legally restrictive definitions. In North Carolina, using the term *juvenile* or *delinquent* necessarily distinguishes individuals within the criminal justice system, since juveniles are classified as individuals between the ages of 6 and 16 and delinquency requires a formal adjudication within the juvenile court system. By using *law-violating*, rather than the vague term *deviant* or the legally restrictive term *delinquent* as a conceptual component, the study was able to identify a wider age range of individuals involved in collective youth crime, as well as a broader classification of crimes committed. Furthermore, utilizing the term *group* rather than *gang* as a key conceptual component also provided a number of other advantages. As discussed in the previous chapter, the greatest proportion of collective youth crime is committed by groups and not gangs. Restricting the systematic analysis of collective youth crime to gangs — which are typically larger, more organized, and often more conspicuous — would eliminate or discount the less formalized groups, cliques, and assemblages that are responsible for a larger proportion of criminal activity (Miller, 1982). Moreover, the previous discussions regarding the difficulty in establishing a formal definition of gangs and gang-related incidents demonstrates the problems that would be faced if *gang* were adopted as the only unit of analysis. Collective criminal activity does not necessarily require simultaneous participation in particular acts, but does require the cooperation and moral support of colleagues. This is the essence of becoming involved in group-oriented criminal activity. In many cases, the key criminal act, such as theft or assault, may only be executed by one individual, but quite often these acts are planned, encouraged, and supported by other members within the group.

Out of the twenty subtypes of law-violating youth groups identified by Miller (1982), only three were designated as youth gangs, with the others falling somewhere between loose-knit and more organized cliques or groups. These distinctions have very significant policy and research implications, particularly in the present study. According to Cohen's (1969) research findings that differentiated between gangs and groups, he concluded that "gang and group delinquency are different forms of juvenile deviance and should be approached etiologically, as well as for purposes of treatment and prevention, from different starting points" (p. 108). An understanding of how gangs and groups differ has only been examined in a few other research projects in recent years (see Kornhauser, 1978; Morash, 1983; Curry and Spergel, 1988). A comprehensive analysis of the criteria that distinguish gangs from other groups in North Carolina, the differences in the perceived scope and nature of their activities, and their prevalence across the State, is the heart of this research endeavor. It is important to note that the gang subtype in the present research was in the minority according to the number of respondents who self-reported problems. If the study had focused only on the perceived scope of the *gang* problem, this would have limited the findings and precluded the valuable data derived from the comparative analysis of gangs and groups. In an effort to avoid limiting the analysis in the present research, Miller's (1982) definition of law-violating youth group was adopted to help establish the research parameters and the general conceptual model for conducting the study:

> A law-violating youth group is an association of three or more youths whose members engage recurrently in illegal activities with the cooperation and/or moral support of their companions (p.18).

Curry and Spergel's (1988) conceptualization of the youth gang further aided in the analysis of respondent definitions. According to these researchers, the gang operates within a structured framework of communal values, is complexly organized with leadership and rules of conduct, maintains a tradition of turf, colors, and symbols, and engages in activities that involve mutual support and conflict with other gangs. The criteria or elements that respondents most often cited to distinguish gangs from other youth groups were quite similar to the above definitions.

Despite the anomalies in defining the perceived nature of the problem by some respondents, there was a sufficient degree of consensus to form a rudimentary conception of youth gangs in order to classify and differentiate them from the other law-violating youth groups self-reported by respondents. However, there were some cases where the respondent used definitional criteria that would appear to indicate a gang problem, yet they self-reported their problem as nongang in nature. This demonstrates that there was some disagreement on the parameters of what constitutes a gang, particularly where characteristics may not be readily apparent. This fact makes is difficult to compare the scope and nature of the problem *across* jurisdictions; in other words, comparing the perceived scope and nature of the problem in two different cities cannot be easily accomplished because of the strong likelihood that the definitions used to frame the problem were not consistently applied by all respondents, even if the respondents were from the same organizational orientation. And even if there were a strong consensus on the key definitional concepts used to define the problem, there is not sufficient verifiable data on gang or group-related incidents to make concise conclusions or comparisons of the true scope and nature of activities (see e.g. Maxson and Klein, 1990).

C. Conclusion

In order to obtain information on the problem of law-violating youth groups in North Carolina, a survey instrument derived from two previous national-level gang projects was designed and forwarded to 410 potential respondents. A primary objective was to geographically cover as much of North Carolina as possible and gather information from a variety of sources who have substantial knowledge of youth crime and activity. Respondents were classified into the three broad categories of Law Enforcement, Youth Services, and Education. A major difference between the present study and the previous national-level gang studies, and a recognized limitation, is the focus on respondents from only three professional fields. There is undoubtedly a wealth of information that can be gathered from other public and private organizations familiar with collective youth crime. In particular, it would have been beneficial to identify and survey grass roots organizations, local government criminal justice councils and other planning and coordinating agencies, private outreach and youth groups, academics, and legislative organizations. This effort could have provided an even broader perspective from which to base the study's analysis and possibly increased the general reliability and validity of findings.

The initial sample universe did include district attorneys, public defenders, and district court judges (N=143) who processed and tried juvenile cases, but because of the extremely low response rate (12.5 %), whether due to lost or misplaced surveys or other reasons, the sample universe was later modified and narrowed to the three categories of Law Enforcement, Youth Services, and Education. With a sample response rate of 62.7% for all respondent categories, the largest category of respondents was represented by the Law Enforcement field, constituting 47.6% of all respondents in the study. The diversity of perceptions among respondents posed a number of analytical challenges, since very few respondent organizations utilized official gang definitions and only sporadically recorded incidents that qualified as gang-related. Therefore, by gathering information from a variety of sources (e.g. official reports, studies, and intelligence data) and using other methods to supplement the data gathered via the survey instrument (e.g. interviews)—the validity and reliability of the information provided by respondents could, to some extent, be verified.

This chapter also addressed the important issues of bias and sampling error. In spite of trying to maintain a rigorous and systematic method for obtaining and evaluating information, there were a number of problems that could not be easily overcome. The lack of substantial corroborative and supporting data on youth gangs and groups in the State required placing emphasis on the information provided by respondents. Even though there is reasonable evidence that most of the respondents were acting within an official capacity when they answered the survey questions, their views, perceptions, and characterizations of the problem were still subject to personal biases, affected by such factors as prejudice, experience, and knowledge. Furthermore, the information provided by respondents was probably affected by their professional orientation, which influenced the perspective from which they framed, perceived, and responded to the problem.

The fact that respondents were from many different agencies and locations across the State leads to the proposition that there were probably interdepartmental differences in how information on gangs and groups was collected and maintained. The lack of standard reporting and collection procedures and practices across organizations likely had some effect on the overall reliability of data, since some organizations maintained records and frequently updated information, while others did not. Two other potential biases that were discussed involved how the survey information was coded and analyzed, and the effect of nonresponse on the findings and conclusions. Special procedures and reliability checks were utilized to ensure that the data were coded consistently, but there was still some degree of researcher subjectivity in coding the responses that was not altogether clear. In general, nonresponse bias appeared to be most influential if the nonrespondents were from cities and counties from the three smallest population tracks, since respondents from cities and counties in the same population tracks reported problems at modest levels. The collective youth crime problem (gang and group), therefore, may have been more serious or prevalent in the smaller cities and counties than reported. Since it is important always to keep in mind the threats to data reliability, many of the aforementioned points are again discussed in forthcoming chapters.

3

Definitions of
Law-Violating Youth Groups

A. Introduction

The term *law-violating youth group* connotes a wide variety of activities by a collective of individuals who may share similar or disparate social backgrounds, demographic characteristics, and criminal propensities. The difficulty is at what point youth gangs are differentiated from the larger body of other law-violating youth groups. Earlier conceptions of youth gangs (Shaw and McKay, 1931; Whyte, 1943) often used the terms gang and group interchangeably or only implicitly recognized the differences between the two phenomena, but in most cases, these collectives did not engage in serious criminal activities. Thrasher's (1936) youth gang definition,[1] one of the most frequently cited definitions, exemplified the earliest ideas of what constituted a youth gang. But it was not until Cartwright et al. (1975) amended the definition to include the notion that a gang is "considered an actual or potential threat to the prevailing social order" (p.4) that it became much more restrictive, providing the criterion that would assist in differentiating youth gangs from other delinquent groups. A shift in the perceptions of gangs—precipitated by the evolutionary modification of gang definitions by academics, youth counselors, prosecutors, judges, police, and other professionals in a variety of fields—can be attributed to contemporary research findings, as well as media reports, that gangs have not only become more persistent and lethal in recent times, but have also demonstrated greater criminal propensities than other law-violating youth groups. However, solely relying on the criteria of general criminal activi-

---

1. A gang is an interstitial group, originally formed spontaneously and then integrated through conflict. It is characterized by the following types of behavior: meeting face to face, milling, movement through space as a unit, conflict, and planning. The result of this collective behavior is the development of tradition, unreflective internal structure, esprit de corps, solidarity, morale, group awareness, and attachment to local territory (Thrasher, 1936).

ties for the purpose of distinguishing gangs from other groups is inadequate, since nongang crime has also become more widespread and problematic in many cities.

A number of researchers (Miller, 1982; Spergel, 1984; Short, 1989; Curry and Spergel, 1988) established definitional characteristics, albeit conceptual in nature, to distinguish gangs from other forms of law-violating youth groups. Youth gangs were characterized as having unique organizational features (e.g. complex and diffused structures, core and peripheral members, rules and traditions), identifiable leadership (established and situational) and group characteristics, a sense of turf or territory, and goals and purpose. Cohen (1969) concluded that gang offenders were generally older, more homogeneous (in age, sex, and race), and more violent than youth groups. Youth group delinquency, assert Curry and Spergel (1993, p. 275), is "law violating behavior committed by juveniles in relatively small peer groups that tend to be ephemeral, i.e., loosely organized with shifting leadership." In fact, youth gangs and groups quite possibly represent two distinct social phenomena based on differential criminal patterns (Curry and Spergel, 1988).

Miller (1982), in adopting a broad approach to assess "collective youth crime," also felt it was necessary to distinguish gang behavior — as one form of group delinquency — from other forms. Miller's concept of "law violating youth group," defined as "an association of three or more youths whose members engage recurrently in illegal activities with the cooperation and/or moral support of their companions" (p. 20), is clearly distinguishable from gangs because the definition fails to include such important concepts as organization, structure, turf, and colors. Utilizing triangulation methodologies, the widely accepted gang definition (below) produced by Miller reduced any occupational bias by incorporating definitional elements from practitioners in a variety of fields. By combining six elements,[2] on which 85% of the respondents concurred, Miller constructed the following definition of gangs:

> A youth gang is a self-formed association of peers, united by mutual interests, with identifiable leadership and internal organization, who act collectively or as individuals to achieve specific purposes, including the conduct of illegal activity and control of a particular territory, facility, or enterprise (1982, p. 21).

Based on Miller's definition, it may be inferred that gangs require a certain degree of cohesion to maintain such a structured organization — even if only loosely — with leadership and lines of authority; furthermore, in order to maintain such an organization, membership stability would appear

---

2. organized, identifiable leadership, identifiable territory, continuous association between members, specific purpose, and engagement in illegal activities.

important. The notion that youth gangs are well-organized and cohesive has been considerably debated in the literature over the past thirty years (see for instance the diverging views of Yablonsky, 1962; Klein, 1971; Miller, 1982; Skolnick et al., 1988; Taylor, 1990; and Jankowski, 1991). Characterizations of gang structure have come in a variety of forms during this period, ranging from loose-knit amorphous masses (Klein, 1968b), "near-groups" (Yablonsky, 1965), and "loosely structured sets of companions" (Gold and Mattick, 1974, p. 335), to informally organized (Moore, 1978) and highly organized collectives (Jankowski, 1991; Taylor, 1990). Whether gangs are loosely-knit or well-structured appears to be influenced by many interdependent factors—individual, cultural, and social structural. And as Spergel (1995, p.74) asserts, "[i]t is likely that the loosely knit characterization refers to the gang member's diffuse and seemingly erratic pattern of interaction with other gang members, while the well-organized characterization refers to the large membership size of certain gangs, their location in different streets or sections of the neighborhood or city, their supposed hierarchical organization, or simply gang longevity." Lastly, gangs have also been broadly classified as having a vertical or horizontal structure; while the vertical structure is considered the more common organizational characteristic of "traditional" youth gangs (e.g. age-graded cliques, centrally located), the horizontal structure may be a later form of gang structural development, in the sense that the gang becomes more diffuse across communities and cities over time. The implication is that as the gang develops, it may function to provide increasing sources of criminal economic opportunities (Spergel, 1995).

Regardless of the actual gang structure, a commitment to the particular life-style and a substantial degree of cohesiveness—which is often absent in nongang group formations—are required to motivate members and the gang to congregate recurrently and to initiate concerted activities. The central influences on gang structure have been defined in the research in terms of internal cohesion—the attraction members feel toward one another and the gang as a unit, member motivation to participate in the gang's activities and contribute to its goals, and the coordination of gang member activities—and external cohesion, such as poverty and dysfunctional family relationships (Klein and Crawford, 1967; Goldstein, 1991). Cohesiveness is a primary characteristic of all group development (delinquent or not), but appears to be an especially powerful influence on the nature of youth gang activity, the quality of member interaction (group processes), and the collective's structure; it may also serve as a major determinant of whether the gang successfully achieves its goals. Thus, in the general perception and definition of the problem, organization and structure appear to be two of the most important criteria for distinguishing youth gangs from other criminal and delinquent youth groups.

In light of the previous discussion, this definitional exercise becomes important for a number of reasons: first, it will aid in identifying the key distinguishing characteristics of gangs and groups in order to understand the perceived scope and nature of the problem; second, it will assist later in developing and implementing appropriate prevention and intervention strategies that can be comparably assessed over time; and third, the analysis of definitions provides a context for interpreting and comparing the data that is presented in subsequent chapters (see Spergel et al., 1990). From a criminal justice policy perspective, this analysis not only facilitates a more informed understanding of what constitutes youth gangs and groups, it also highlights the need for greater definitional consensus so that the problem can be more accurately assessed and adequately addressed in the future.

In order to gain the best possible understanding of the definitions provided by respondents, a variety of statistical procedures, including factor analysis and descriptive statistics, were used to demonstrate not only the degree of consensus in the concepts used, but also the significant degree of diversity and variability between respondent categories. Descriptive statistics — which involved measures of central tendency, variability, and simple correlation — assisted in summarizing and characterizing the large set of raw data generated by the questions. However, because simple correlations among the variables were too large and difficult to summarize in many instances, factor analysis was employed to determine if a smaller number of underlying constructs accounted for the major sources of variation (Huck et at., 1974; Stevens, 1986). Through the use of factor-analytic techniques, smaller sets of variables are typically identified and used as operational representatives of the larger set of variables (Gorsuch,1983). But in this case, the factor analyses were performed primarily to demonstrate the significant degree of variability found in definitions, and to also point out that there may be other concepts — which could not be accounted for in this analysis — that may go into definitions.

B. Defining Youth Gang and Youth Group

A content analysis was conducted on the information provided by all respondents — regardless of whether they had a collective youth crime problem or not — who attempted to define youth gang or youth group. The questions from Section III (Definitional Criteria) of the survey (see Appendix) elicited specific information regarding the definitional criteria, including key organizational and behavioral characteristics, that go into defining youth gang and youth group. Respondents were explicitly asked if their respective organizations distinguished between youth gangs and groups, and if so, how. Because 84.5 percent of all respondents specified that their organizations did make the distinction (Appendix, Section III), it became particularly important to discern what key activity or behavior made these collectives a concern or relevant to the respondents' organizations. Data from the following key survey questions provided the information for the analysis of youth gang and group definitions:

What is your definition of youth gang? Youth group?

What key activity or behavior makes youth groups or youth gangs a concern or relevance to your work?

The open-ended questions provided the opportunity for respondents to include any terms, concepts, or ideas regarding how their organization formally defined gangs and groups. The open-ended questions had a number of advantages over using a limited number of previously determined terms and concepts from which respondents could have chosen: first, it was a matter of avoiding being overly inclusive or exclusive in the selection of terms and concepts, enabling definitions to remain more subjective and pluralistic; secondly, open-ended questions precluded the use of theoretically dominant or popular terms and concepts, which could have forced respondents into choosing terms haphazardly or simply out of convenience. Though it may have been much more laborious to define the problem, the respondents at least had the opportunity to articulate terms and concepts that were most applicable to their unique situation. More importantly, unprompted responses reduced the risk of researcher bias and ensured there was a reasonable degree of neutrality.

Following a content analysis of definitional responses, information was classified into 45 empirically anchored components or concepts (Table 3.1) that reflected the theoretical considerations discussed in the literature (particularly Cloward and Ohlin, 1960; Short and Strodtbeck, 1965; Cohen, 1969; Miller, 1982; Curry and Spergel, 1988; Spergel et al., 1990; Spergel and Curry, 1990; Sanders, 1994) and the frequency of their use by respondents. These 45 components were further classified into eleven broad conceptual rubrics — e.g. general group characteristics, noncriminal activities, crimes of violence, property crimes, and symbolic characteristics — for analytical simplicity (see methods used in Spergel et al., 1990).

Since a primary analytical consideration in the present analysis was to identify the perceived difference and variations between youth gangs and groups, the adoption of a broad structural and behavioral framework that might fit both gangs and groups was important. A less restrictive definition of gangs (e.g. Klein, 1971; Cartwright, 1975), rather than one that was more precisely and succinctly defined (e.g. Miller, 1982; Sanders, 1994) assisted in establishing the conceptual components of the first definitional rubric, *general group characteristics*. The gang, as posited by Klein (1971, p. 111) is "any denotable adolescent group of youngsters who (a) are generally perceived as a distinct aggregation by others in the neighborhood; (b) recognize themselves as a denotable group; and (c) have been involved in a sufficient number of delinquent incidents to call forth a consistent negative response from neighborhood residents and/or enforcement agencies."

Table 3.1
Frequency of Cited Dichotomous Variables Derived from Content Analysis of
Youth Gang and Youth Group Definitions (N=257)

Variables / Subcomponents	Gangs		Groups		
	N	%	N	%	(t)
1. *General Group Characteristics*	223	86.4	180	70.0	**
Leadership					
Regular Association					
Certain Number of Members					
Loosely-knit					
Common Behavior					
2. *Group Organizational Characteristics*	207	80.5	147	57.1	**
Affiliation with other gangs/groups					
Goals and Purpose					
Rules					
Maintain unity					
Conflict with others					
Established identity					
Organized structure					
Recruitment					
Exclusiveness					
3. *Non-criminal Activities*	40	15.6	37	14.4	ns
Protection					
Sports					
Recreation					
Non-violent activities					
4. *Drug Crimes*	178	69.2	179	69.6	ns
Drug use					
Drug Trafficking					

5. *Crimes of Violence* Robbery Intimidation General violence Rape Armed Assault Shootings	234	91.1	215	81.7	**
6. *Property Crimes* Vandalism Theft/Larceny Burglary Breaking & Entering	119	46.3	151	58.6	**
7. *General Criminal Activity* (nonspecific)	219	85.2	189	73.5	**
8. *Collective Symbols* Name Colors Graffiti Initiation Logos Rituals	177	68.9	97	37.8	**
9. *Personal Symbols* Tattoos Clothes Hand Signs Nicknames	81	31.5	43	18.7	**
10. *Adult Members*	186	72.4	210	81.7	**
11. *Reside in Same Locale*	129	50.2	141	54.9	ns

$p \leq 0.05$* $p \leq 0.01$** $p \leq 0.001$*** ns=not significant

The next major rubric, *group organizational characteristics*, encompassed the structural-behavioral concepts researchers have consistently used to distinguish youth gangs from groups (Cohen, 1969; Miller, 1982; Spergel, 1984; Curry and Spergel, 1988; Sanders, 1994). The key terms and concepts used and advocated by these researchers—e.g. goals and purpose, established identity, rules and traditions, maintain unity, complexly organized, and leadership—served as the significant conceptual identifiers for this rubric. It was hypothesized that components within this rubric would be cited more frequently and achieve greater consensus among respondents as youth gang characteristics, but would be less significant components in defining youth groups. The underlying argument is that youth gang structures facilitate unique group processes that do not occur to the same extent in youth groups (Miller, 1982; Spergel et al., 1990; see also Thornberry et al., 1993, 1994).

Research has indicated that the organizational features of youth gangs are particularly conducive to criminal behavior (Spergel, 1990; Covey et al., 1992; Thornberry et al., 1993), and that one of the most prevalent forms of criminal behavior that manifests in the gang setting involves violence (Cohen, 1969; Friedman et. al. 1975; Jankowski, 1991; Reiner, 1992; Sanders, 1994) and, to varying degrees, drug use and drug trafficking (Fagan, 1989, 1990; Moore, 1978)—even though drug activities may take place outside the gang setting (e.g. Klein et al., 1991; Moore, 1991). Furthermore, research has, with great consistency, demonstrated that youth gang criminal activities have been more serious in nature when compared to youth groups and other non-gang delinquents (see Rand, 1987; Tracy, 1982, 1987; Tracy et al., 1990). Less serious criminal activities, conversely, appear to be more characteristic of delinquent youth groups (Cohen, 1969). Therefore, in order to determine the general scope and nature of youth gang and group activities, and any variation that may exist between these collectives, a set of criminal activities comprising four subcategories of dichotomous variables was designated: these descriptive categories included *drug crimes, crimes of violence, property crime,* and *general criminal activity* (Spergel et al., 1990). Because not all youth gang and group activity is illicit (Whyte, 1943; Moore, 1978; Horowitz, 1990), the category *noncriminal activities* was also designated for this analysis.

Two categories regarding the use of symbols, designated as *collective symbols* and *personal symbols,* were very important for differentiating youth gangs and groups. According to Jackson and McBride (1985), communication through the use of colors, graffiti, logos, handsigns, tattoos, and clothing are critically important for youth gangs, since "a gang's image and reputation depend on recognition" (p. 59). According to Spergel (1995), special clothing or dress, signs and mannerisms, are often identifiers of a particular gang and youth in search of status, honor, or reputation—invariably within the gang domain and its social processes. Moreover, "Graffiti and criminal activities are not only distinctive in particular gangs, ethnic and racial cultures, and communities, but evolve over time and reflect the changing character and interests of gangs and their members to prove they are different..." (p.98). If this assertion is correct, it may be argued that youth gangs and their members need recognition and reinforcement of belonging in more direct and explicit ways than youth groups; therefore respondents should cite more frequently, and demonstrate with greater consensus in their definition of youth gangs, the components of collective and personal symbols.

The last two rubrics—designated as *adult member involvement* and *reside in same locale*—were included in this analysis but were not combined with any of the other variables (see Spergel et al., 1990). The presence of adult members in both youth gangs and groups has a number of implications: adult involvement may have an impact on the scope and nature of criminal activities committed by the collective; and it may also demonstrate that gang and group involvement possibly perpetuate membership and further influence the extent and seriousness of a criminal career (e.g. Tracy, 1982). Maxson et al. (1985), Horowitz (1983), and Spergel (1983) discovered that the most serious gang-related offenses, namely homicide and aggravated assault, were most commonly perpetrated by individuals in their late teens to early twenties. Even though the modal frequency for arrested youth gang members has most often been the reported age of 17, and for youth group members a slightly lower 15 years of age, the findings in the available research have generally reported that older youth gang and group members (e.g. 17 years and older) were not only more actively involved in criminal offenses, but their criminal activities were also more seriousness in scope and nature (Cohen, 1969; Miller, 1975, 1982; Spergel, 1986; Torres, 1980; Klein et al., 1991). A number of studies have reported adult involvement in youth gang drug-trafficking activities (see in particular Spergel et al., 1990; Fagan, 1990; and Klein et al., 1991), but whether this integration makes the collective generally more criminogenic is difficult to discern. Therefore, the interrelationship between violence, drug activities, and age will be examined in greater detail in forthcoming chapters.

Lastly, members of youth collectives who *reside in the same locale* may designate their neighborhood as territory, which, according to Spergel (1995, p. 87), is "a critical factor in determination of the purpose, structure, motivation, and frequency of gang conflict." However, the "territorial imperative" has likely been modified in recent years due to more mobile youth; youth collectives, especially gangs, may seek to control physical, social, as well as economic interests in different sections of a city or town (Spergel, 1995). This expanded conceptualization of turf not only complicates prevention and intervention strategies, but may also raise a number of theoretical issues regarding traditional concepts of youth gangs and groups. Therefore, an analysis of these two rubrics became necessarily important. By coding the key terms and concepts of the definitions provided by respondents into the previously mentioned conceptual categories—using the key words and concepts as guidance (Table 3.1)—there was an opportunity to analyze the definitions using factor analytic, as well as other statistical methods (see Spergel et al., 1990). Each conceptual category could therefore be considered a statistical variable or component in the larger analytical framework.

1. Factor-Analysis

The frequency in the use of particular definitional terms and concepts by respondents provides some idea of their importance—especially the differences between youth gangs and groups—but does not necessarily provide helpful information regarding how the terms and concepts are combined to formulate definitions. Because a significant degree of diversity existed in the way respondents defined youth gang and group, a more sophisticated statistical procedure that provided more precise qualitative and quantitative distinctions between variables (terms and concepts) was employed. In order to parsimoniously describe data that may be broadly disparate, and where very little generalization can be adequately made, factor analysis, represented with factor loadings, was employed to measure the degree of generalizability found between variables. Through factor-analytic techniques, the large number of diverse variables provided by respondents in their definitions could be reduced and more easily summarized, while simultaneously maximizing the amount of information for the analyses. The factor analysis, in other words, produced a set of linear combinations that reduced the original set of variables into smaller, more interpretable representatives or dimensions; the smaller set of variables, in theory, accounted for the greatest proportion of reliable variance.

The primary purpose for the use of this technique in the analyses of definitions (in this and subsequent sections of this chapter) was not only to increase the comprehensibility of the extensive and sheer amount of available data, but to also narrow substantially the conceptual framework and increase the understanding of the complex and diverse perceptions of respondents (Gorsuch, 1983; Stevens, 1986; see also Spergel et al., 1990). In general, the factor analyses demonstrated that there were numerous combinations of variables—as demonstrated in the separate factor loadings—that actually go into definitions, particularly for the definitions of youth gang and group. To wit, even though there were common concepts and terms identified by respondents in their definitions, not all of these concepts were emphasized or articulated by all respondents.

In determining how many principal components to retain for the analyses, graphic scree tests were conducted to ascertain the factors that should be retained. Stevens (1983) recommends retaining components whose variance or eigenvalues are greater than one, thus ensuring the retention of components which account for the largest amounts of variance. The explanatory strength of each factor and the combined factors depends on the total variance that can be individually and collectively explained; it is most ideal to have a combined set of factors that accounts for 75 percent or more of the total proportion of variance. However, it is also acceptable to retain factors with smaller eigenvalues — which, in turn, will likely produce lower individual and collective variance — when the primary purpose of the analysis is exploratory, rather than confirmatory (Gorsuch, 1983).

Table 3.2 demonstrates that for youth gang definitions four factors emerged that accounted for 52.8 percent of the variance. Of all the factor analyses performed in this chapter, the factors derived from the definition of youth gangs not only provided the highest degree of communality among the factors, it also illustrates that there were a number of methods — gauging by the number of factors and their respective loadings on the most significant variables — used by respondents to conceptualize and frame their definitions. To increase the interpretability of components, it was necessary to conduct an oblique rotation (SAS Promax) of correlated factors. In general, the initial principal factor solutions and principal component analyses, derived from extracting factors from correlation matrices, were not sufficiently informative nor helpful, therefore more sophisticated factor models were deemed necessary for this and subsequent definitional analyses.

Table 3.2
Promax Rotated Factor Matrix from Factor Analysis of
Correlation Coefficients of Youth Gang Definition Characteristics (N=233)

Variable	Factor 1	Factor 2	Factor 3	Factor 4
Crimes of Violence	.619	-.363	.167	-.247
Group Organization	.587	-.253	-.270	-.380
Personal Symbols	.549	.269	.439	.235
Reside in Same Locale	-.628	.533	.097	.189
Collective Symbols	.049	.140	.551	.207
Drug Crime	-.108	-.052	-.466	.577
Adult Involvement	.269	.040	-.334	.516
Noncriminal Activity	-.207	.332	-.591	-.021
General Criminal Activity	-.135	-.774	.216	-.130
Property Crimes	.226	.381	.145	-.429
General Group Charact.	.225	.271	.361	.161
Eigenvalues	1.67	1.50	1.47	1.17
Variance Explained	(15.2%)	(13.6%)	(13.4%)	(10.6%)
Total Variance (52.8%)				

As Table 3.2 indicates, crimes of violence, organizational characteristics, and personal symbols loaded heaviest on the first factor. This factor characterizes the youth gang as a relatively organized and serious collective with established identities; gang identities were achieved primarily through the display of personal rather than collective symbols, and the most prevalent form of behavior was violent in nature. It may be inferred that, because of the negative loadings on drug crimes and general criminal activity, respondents were more concerned about violent criminal behavior and personal safety, rather than the other criminal propensities of gangs. The heavy negative loading on reside in same locale indicates that youth gangs were not necessarily perceived, to any significant degree, as turf-oriented within particular neighborhoods, which is contrary to the findings in much of the gang literature (see Miller, 1982; Taylor, 1990; Sanders, 1994; and also general discussions in Spergel, 1990 and Covey et al., 1992). These loadings, however, implicitly support Klein and Maxson's (1989) suggestion that gangs are more prone to violence, and Jackson and McBride's (1985) findings that the use of symbols serves as an important communication medium within the gang context.

The second factor, Factor 2, represents the classical definitions found in earlier gang studies (Whyte, 1943; Short and Strodtbeck, 1965). The heaviest loading on the residential locality of members — in addition to the moderate loading on noncriminal activities, and especially the negative loadings on general criminal activities and crimes of violence — indicates a collective of youth that gathers in a particular neighborhood, primarily for mutual companionship, friendship, and support. This factor defines youth gangs as less serious problems within the community, even though there may be some criminal inclinations in the form of property offenses. The use of personal and collective symbols loaded heaviest on the third factor, Factor 3, with a light loading on general criminal activities and general group characteristics. There were also moderate negative loadings on adult involvement in gang activities and involvement in drug crimes. This factor probably conceptualizes youth gangs as unique collectives involved in a wide variety of criminal activities, but not heavily involved in any particular type of crime. The loading pattern for this factor places greater emphasis on group identifying characteristics, rather than specific behavioral activity of gangs; it also demonstrates a concern for a collective of youth that has the potential of becoming a more serious threat to the community (Spergel et al., 1990).

Drug crimes and the involvement of adult members in youth gang activities loaded heaviest on the last factor, but loaded negatively on all of the other crime categories (violent and property crimes, and general criminal activity). This factor characterizes youth gangs more as instrumental (Huff, 1989) or gain-oriented (Miller, 1982) entities, rather than the traditional conception of collectives involved in violent and other general criminal behavior. These loadings inferentially demonstrate that there may not be a clearly perceived association between drug use and distribution and violent activity. It could also be argued that youth gang violence occurs independent of involvement in drugs (Klein et al., 1991; Fagan, 1989).

For youth groups, three factors emerged that accounted for only 26.5 percent of the variance (Table 3.3); therefore, the interpretive strength for this analysis on youth group definitions is significantly weaker than that found in the previous analysis of gang definitions. Property crimes, followed closely by general group characteristics and general criminal activity, loaded heaviest on the first factor. The heavy loading on property crimes further supports Cohen's (1969) assertion that youth groups have a greater tendency to engage in these types of offenses. The moderate loadings on general group characteristics, combined with the weak loading on group organizational characteristics, indicate that groups were not considered well-organized or structured. This factor conceptualizes youth groups as loose-knit collectives involved in a variety of criminal activities, but not significantly in crimes of violence.

Table 3.3
Promax Rotated Factor Matrix from Factor Analysis of
Correlation Coefficients of Youth Group Definition Characteristics (N=207)

Variables	Factor 1	Factor 2	Factor 3
Collective Symbols	.107	.338	-.169
General Criminal Activity	.483	.176	.165
Noncriminal Activity	-.095	.013	.080
Adult Involvement	-.222	-.138	-.103
Property Crimes	.622	.022	-.099
Crimes of Violence	.157	.195	.485
Personal Symbols	.273	.194	.487
Reside in Same Locale	-.196	-.056	-.570
General Group Charact.	.389	.568	.153
Group Organization	.123	.509	.271
Drug Crimes	.002	-.350	-.039
Eigenvalues	.984	.970	.960
Variance Explained	(8.95%)	(8.82%)	(8.73%)
Total Variance (26.5%)			

General group characteristics and group organizational characteristics loaded heaviest on the second factor, Factor 2, and also moderately in the negative direction on involvement in drug-related crimes. There was also a positive loading on the use of collective symbols. These loadings indicate that group characteristics were more important identifiers than the specific behavioral or offense patterns. This factor defines youth groups as relatively stable collectives, but not necessarily serious threats to the public order. Crimes of violence and the use of personal symbols loaded heaviest on the last factor, Factor 3, with general group characteristics demonstrating weak loadings. This factor conjures the image of a loose-knit collective of youth primarily involved in assaults and intimidation. The moderately strong negative loading on residential locality of members indicates that these collectives were most likely not indigenous to any particular neighborhood. If a respondent scored high on this dimension, key concerns for youth groups probably included the seriousness of the crime members individually or collectively committed, and their potential for becoming more criminogenic.

In sum, all of these factors, generated from covariance patterns among the eleven broad definitional rubrics identified earlier, provided information on the extent to which definitional variables or components could be attributed to common factors. The factor analysis was employed primarily to summarize the interrelationships among the strongest variables and to highlight the diversity in the definitions provided by respondents. As noted, there were a number of different ways in which respondents characterized youth gangs and groups, despite the general emphasis on certain terms and concepts identified early in the analysis. According to the data produced in the factor analysis, youth gangs were considered much more organized and structured than youth groups, and typically, but not always from the same neighborhood. It was also more characteristic of youth gangs to display distinguishing symbols and to participate more frequently in crimes of violence. However, youth gangs could also be characterized as less serious collectives in neighborhoods, even though criminal inclinations may be present; or as unique collectives involved in a wide variety of criminal activities. Youth groups could best be defined as loose-knit, though stable, collectives involved in a variety of less serious criminal activities, such as drug and property crime, but posing little threat to the public order. The interpretive strength of the derived factors for youth gangs was not substantially strong, but for youth groups it was particularly weak; the factor analysis could not account for approximately 50 and 75 percent of the variance that went into defining gangs and groups, respectively. The high degree of unaccounted variance forces the analyses into a different direction.

2. Analysis of Definitional Consensus

According to Spergel et al. (1990), a consensus on definitional components may provide a more informed idea about what influences their selection. It was quite possible that the professional orientation of respondents (e.g. police, probation) or the geographic area in which respondents were located had a more significant influence on the selection of key terms and conceptual components used to define youth gangs and groups. Spergel at al.'s (1990) research findings concluded that the definitions of youth gang, gang member, and gang-related incidents varied across different types of organizations as well as by area, but the greatest level of consensus on definitional concepts and components was more closely linked to area, rather than the respondents' professional discipline or organizational affiliation. The study also discovered that the seriousness of the gang problem—whether it was chronic or emerging—also had an effect on definitions. For example, there was a greater emphasis on anti-social behavior and criminal activities in cities with chronic gang problems, but where the problem was less serious or emerging, the emphasis was on the organizational and symbolic aspects of the gang.

Similarly, Needle and Stapleton (1983) discovered in their survey of police organizations that violent behavior was the key criterion most often cited for not only defining gangs, but also for distinguishing youth gangs from groups. How broadly police and other criminal justice organizations apply definitions may also depend on the size of their respective cities or jurisdictions; and moreover, whether the perception of the problem is serious may depend on the number, size, and type of youth collective, and the proportion of illicit activities attributed to these groups relative to total crime in their particular jurisdictions (Spergel, 1990). By contrast, community oriented and grassroots organizations, outreach and youth agencies, and even schools—which tend to de-emphasize the criminal aspect of collective youth activities and emphasize symbolic behavior—may view the nature of the problem as less serious based on their definitions and perceptions. As Spergel (1990, p. 177) importantly notes, definitions "become the basis for different policies, laws, and strategies... [and] determine whether we have a large, small, or even no problem." This, consequentially, affects which agencies and organizations receive adequate, if any, prevention and intervention program funding to address the problem.

To ascertain what influence area and professional orientation of respondents had on the selection of key definitional components for both youth gangs and groups, a measure of consensus was conducted. The procedures used in this analysis, which were replicated from Spergel et al.'s (1990) research, aimed to demonstrate the extent to which respondents nominated the key definitional components (based on professional orientation and area). To determine the consensus of definitions by area, only those locations where multiple respondents (typically two) provided surveys were retained. There were only 12 cities (20.6%) and 36 (36.0%) counties where multiple responses were available for this analysis. For the 12 cities, the two respondents were the city police agency and the city's central school system organization; for the counties, the two respondents were the county sheriff's department and the county school district organization. Because court counselor agencies are responsible for jurisdictions that range from one to seven counties, there was a procedural dilemma in determining how to incorporate these respondents into the county analysis. It would have been too arbitrary to include court counselor responses with one set of county responses and not another where there were multiple counties within the agencies' jurisdiction. Furthermore, it would have raised validity issues had the same court counselor responses been included (duplicated) in the analysis of several counties (assuming there were multiple responses from all counties within an agency's jurisdiction). In light of these validity concerns and also for analytical considerations, responses from court counselor agencies and correctional organizations were excluded from the area analysis, but were included in the organizational analysis.

The measure of consensus that was utilized for this analysis was conducted using the following techniques: 1) If both respondents in each location (city and county) used one of the terms or concepts listed in Table 3.1, the value for the particular rubric—e.g. general group characteristics, drug crimes, crimes of violence—would equal 1.0; 2) If neither respondent used any of the terms and concepts found within each particular rubric, the value for the rubric would equal zero; 3) If only one of the two respondents utilized any of the terms in a particular rubric, the value would equal .5 for that rubric. The values for all twelve rubrics were then averaged and scaled on a continuous interval in order to obtain the scores by area. Similar techniques were used to determine the degree of consensus among all five respondent categories for each rubric, however the value given to each definitional category for each respondent could only be 1.0 (at least one of the terms or concepts was used) or zero (not used). Lastly, the average scores for all twelve rubrics for each respondent (again using similar techniques) were averaged with all the other respondents within the same organizational category to determine the organizational consensus scores. The consensus scores could then be used to compare and analyze the similarities and variations that may exist between areas, in the use of definitional rubrics, and between respondent categories.

A number of important steps were taken in the present analysis of youth gang and group definitions—and also for the other definitions discussed later in this chapter and for the classification of localities in subsequent chapters—to determine what key components and concepts were commonly used by all respondents, regardless of area and occupational orientation, and what variations may exist across areas and between respondents. Even though there have been many diverse conceptions of gangs through the years (contrast for example Thrasher's [1936] conceptualization with the more recent definitions of Miller [1982], Curry and Spergel, [1988], and Sanders [1994]), there appears to be a broad consensus among contemporary researchers, practitioners, and within the larger body of literature on gangs, that certain components are particularly important for differentiating gangs from other delinquent and criminal youth groups (refer back to the earlier discussion in this chapter).

The present research endeavored to determine which components could be included to formulate a "consensual definition" of youth gangs (see Miller, 1982, p. 19), so that analytical parameters differentiating youth gangs from other nongang groups could be more clearly established. This exercise furthered the analysis in two ways: first, the consensual definition could be compared and contrasted to those definitions commonly found in the literature, thus providing some general idea of how practitioners in North Carolina conceptualize and define the problem; and second, the consensual definition could be used to determine — by directly asking respondents who self-reported youth gang or group problems — whether the definition characterized the nature of their problem. In other words, if respondents agree that the definition reflects the problem in their communities or jurisdictions, and they also self-reported youth gang problems, the validity and reliability of their assessments may be arguably strong; however, if respondents disagree with the definition, the validity of their assessments becomes a greater concern. Since it was a goal of this project to determine the areas that were having actual or perceived youth gang and group problems, ascertain their prevalence across communities, and define the perceived scope and nature of their criminal activities, this particular definitional exercise was important.

The method chosen for establishing the consensual youth gang definition came from the ideas and procedures discovered in Miller's (1982) survey research. His definition of youth gang was derived from concepts and terms (described as elements) provided by an array of respondents (309 from a variety of organizations such as police, probation, grassroots, community service, and schools) from 121 agencies in 26 cities across the United States. Miller discovered that there was an 85 percent consensus on six definitional elements, which thus provided the opportunity to conceive a definition of youth gangs (see earlier discussion) and then to subsequently identify some twenty different categories and subcategories of law-violating youth groups (of which only three were actual "gangs": turf gangs, fighting gangs, and gain-oriented gangs). The forthcoming analysis highlights the consensus of definitions: first by area where there were multiple respondents, then by definitional criteria across areas and categories, and lastly by definition for all respondent categories.

The information in Table 3.4 identifies the cities (N=12) and counties (N=36) where there were multiple respondents who self-reported youth gang or group problems, or were uncertain. The table also reports the degree of consensus discovered between respondents for the eleven definitional criteria used to characterize youth gangs and groups. Again, the scores for each location were calculated by first determining the degree of consensus between respondents in each area for each of the eleven gang/group definitional rubrics (e.g. 1.0, .5, 0), and then calculating the average for all eleven scores. In order to classify the nature of the problem in each locality (gang, group, both, unsure), both respondents from each jurisdiction had to self-report gang or group problems in the questionnaire. For the 12 cities identified for this analysis, there were six (50 percent) that could be tentatively classified as having youth gang problems (incidentally, respondents in all of these cities also reported nongang groups within their localities), and three (25 percent) classified as having only youth group problems. In the remaining three cities (25 percent), respondents reported uncertainty about the nature of their problems. There were ten counties (27.8 percent) where multiple respondents cited youth gang problems, 13 (36.1 percent) where the problem reportedly involved only youth groups, and six (16.7 percent) where there was uncertainty. For the remaining seven counties (19.4 percent), there were no self-reported youth gang or group problems, nor uncertainty that a collective youth crime problem existed. Among the areas that were classified as experiencing youth gang problems, there were generally higher consensus scores between respondents for the definitions of youth gang when compared to areas where youth groups were the problem, or for those areas where uncertainty or no problem was reported. Interestingly, there was no discordance in the consensus of the problem for each jurisdiction with multiple respondents, even though there may have been some minor differences in the criteria used to define the problem; in essence, there was 100 percent concurrence on the self-reported nature of the problem and the consensual definition by area. Therefore, the classification of the areas that had multiple respondents must generally be considered more valid than those localities where there was only one respondent[3] (79.4 percent). This does not necessarily imply that the local-

---

3. The following chapter identifies all the locations where respondents cited youth gang and/or group problems, regardless of whether there was one or multiple responses from each respective location. The central purpose of the present analysis is to examine levels of consensus.

ities where only one response was available makes the information provided automatically suspect (the uncorroborated data may in fact be accurate), but it does in effect limit the strength of any conclusions that can be drawn.

There was a moderate pattern in consensus scores based on the populations of the areas: Charlotte, Durham, Fayetteville, and Greensboro — all relatively large urban areas — had the highest consensus scores in the city sample; Mecklenburg, Forsyth, Gilford, Buncombe, and Cumberland Counties (four of the five largest in the State) attained the highest scores within the county sample. Beyond these areas, the consensus scores followed no distinct patterns. This pattern is not all that surprising, since respondents from the more populated areas also generally reported more serious and persistent youth gang and group problems. It may be reasonable to assert that the organizations within these areas may have a more informed understanding of the problem (or a least a more ingrained conceptualization of the problem). Spergel et al. (1990), by comparison, found slightly higher consensus scores for areas experiencing emerging gang problems when compared to those areas that were experiencing chronic, or more serious, problems; however, the authors admitted obtaining more respondents from the larger cities with chronic gang problems.

Table 3.4
Average Degree of Consensus on
Gang and Group Definitional Criteria by Area
(Multiple Responses)

Cities (N=12)

	Gang	Group
Albermarle**	.59	.56
Ashboro	.46	.41
Charlotte*	.73	.68
Clinton**	.55	.50
Durham*	.68	.64
Fayetteville*	.64	.55
Graham**	.55	.59
Greensboro*	.59	.50
Lenoir*	.55	.50
Mt. Airy*	.55	.46
Shelby	.50	.36
Thomasville	.46	.41

Counties (N=36)

	Gang	Group		Gang	Group
Alexander**	.59	.50	Hoke*	.59	.50
Avery**	.55	.55	Iredell**	.64	.59
Bladen	.55	.46	Johnston	.59	.55
Brunswick**	.59	.50	Lee***	.50	.55
Buncombe*	.68	.55	McDow.***	.50	.50
Burke***	.55	.46	Mecklnbg*	.69	.59
Caldwell*	.64	.59	Montgom.	.55	.50
Catawba**	.50	.55	Onslow**	.64	.55
Chatham**	.59	.55	Orange	.46	.50
Columbus	.55	.41	Randolph	.50	.41
Cumberland*	.64	.59	Richmond	.41	.36
Duplin**	.55	.41	Rocking.**	.50	.54
Edgecombe*	.59	.46	Sampson***	.46	.46
Forsyth*	.68	.55	Union**	.55	.59
Gilford*	.64	.59	Wake*	.68	.64
Harnet**	.59	.55	Wilkes**	.55	.46
Haywood***	.50	.41	Wilson***	.50	.41
Hertford*	.55	.46	Yadkin**	.59	.50

multiple respondents reported youth gang problems*
multiple respondents reported youth group problems only**
multiple respondents reported uncertainty***

The discussion now turns from the general consensus scores by area to the specific consensus scores for each of the eleven definitional rubrics. Listed in the first column of Table 3.5 are the definitional criteria followed by the consensus scores for each criteria based on area and the five professional orientations of respondents. The data in this table indicate a very significant pattern: there was greater consensus of the definition of youth gang and group across areas when compared to respondent categories. This finding demonstrates that the professional orientation and agency affiliation of respondents may have been less influential than the location from which duties were performed. A geographical effect and physical proximity, as Spergel et al. (1990) also discovered, may ostensibly have a stronger influence on gang and group definitions than the effect of professional network.

Table 3.5
Average Degree of Consensus Across 48 Areas and Five Respondent Categories
(Gang and Group Definition Criteria)

	Area		Respondents (N=257)	
	Gang	Group	Gang	Group
General Group Charact.	.70	.66	.55	.41
Group Org. Charact.	.68	.39	.45	.37
Non-Criminal Act.	.25	.20	.25	.29
Drug Crimes	.66	.59	.60	.55
Crimes of Violence	.69	.43	.61	.47
Property Crimes	.33	.66	.39	.58
General Criminal Act.	.45	.42	.37	.41
Collective Symbols	.66	.28	.56	.32
Personal Symbols	.66	.20	.41	.20
Adult Member Involv.	.79	.66	.66	.56
Reside in Same Locale	.42	.30	.33	.21
Over all areas/categories:	.57	.44	.47	.40

Across areas, the definitional rubrics that had the highest consensus scores (at least 66 percent) for the definition of youth gang included general group characteristics, group organizational characteristics, crimes of violence, drug crimes, collective and personal symbols, and adult involvement. Whereas for youth groups, the key defining characteristics were general group characteristics, drug crimes, property crimes, and adult member involvement. These general differences appear to comport to established research that examined collective youth crime from an activity and structural perspective (e.g. Cohen, 1969; Curry and Spergel, 1988; Miller, 1982; Sanders, 1994; Klein and Maxson, 1989), rather than from behavioral and theoretical perspectives (Moore, 1988; Hagedorn, 1988; Horowitz, 1990). However, the low consensus scores for *reside in same locale* (for gangs) may be further indication that the traditional sense of turf or territory within the neighborhood has become less important. "A gang may now hang out, socialize, or do business in different parts of the neighborhood, city, or county. It may no longer need — as much — a specific location or the same center or building as a point of identification or control for each of these purposes" (Spergel, 1995, p.88); thus, the introduction of other dimensions, such as social and economic concerns (e.g. illicit opportunities), potentially complicates the original ideas of territoriality — control and symbolic identification.

Defining gang and group did not appear to be as problematic across areas, since the higher consensus scores in the most important distinguishing characteristics (group organizational characteristics, crimes of violence, property crimes, and collective and personal symbols) appear to indicate that respondents could differentiate between these two types of collectives in their cities and counties. However, after examining the data across the five respondent categories, there appears to be less certainty in distinguishing these collectives. Even though the consensus scores were somewhat higher for the characteristics that go into defining youth gangs, the differences were not as pronounced. In light of the data presented in these tables, it may be appropriate to conclude that there was greater disagreement on definitions based strictly on professional orientation, but there was greater agreement between respondents (regardless of professional orientation) located in the same cities and counties. These findings complicate and make more difficult the ability to comparably and accurately assess the scope and nature of the problem by respondent category, but it does provide the opportunity to assess the problem using area consensus data.

The average degree of consensus for each respondent category on all definitional variables is illustrated in Table 3.6. There was a higher degree of consensus among respondents on what characteristics constitute a youth gang, although the difference was only statistically significant at the .05 level. The highest definitional consensus for youth gangs and groups was provided by respondents from sheriffs' departments and corrections; the most significant statistical variations between consensus scores — for the definitions of youth gang and group provided by each respondent categories — were demonstrated by sheriffs' departments and juvenile services (court counselors). Based on these descriptive statistics, it may be inferred that respondents from sheriffs' departments and juvenile services found greater distinction between youth gangs and groups, or at least had a better idea of what constitutes a youth gang. But for the other respondent categories, the distinguishing characteristics may have been more difficult to discern. Recent research on youth gangs (Spergel et al., 1990) noted a similar pattern in the consensus of definitions among a wide array of respondent categories, namely higher consensus among law enforcement and corrections, and less consensus within academic, grassroots, and community/youth services settings.

Table 3.6
Average Degree of Consensus on Definitional
Criteria for Youth Gang and Youth Group
by Respondent Category

Respondent Category	Youth Gang		Youth Group	
	(N)	(%)	(%)	(t)
Police	59	.62	.49	ns
Sheriff	62	.67	.51	*
Schools	86	.47	.43	ns
Juvenile Serv.	32	.59	.46	*
Corrections	11	.61	.55	ns
Average over five areas:		.58	.49	*

$p \le 0.05^*$ $p \le 0.01^{**}$ $p \le 0.001^{***}$ ns= not significant

Based on the information provided by respondents and the analysis in this section, respondents from all categories commonly characterized youth groups as loose-knit networks composed of individuals who regularly associated with each other and participated in general criminal activities, but typically absent were some of the key elements they used to characterize gangs, such as specific criminal activities, an established identity (e.g. names), and some sense of structure and organization. Though some youth groups may have been very capable of maintaining unity and some type of structure, most groups were best characterized as ephemeral and lacking cohesion, which militates against the groups' abilities to perpetuate, particularly when exposed to external pressures (Cohen, 1969). Thus, by using the criteria where at least two-thirds of the respondents across 48 areas agreed, the consensual definition of youth gang for this study can be generally defined as :

> a collective of youths — most likely young adults (16 and over) — that has a discernible organizational structure, whose members recurrently interact and congregate in particular areas or neighborhoods, use collective and individual symbols for identification purposes, and engage predominantly in acts of violence (including threats and intimidation) and drug-related crimes.

Conversely, a youth group displays only general group characteristics with no discernible structure, and is most likely composed of adults whose primary criminal activity involves property and less serious offenses. The extent to which respondents in gang problem areas agree with the above consensual gang definition will be revisited in the following chapter on the prevalence and location of law-violating youth groups.

Generally, respondents from corrections, police agencies, and sheriff's departments, especially those agencies experiencing actual or perceived youth gang problems, emphasized the criminal elements within their definitions—i.e. references were quite often made about violent criminal activities, drug activities, and other general criminal patterns—and the organizational structure of gangs. Respondents from the other two organizational categories—court counselors agencies and schools—emphasized general group characteristics and organization, general criminal activities, and the use of collective and personal symbols, regardless of whether their respective areas were experiencing youth gang problems or not. The use of symbols was widely reported by all respondents, but it was perceived as a more common trait or characteristic in the larger towns and cities. The use of symbols, according to Jackson and McBride (1985, p. 71), is "an essential communication medium that advertises [the gang], describes its social structure, records its conflicts, and exalts its lifestyle." A similar pattern was also discovered in the use of gang names; respondents, particularly law enforcement organizations, were more likely to identify youth gangs by names where the nature of the problem was perceived as more serious, and quite often, many of the most serious problems occurred in the larger cities. The display of colors, predominantly in the wearing of team sport jackets and jogging suits, was perceived as most prevalent among black youth gangs. Less uniformity was reported for white, Hispanic, and Asian youth gangs; the most common characteristic included pierced ears, the wearing of oversized or baggy clothes, and wearing baseball caps backwards. Youth groups displayed far fewer personally distinguishing symbols—symbols that invariably tie an individual to a certain group.

Finally, the two most important criteria respondents used to distinguish youth gangs from groups across areas pertained to organizational and structural characteristics. Organization and structure are particularly important for understanding youth gangs, since these two characteristics have a significant influence on gang development and behavioral patterns (e.g. group processes, criminal activities). The extent of gang organization in different communities, whether perceived to be loosely knit or more cohesive in nature, may have influenced the approaches used by organizations to mitigate and control the problem. Because it is important to understand the correlations between the characteristics of the problem (e.g. gang versus group) and the steps taken by organizations to deal with it, this topic will be discussed in greater depth in a forthcoming chapter.

C. Identifying Youth Gang and Youth Group Members

In its essence, a youth gang or group member is an individual who associates with and participates in a known and identifiable gang or group within the community. However, the research literature has emphasized that individual-level participation within youth collectives may vary widely, where involvement may be more or less frequent and serious. Membership terms such as "wannabe," core member, core cliques, leader, floater, regular, associate, and veteran have evolved to differentiate the levels of participation and commitment within youth collectives (see e.g. Cohen and Short, 1958; Cloward and Ohlin, 1960; Short and Strodtbeck, 1965; Cohen, 1969; Klein, 1971; Gold and Mattick, 1974; Hagedorn, 1988; Taylor, 1990). From a public policy perspective, it is important to know what different positions and roles youth gang and group members play within the local gang and group context; since it has been argued that the more committed the member (e.g. core, regular, or leader), the greater level of participation in gang and group activities, including crime and deviance (Klein, 1968b; Pitchess, 1979; Sarnecki, 1986; Vigil, 1988).

Different organizations within the community have different strategic and tactical reasons for identifying different types of gang and group members: law enforcement typically focuses on the hardcore members and leaders for crime control purposes, even though they may make up only a small proportion of the collective; while on the other hand, social agencies and school officials are generally more concerned with fringe or "wannabe" members and issues of prevention (Spergel, 1995). Because members may move from fringe or peripheral positions to regular, hardcore positions (or vice-versa), it becomes important that organizations have a method for identifying and monitoring gang and group members and their activities. The purpose of this particular analysis, therefore, was to present information on the most commonly used methods or techniques for identifying members. The methods and techniques used—whether they are systematic or not—likely has some effect on the organizations' capabilities to apprehend the most serious members, make estimates on the size and seriousness of the larger groups and gangs to which they belong, and target the individual member and their collectives for prevention and intervention purposes.

Analytical procedures used to define and differentiate youth gangs from groups were similarly used to examine how respondents identified gang and group members. A number of dichotomous variables, produced by the content analysis of responses to the following open-ended question (Appendix, Section III), emerged to illustrate the diversity of methods used by respondents (Table 3.7):

What are your organization's principal ways of identifying a youth group or gang member?

These methods included knowledge of member residence, the group locale, using formal identification procedures, criminal investigation, group association, and general observance. There were no differences in the ordering of the methods, insofar as the frequency of their selection, based on the perceived nature of the problem, and there was only one statistically significant variation in the frequency of methods used. Respondents relied more heavily on *group association* to identify youth gang members, most likely because gang youth used more conspicuous ways of identifying themselves as members, such as in the use of certain colors and clothing.

The most frequently cited method was *formal identification*, followed closely by *investigation*. These two methods are somewhat related. The former is much broader in scope and applies to methods that could have been used by all respondents, regardless of organizational orientation; whereas the latter method refers more specifically to formal investigations of criminal violations or infractions within the justice system (e.g. probation violation). These two methods involve the most systematic processes for identifying members, primarily because organizations are more likely to adhere to formalized procedures and guidelines. The next most frequently cited method, *general observation*, was the designation used by respondents who did not articulate specific methods. However, it was quite possible that respondents used a number of more general and less systematic methods for identifying members.

Table 3.7
Frequency of Dichotomous Variables derived from
Content Analysis of Youth Gang and Youth Group Member Identification Methods
(N=257)

Variable	Youth Gangs		Youth Groups		
	(N)	(%)	(N)	(%)	(t)
Formal Identification	145	56.4	161	62.6	ns
Investigation	118	45.9	133	51.8	ns
General Observation	108	42.0	127	49.4	ns
Group Association	68	26.5	44	17.1	**
Other (e.g. informants)	40	15.5	35	13.6	ns
None	35	13.6	34	13.2	ns
Group Locale	26	10.1	18	7.0	ns
Residence	21	8.2	18	7.0	ns

$p \leq 0.05^*$ $p \leq 0.01^{**}$ $p \leq 0.001^{**}$ ns=not significant

The three least cited methods were *group association, group locale*, and *residence. Group association*, which comports to some of the propositions implicit in the variable group locale, assumes that individuals who are frequently observed in the presence of other gang and group members — particularly if the individual member displays symbols (e.g. sport jacket, hats, colors) — may also be members of the collective. Yet, "guilt by association" may lead to labeling and the over-identification of the problem. *Group locale*, presupposes that youth collectives claim certain parts of a neighborhood or particular hang-outs as territory; thus, individuals who frequent these known areas may be considered part of a youth gang or group. This method may be problematic, however. Without corroborative information, organizations may erroneously label youth as members, when in fact the youth may only be friends of true members and may not even participate in gang and group activities.

The least cited method for identifying both gang and group members was *residence*. Covey et al.(1992) assert that residential proximity, or what they term critical mass, is necessary for the formation of delinquent subcultures, therefore residence — particularly low-income, public housing areas (Curry and Spergel, 1988) — should serve as one general method for identifying members. In other words, knowledge of the neighborhoods where gangs and groups persist may serve as a clue for locating their members. This last method may be beneficial in identifying problem neighborhoods, but may be too general to identify members effectively. Lastly, for respondents who cited other, infrequently used methods and techniques, such as self-admission and informant identification, or did not specify any methods whatsoever, the variables *other* and *none* were used to categorize these responses.

1. Factor Analysis

The eight variables, which include two nondescriptive variables, were subjected to a factor analysis using the promax oblique rotation procedure. This procedure, conducted on the 257 respondents who addressed the issue, increased the interpretability of this modest set of variables. The rotated factor analysis resulted in two factors that accounted for 24.0 percent of the variance for youth gang member identifiers, and two factors that accounted for 24.1 percent of the variance for youth groups. The explanatory power was therefore quite weak for both youth gang and group categories. There were apparently other underlying techniques and methods used by respondents that were not brought out in the factoring of the principle components.

Table 3.8 indicates that there were two main methods for identifying youth gang members. Group association loaded most heavily on the first factor, but formal identification methods also loaded moderately on this factor. Because the large proportion of respondents were from the law enforcement category (police and sheriffs' organizations), the loading on these two methods was not surprising; law enforcement organizations, more so than offices and agencies found in any of the other professional categories, actively employ surveillance techniques and gather intelligence on suspects and criminal groups; therefore, these organizations most likely scored high on this factor. Respondents from organizations that rely on information provided by secondary sources (e.g. schools, probation), conversely, received low scores. Factor 2 was dominated by the loading on group locale, though there were light positive loadings for group association, residence, and formal investigation. This factor identifies individuals as youth gang members if they frequented known gang locations, such as street corners, parks, neighborhood lots, and certain locations within schools.

Table 3.8
Promax Rotated Factor Matrix from Factor Analysis
of Correlation Coefficients of Youth Gang Member
Identification Methods (N=216)

Variable	Factor 1	Factor 2
Group Assoc.	.622	.227
General Observ.	.274	-.215
Formal ID	.490	.103
None	-.568	.057
Group Locale	.047	.665
Residence	.067	.254
Investigation	.303	.304
Other	.013	-.302
Eigenvalues	1.12	.800
Variance Explained	(14.0 %)	(10.0%)
Total Variance (24.0 %)		

Table 3.9
Promax Rotated Factor Matrix from Factor Analysis
of Correlation Coefficients of Youth Group Member
Identification Methods (N=157)

Variable	Factor 1	Factor 2
General Observ.	.536	-.327
Formal ID	.484	.248
Group Assoc.	.351	.000
None	-.679	.014
Group Locale	.040	.555
Residence	.030	.372
Investigation	.294	.311
Other	.045	-.169
Eigenvalues	1.19	.741
Variance Explained	(14.0%)	(10.1 %)
Total Variance (24.1%)		

There was only a slight variation on the factor loadings for the two main methods that were used to identify youth group members (Table 3.9). General observation, albeit moderate in weight, loaded heaviest on the first factor, with formal identification and group association also receiving moderate and light loadings, respectively. This factor indicates that there were multiple identification methods, such as the following ones provided by a respondent from a large metropolitan police department: direct association with known gang and group members, confidential source information, graffiti identification by specially trained members, and information from uniform patrol and school liaison officers. Group locale, as discovered in the youth gang analysis, also loaded positively on the second factor; however, the loadings on formal identification and residence were slightly heavier.

2. Analysis of Consensus of Identification Methods

In order to gain a greater understanding of these variables—the conditions under which an individual is identified as either a youth gang or group member—a measurement was again conducted to determine the extent to which the member identification methods were nominated by respondents. This analysis examines the degree of consensus for each member identification method across all areas where there were multiple respondents; then by each identification method for all five respondent categories; and lastly, by identification method based on each respondent category. Once again, the procedures utilized in this analysis were replicated from the study conducted by Spergel et al. (1990). For the first analysis, only those areas where multiple respondents provided surveys were included — 12 cities (20.6%) and 36 (36.0%) counties. City police agencies and the city central school system organizations were the two respondent categories used in the city analysis; county sheriff's department and the county school district organizations were used in the county analysis.

The area-level data (Table 3.10) indicate that there was greater consensus on the methods used to identify members, both gang and group, in areas that were experiencing youth gang problems. In general, there was a slightly higher degree of consensus across areas in methods used to identify gang members compared to group members. Because of the more serious nature of gang activities, respondents may have discovered that certain methods, such as investigation and formal identification, were more effective than others for identifying and monitoring gang members. There was a higher degree of consensus in the most populated cities of Charlotte, Fayetteville, Durham, and Greensboro when you compare these cities to the others in this analysis. However, the consensus scores for the three largest counties — Mecklenburg, Forsyth, and Guilford — were only slightly higher in comparison to counties with smaller populations. Population does not appear to have a significant influence on whether county-level organizations adopt similar approaches and methods for identifying members, despite the fact that more serious problems tend to manifest in the more populated areas, but it does ostensibly influence city-level organizations.

The analysis again turns from the general consensus scores by area to the specific consensus scores for each of the member identification methods. The first column of Table 3.11 identifies the identification methods followed by the consensus scores for each method based on area and the five professional orientations of respondents. The data demonstrate a moderate pattern: the consensus on methods for identifying youth gang members across areas and respondent categories was somewhat higher compared to methods used to identify group members. There were very few differences in scores when comparing area and respondent categories. Neither professional orientation and agency affiliation of respondents nor the location from which duties were performed had an overriding influence on the methods adopted. Geographical effect and physical proximity had only a slightly stronger influence on member identification methods than the effect of professional network.

Table 3.10
Average Degree of Consensus on Gang and Group Member
Identification Methods
(Multiple Respondents)

Cities (N=12)

	Gang	Group
Albermarle**	.50	.44
Ashboro	.38	.31
Charlotte*	.56	.50
Clinton**	.38	.44
Durham*	.50	.56
Fayetteville*	.56	.44
Graham**	.44	.31
Greensboro*	.50	.44
Lenoir*	.44	.50
Mt. Airy*	.56	.50
Shelby	.50	.37
Thomasville	.38	.31

Counties (N=36)

	Gang	Group		Gang	Group
Alexander**	.50.	44	Hoke*	.63	.56
Avery**	.56	.44	Iredell**	.50	.44
Bladen	.44	.38	Johnston	.56	.50
Brunswick**	.50	.44	Lee***	.50	.56
Buncombe*	.56	.50	McDow.***	.50	.50
Burke***	.50	38	Mecklnbg*	.63	.56
Caldwell*	.56	.44	Montgom.	.50	.38
Catawba**	.50	.50	Onslow**	.50	.44
Chatham**	.50	.56	Orange	.44	.38
Columbus	.56	.50	Randolph	.44	.50
Cumberland*	.63	.56	Richmond	.50	.44
Duplin**	.44	.38	Rocking.**	.44	.50
Edgecombe*	.63	.44	Sampson***	.44	.50
Forsyth*	.56	.50	Union**	.50	.44
Gilford*	.63	.44	Wake*	.56	.50
Harnet**	.44	.50	Wilkes**	.44	.38
Haywood***	.50	.38	Wilson***	.38	.31
Hertford*	.56	.50	Yadkin**	.56	.50

multiple respondents reported youth gang problems*
multiple respondents reported youth group problems only**
multiple respondents reported uncertainty***

Table 3.11
Average Degree of Consensus Across 48 Areas
and Five Respondent Categories
(Gang and Group Member Identification Methods)

| | Area | | Respondents (N=257) | |
	Gang	Group	Gang	Group
Formal Identification	.71	.62	.68	.54
General Observation	.60	.63	.55	.62
Investigation	.52	.54	.50	.53
Group Association	.60	.55	.61	.55
Other (e.g. informants)	.39	.30	.36	.31
None	.37	.30	.36	.31
Locale	.31	.26	.32	.26
Residence	.27	.25	.31	.33
Overall areas/categories:	.47	.44	.46	.43

The final analysis in this section involved determining the level of consensus based on respondent category. The scores (1.0 if the identification method was used or 0 if it were not) for the eight dichotomous identification methods (e.g. formal identification, investigation, general observation) were averaged for each respondent in the respective organizational categories. The calculated average of all eight method scores (for each respondent) were then averaged with all the other respondents within the same organizational category to determine the organizational consensus scores. The results of this procedure are illustrated in Table 3.12. There were no significant statistical variations in the consensus scores within each of the professional categories nor across all categories for both types of collectives. However, the data indicate that there was greatest consensus on the methods of identifying both youth gang and group members within the corrections category. The degree of consensus was significantly greater (p< 0.01) than any of the other categories; this disparity may have been due to the more formalized reporting procedures and monitoring programs established by security regulations and other policy guidelines within the North Carolina Department of Corrections, Youth Services Command, and local facilities. One corrections official stated that the principal way of identifying youth gang and group members was through the collection of Security Threat Group information by staff members, which subsequently gets reported to and compiled by the Security Threat Group Intelligence Officer. According to an Assistant Superintendent for Programs at another facility, special training on information gathering and reporting procedures were available through an Institutional Intelligence Gathering Committee.

Table 3.12
Average Degree of Consensus on
Member Identification Methods used by Respondents

Respondent Category	(N)	Youth Gangs (%)	Youth Groups (%)	(t)
Police	59	.44	.37	ns
Sheriff	62	.48	.35	ns
Schools	86	.54	.43	ns
Juv. Serv.	32	.44	.30	ns
Corrections	11	.90	.38	ns
All categories:		.56	.47	ns

ns=not significant

In general terms, there was a slightly higher degree of consensus across professional categories of methods used to identify youth gang members. With the exception of corrections respondents, the highest degree of consensus was found in the school category, the only non-criminal justice category in the study. The most common method used by school officials to identify members was by group association, followed closely by general observation. There were only minor statistical variations between the consensus scores of the other three professional categories. For all respondent categories, formal identification of youth gang and group members was the most prevalent method cited. In most cases, formal identification entailed a process by which member affiliations and activities were closely monitored by authorities, primarily because of antecedent behavioral or criminal infractions related to group activities. The most significant statistical variation (see Table 3.7) between methods cited was the more frequent use of group association to identify gang members; the earlier finding, that youth gangs more often displayed both collective and personal symbols, most likely influenced this variation. Minimal importance was placed on residence and group locale as identification methods for both types of collectives, which may indicate that youth collectives, especially gangs, do not necessarily manifest in particular neighborhoods nor always operate on designated turf, as previous research (Moore, 1978; Spergel, 1990; Taylor, 1990; Covey et al., 1992) has otherwise indicated.

D. Defining Youth Gang and
Youth Group Incidents

The final analysis in this chapter pertains to defining youth gang and group incidents, which are the most important criteria for determining the scope and severity of the problem in certain localities (Spergel et al., 1990). Identifying an incident as gang or group-related may be simple conceptually, but in reality the distinction is very difficult, since it is not always clear or easy to differentiate individually motivated activities from those that are group-related (Sanders, 1994). In most cases, law enforcement definitions have been used as the standard by which to measure and assess the severity of the problem; the severity of the problem, by implication, depends on the level of criminal activities. Yet, even the criteria the law enforcement community use to designate an incident as gang or group-related has been widely diverse and nonstandard.

Two significantly different procedures have been employed to determine whether a gang or group incident has occurred. The incident can be either *gang or group motivated*, whereby the act requires a gang or group modus operandi or involves specific circumstances that consequently enhance the group's status and function; or the act can be *gang or group related*, where an incident must simply involve a suspect, offender or victim, who has been identified as a gang or group member, regardless of motivation and circumstances. The criteria and procedures an organization adopts will largely determine the scope and serious of the problem. The former procedure focuses on the specific circumstances and situation in which the incident may have occurred, the latter procedure focuses on the individual as a gang or group member (Spergel, 1995). A number of studies have also supported the criterion of criminal activity, particularly violent behavior, as the major component for defining an incident as youth gang-related (see Miller, 1982; Needle and Stapleton, 1983; Sanders, 1994), yet the criteria and conditions under which an incident is designated remain unclear. Far fewer studies have even suggested what activity or criteria defines an incident as youth group-related, though previous research and the earlier findings of this study indicated that group-related activities were generally less serious in nature than gang activities. The most critical issue is distinguishing between gang and group motivated crime, and the crime committed by members that is not motivated or related to the collective (Spergel, 1995).

A content analysis of the definitions provided by the 257 respondents who addressed the following question (Appendix, Section III) revealed five definitional components, or dichotomous variables, used to define both youth gang and group-related incidents (Table 3.13).

What is your organization's definition of a youth group or gang-related incident or case?

For both collectives, the most frequently cited criterion was the involvement of multiple offenders in incidents; this was discovered for all respondents, with the exception of police, who relied more on the involvement of individually known members. The least cited criteria were incident locale and the involvement of rival youth gangs or groups. School officials were the only respondents who used rival gang or group involvement as one of the criteria for designating incidents.

Table 3.13
Frequency of Dichotomous Variables Used to
Define Youth Gang and Group-Related Incidents
(N=257)

Variable	(N)	Youth Gang (%)	(N)	Youth Group (%)	(t)
Multiple Offenders	179	69.6	176	68.5	ns
Known Members	119	46.3	74	28.8	**
Group Motivated	59	42.0	311	2.1	**
Rival Groups Involved	22	8.6	13	5.1	ns
Incident Locale	8	3.1	6	2.3	ns

p≤0.05* p≤0.01** p≤0.001*** ns=not significant

Even though the key criteria for defining incidents were the same for both types of collectives, the frequency for citing the criteria was generally higher for youth gang-related incidents, particularly for *known members* and *group motivated*. These two criteria, which produced the only statistically significant variations between gang and group variables, were particularly important for differentiating gang from group-related incidents. To some extent, this finding may increase the credibility of the index crime estimates provided by respondents in the forthcoming chapters. The heavy reliance on multiple offenders for both gang and group-related incidents may indicate that individually motivated and initiated criminal acts, even if the individual is a known gang or group member, were not necessarily qualified or designated as gang or group-related. Moreover, the reliance on the multiple-offender criterion further suggests that respondents associated gang and group-related crime with co-offending, which may imply group function and motivation. This is despite the fact that a modest proportion of the respondents articulated group motivation (modus operandi) as a key criterion. Secondary importance was placed on knowledge that the individual youth belonged to a youth gang or group, and the locality of the incident and involvement with rival groups as defining criteria demonstrated very little importance.

1. Factor Analysis

The factor analysis identified two types of methods used by respondents to define gang-related incidents, and only one for group-related incidents. In defining gang-related incidents, the factoring of the five variables produced two factors that explained 52.2 percent of the variance among variables, while the one factor for group-related incidents explained 32.3 percent of the variance. The data in Table 3.14 illustrate the loadings for these factors for both collectives. For youth gang-related incidents, the multiple offender variable loaded most heavily on the first factor, with a moderate loading on known individual members; there was also a light positive loading on the group motivation variable and a negative loading on rival group involvement. One respondent—a senior ranking police officer from a large city—scored high on this factor by describing a youth gang-related incident case as one that involved three to four known gang members who aided and abetted one another in the commission of crimes that furthered gang objectives. Respondents who relied on police or informant information received moderate to low scores on this factor. Rival group involvement loaded heaviest on the second factor, with individual known members loading moderately positive, and the other three variables loading negatively. A police criminal investigator, who scored high on this factor, stated that most gang-related incidents resulted from gang rivalries that involved the sale of crack cocaine.

Table 3.14
Promax Rotated Factor Matrix from Factor Analysis
of Correlation Coefficients of Youth Gang
and Youth Group Incidents (N=231)

Variables	Youth Gang Factor 1	Factor 2	Youth Group Factor 1
Multiple Offenders	.775	-.302	.623
Rival Group Involv.	-.358	.704	.105
Group Motivated	.344	-.313	-.321
Known Members	.689	.489	.416
Location	.284	-.300	.145
Eigenvalues	1.40	1.21	1.60
Variance Explained	(28.0%)	(24.2%)	(32.3%)
Total Variance		(52.2 %)	(32.3%)

The only factor that emerged for youth group-related incidents was dominated by the multiple offenders variable, but there was also a moderate positive loading on known members; the other three variables received statistically light loadings. Many respondents characterized youth group-related incidents as those collectively perpetrated by small, indistinguishable groups. A juvenile criminal investigator's comments on the recent rise in auto thefts and burglaries in his jurisdiction serves as an excellent, if not typical, case in point: "It has been our experience that most of these break-ins are being committed by juveniles, operating in small to medium groups. Our office has charged approximately 35-40 individuals over the past two years with vehicle break-ins, most of these [perpetrated] in groups of three to ten members."

2. Analysis of Definitional Consensus

This final section, in maintaining the consistency of the analysis presented up to this point, examines the extent to which respondents nominated the methods used to identify gang and group-related incidents. The consensus scores across areas are examined, followed by an aggregate analysis of methods utilized by all respondents; the discussion concludes with an analysis of methods used based on respondent category. Across cities and counties where there were multiple respondents, there was once again stronger consensus found for those methods used to identify youth gang-related incidents (Table 3.15). The greatest differences in the consensus scores, when comparing areas where gangs and groups were present, were generally found in the most populated cities and counties, particularly the cities of Charlotte, Durham and Fayetteville, and the counties of Guilford and Forsyth. In these areas, respondents appeared to have the best or clearest idea of what factors need to be present in order to classify an incident as gang-related; conversely, respondents were only able to agree on a few methods or factors that were necessary to classify an incident as group-related. Compared to the analysis and findings in the other sections, particularly in the cities and counties just mentioned, the consensus score patterns were remarkably similar, in that the most populated areas had the highest scores and for all areas the scores were generally higher for definitions and identification methods as they related to youth gangs. Ostensibly, it was easier for respondents to reach a consensus where the problem manifested in the most serious form, perhaps because of more systematic identification methods and better information systems for dealing with gang problems (see e.g. Spergel et al., 1990).

Table 3.15
Average Degree of Consensus on Methods for Identifying
Gang and Group-Related Incidents
(Multiple Respondents)

Cities (N=12)	Gang	Group
Albermarle**	.50	.40
Ashboro	.40	.40
Charlotte*	.70	.50
Clinton**	.40	.30
Durham*	.60	.30
Fayetteville*	.60	.40
Graham**	.40	.40
Greensboro*	.50	.30
Lenoir*	.60	.50
Mt. Airy*	.50	.40
Shelby	.40	.40
Thomasville	.30	.30

Counties (N=36)

	Gang	Group		Gang	Group
Alexander**	.50	.50	Hoke*	.60	.40
Avery**	.40	.40	Iredell**	.50	.50
Bladen	.40	.40	Johnston	.40	.40
Brunswick**	.40	.40	Lee***	.30	.30
Buncombe*	.60	.50	McDow.***	.40	.30
Burke***	.40	.50	Mecklnbg*	.60	.50
Caldwell*	.60	.50	Montgom.	.40	.40
Catawba**	.50	.40	Onslow**	.50	.30
Chatham**	.50	.50	Orange	.50	.50
Columbus	.40	.50	Randolph	.40	.50
Cumberland*	.60	.60	Richmond	.50	.40
Duplin**	.50	.60	Rocking.**	.40	.30
Edgecombe*	.50	.50	Sampson***	.40	.30
Forsyth*	.60	.40	Union**	.40	.30
Gilford	*.60	.40	Wake*	.60	.60
Harnet**	.40	.30	Wilkes**	.50	.50
Haywood***	.50	.40	Wilson***	.50	.40
Hertford*	.60	.50	Yadkin**	.40	.30

multiple respondents reported youth gang problems*
multiple respondents reported youth group problems only**
multiple respondents reported uncertainty***

There was greatest consensus among respondents, across all areas and by category, that *multiple offenders* was the key criterion for identifying incidents as gang and group-related (Table 3.16). An incident must involve the direct cooperation, support, and complicity of others during the actual commission of a crime for it to be considered gang or group-related. This finding may substantially strengthen the respondent estimates of index crimes attributed to collectives, since solo-offending, even if the individual belonged to a gang or group, may not have necessarily constituted a gang or group-related incident. In other words, knowledge that an individual belonged to a gang or group was important, but it did not mean that respondents automatically classified an offense committed by a known member as gang or group-related.

Table 3.16
Average Degree of Consensus Across 48 Areas
and Five Respondent Categories
(Gang and Group Incident Identification Methods)

| | Area | | Respondents (N=257) | |
	Gang	Group	Gang	Group
Multiple Offenders	.75	.67	.70	.61
Known Members	.66	.60	.64	.59
Group Motivated	.53	.31	.53	.34
Rival Groups Involv.	.51	.27	.44	.26
Incident Locale	.44	.42	.42	.41
Overall all areas/categories:	.58	.45	.54	.44

However, group motivated and rival group involvement were particularly important criteria for identifying incidents as gang-related. As mentioned earlier, the group motivation criterion focuses attention on the circumstances of the incident, which may not only provide a more precise understanding of the scope of the problem, but also may provide a more valid measurement. The stronger score on this criterion as it related to gangs may demonstrate that a large number of respondents found it important to distinguish between gang and non-gang motivated offenses. Respondents, to some extent, may have been able to discern, or they at least made some effort to differentiate, between crimes that had some larger gang interest and those that did not. Spergel (1995), for example, identifies gang-related incidents as those that enhance the status or function of the gang, such as intergang violence, turf protection, intimidation, and recruitment. Since rival group involvement also received modest consensus scores as a criterion in the gang analysis, there is evidence that respondents were at least identifying, if not necessarily using, key criteria for differentiating gang from non-gang motivated crimes. The least significant criterion was the location of the incident, demonstrating that most respondents did not rely on spatial nor geographical factors in determining whether an incident was related to gangs or groups. Unlike the analysis found in previous sections, there were no notable differences in the scores based on area and organizational category, which indicates that neither the location of the respondents nor the respondent category had a greater influence over the other with regard to the criteria used to identify incidents.

Table 3.17
Average Degree of Consensus on Methods for Identifying
Youth Gang and Group-Related Incidents
by Respondent Category

Respondent Category	(N)	Youth Gang (%)	Youth Group (%)	(t)
Police	59	.52	.33	*
Sheriff	62	.50	.33	*
Schools	86	.47	.35	ns
Juv. Serv.	32	.33	.28	ns
Corrections	11	.65	.62	ns
All categories:		.50	.38	ns

$p \leq 0.05*$ $p \leq 0.01**$ $p \leq 0.001***$ ns=not significant

Finally, the five components were scaled to determine the average degree of consensus within each respondent category (Table 3.17). Generally, there was greatest agreement on the criteria used to identify youth gang-related incidents, but an additional test indicated that the two law enforcement categories demonstrated the only statistically significant variations in scores. The average degree of consensus among respondents for both types of collectives was greatest for the corrections category, where it was once again discovered that standardized reporting procedures, information gathering, and written guidelines significantly influenced consensus scores. Court counselors had the lowest scores, which, conversely, may indicate a need for standardized reporting practices or awareness training. There were higher consensus scores on the criteria used to define youth gang-related incidents for all respondent categories, with police organizations exhibiting the widest variation in scores when comparing the two collectives. Police organizations most frequently cited the criterion of individually known members as a defining feature for gang-related incidents, and coupled with a greater emphasis on the group motivated criterion, it could be inferred that police used the strictest criteria to define youth gang-related incidents.

In summarizing the key points in this section, respondents cited five criteria — multiple offenders, known individual members, group motivated, involvement of rival groups, and incident locale — for identifying incidents as either gang or group-related. The analysis further revealed that, for both youth gang and gang-related incidents, the most important criterion was the involvement of multiple offenders. The factor analysis initially demonstrated this finding, and the subsequent analysis of consensus across areas, by criteria, and by respondent categories also provided supporting evidence. However, two other factors, group motivation and rival group involvement, did not attain significance in the factoring procedure, but proved to be important criteria in the analysis of consensus, particularly for identifying gang-related incidents. To establish the consensual definition of gang-related incident for this study, it was again necessary to include the criteria where at least two-thirds of the respondents across 48 areas agreed. However, because group motivation is a critical criterion for differentiating gang from non-gang and other group-related incidents, this criterion was also included in formulating the study's operational definition. In considering all three criteria that attained some degree importance in the analysis (multiple offenders, known members, and group motivated), the consensual definition of gang-related incident can be defined as:

> *a violation of the criminal law—involving multiple offenders whose gang affiliations have been established and are known to authorities —for the purpose of enhancing the status, functions, or interests of the gang.*

Establishing this consensual definition provided the framework for evaluating the estimates provided by respondents of the proportion of index crime they attributed to youth gangs. In the absence of crime statistics on youth gangs, the criteria respondents used to make their estimates becomes critically important for validity reasons. By using an operational and standardized definition of youth gang-related incident, it became possible to determine the extent to which respondents agreed or disagreed with the definition. In other words, a respondent's index crime estimates could be questionable if they did not agree with the definitional parameters established by consensus. Conversely, if there is a high concurrence on the definition, there may be reason to believe that the crime estimates were reasonably accurate.

E. Conclusion

The primary objective of this chapter was to examine the key components of the definitions that constitute youth gang and groups, gang and group members, and gang and group-related incidents. Rather than focus attention on one or the other phenomenon, the methods and procedures used provided the opportunity to identify any variations between the two types of collectives. Using an analytical method for evaluating and establishing working definitions—versus a more abstract approach, such as defining the problem within a social context—the salient organizational and operative properties found in respondent definitions of gangs and groups could be established, analyzed, and compared (see Ball and Curry, 1995). Awareness of the distinctions between youth gang and group definitions was necessarily important, since the components and characteristics that emerged through both the factor-analytic and descriptive statistical procedures established the parameters by which the scope and nature of the problem could be reasonably assessed. Specifying an area or locality as one that is experiencing a youth gang or group problem is critically important for prevention and intervention programming: each type of problem calls for a different strategy based on valid, theoretical considerations (Miller, 1990; Curry and Spergel, 1993).

A variety of definitions were offered by respondents, therefore it was necessary to use factor analysis to provide the initial insight into the underlying structure of very complex sets of data. Because the primary purpose was to discover a common structure underlying the data, rather than to confirm or negate a hypothesized structure, the factor analysis was considered exploratory rather than confirmatory (see Dillon and Goldstein, 1984). For all the factors derived using this model, the greatest explanatory strength—those factors that could cumulatively explain at least the majority of the variance (Stevens, 1986)—came from the definitions of youth gang and the definition of youth gang-related incident. The factors derived from the variables in the other definitions could only account for 18.3 to 34.5 percent of the variance, which indicates only limited explanatory power for those definitions. In fact, the factor analysis, employed with the intention of summarizing the interrelationships among the strongest variables, actually illustrated the diversity in the definitions provided by respondents. This was particularly true for the definitions of gang and group, but less so in defining member and identifying the criteria used to designate incidents as gang or group-related.

Because of the limitations discovered in the factor analyses, a measure of consensus was necessary to gain a better understanding of what may have affected the diversity of definitions. One of the premises explored involved ascertaining whether the definitions were influenced by the professional orientation of respondents or perhaps by their geographic location across North Carolina. For the definitions of gang and group, the geographical proximity of respondents was the more influential factor, which demonstrates that, regardless of the respondents' professional background, distinguishing and defining the problem was more directly affected by local gang and group characteristics. The criteria for identifying members and incidents, however, were almost equally influenced by geography and the professional orientation of respondents. The information derived from the analysis of consensus was helpful in establishing the operational definitions of youth gang and gang-related incident, both of which will be used for examining the problem in greater detail in the remainder of this study.

In general, respondents characterized youth gangs as organized (albeit loosely) collectives whose members often displayed personal and collective symbols; these collectives were also perceived as heavily involved in violence—though not necessarily manifesting from turf-protection—and drug-related activities. Gang members were typically identified by their affiliation with known gangs in the local community and by formal iden- tification by the local authorities. The key criterion used to identify gang-related incidents was the involvement of multiple offenders and knowledge that the individual was an active gang member. Substantial emphasis was also placed on gang motivation (modus operandi) and rival gang involvement as criteria for designating an incident as gang-related. Previous research (Spergel, 1991b, Spergel et. al., 1994b) emphasized the importance of considering motivation, function, and circumstances in designating an incident as gang-related. Had respondents not identified the definitional criterion of *group motivated* as important, it would have been even more difficult to assess the validity of the estimates of gang-related index offenses. While there was no method available for determining whether respondents systematically considered the group motivation factor in their assessments of the problem, there may be some comfort in knowing that the majority of respondents did agree that it was one of the top three most important considerations. In contrast, youth groups were not considered well-organized or even structured, and though considered capable of violent behavior, these collectives were perceived as more actively involved in property crimes and other general criminal activities. General observation, which encompassed a wide variety of practices, was the primary method for identifying youth group members, with moderate importance placed on group association and formal identification methods. As with youth gang-related incidents, respondents also relied on the criterion of multiple offenders to identify youth group-related incidents, but little emphasis was placed on the motivations for committing the offenses.

The complexity and elusiveness of definitional components not only demonstrates the need for caution in assessing the scope and nature of the problem, but that the problem also comes in different forms and appears variable. With the diversity of definitions comes a number of other problems: labeling or mislabeling minor delinquent or criminal acts as youth gang or group-related, when in actuality they are neither, may widen or exaggerate the problem; and conversely, failure to identify a youth gang or group problem in its serious form constitutes denial, and may lead to the growth and development of the problem if it is not addressed (Spergel et al., 1990). Even though there appear to be many variations of the collective youth crime problem, the consensual definitions of youth gang and gang-related incident that were developed in this chapter provide the opportunity to make a more meaningful assessment of the prevalence and location of youth collectives throughout the State and the perceived seriousness of their activities. More importantly, the consensual definitions establish the parameters by which the more serious gang problem areas can be identified and differentiated from the less serious group problem areas, both across locations and over time. Ball and Curry (1995, p. 239), however, caution that "[d]efinitions tend to be based on those aspects of the phenomena in question that were most visible and most salient at the time. As the relative visibility of various phenomenal features change with research progress, and the salience of these various features shifts with new perspectives and purposes, redefinition often becomes necessary."

4

Prevalence and Location of Law-Violating Youth Groups

A. Introduction

The prevalence and location of law-violating youth groups throughout the United States has been well documented in the research literature. Miller's (1982) study from the 1970s discovered the presence of youth gangs in 13 percent of all cities with populations greater than 10,000 and in almost 30 percent of all cities with populations of 100,000 or more. In the 1980s, Needle and Stapleton (1983) reported that gangs were even more prevalent — 39 percent of their sample — in cities with populations that ranged from 100,000 to 250,000. More recently, Curry (1994) discovered that 88.2 percent of the largest U.S. cities reported youth gang problems, and for cities with populations over 25,000, 59 percent reported gang crime problems. Between the period of Spergel et al.'s (1990) 1987 survey and Curry's (1994) research, there has been a 23.8 percent increase in the number of cities reporting gang problems. Curry's (1994) survey was the first tabulation of national gang statistics that relied specifically on police records, and by his estimates, the number of gangs and gang members had increased substantially since the 1987 study. These statistics, however, do not provide any indication of how serious the problem is within the different settings, but merely point out the proliferation across the country. The actual seriousness of the problem is difficult to discern without information pertaining to the size of gangs and the frequency and seriousness of their criminal activities.

A number of other important studies have revealed a significant presence of youth gangs in particular settings. In a national survey of 368 district attorneys' agencies, the Institute of Law and Justice (1994) discovered that 84 percent of the prosecutors in large jurisdictions (greater than 250,000 people) and 46 percent in smaller jurisdictions (50,000 to 250,000 people) reported youth gang problems. According to Camp and Camp's

(1985) research findings on youth gangs in state and federal penal institutions, 33 of the 48 state systems they surveyed had gang problems. Within school systems, a national survey of junior high and high school students (age 12-19) discovered that 15 percent (21.5 million) of the students reported gang problems within their schools (Bastian and Taylor, 1991).

The estimate of the size of the problem in any particular city or region and the definition of the problem largely depends on the organization or agency that is relied upon to provide the information. But to ascertain the size *and* seriousness of the problem, criminal justice agencies may be the best source for reasonably reliable data, since they are required to collect and maintain arrest and offense related information. Morales (1992) relied on police recorded data to determine the scope and seriousness of the youth gang problem in Texas; Spergel et al.'s (1990) and Needle and Stapleton's (1983) national level studies relied on law enforcement data and information for assessing the cities in their respective surveys, and Maxson and Klein (1993) relied on law enforcement information to determine the extent of gang migration across the country. State-level studies in New Mexico (Governor's Organized Crime Prevention Commission, 1991), Virginia (Virginia State Crime Commission, 1991), and Arizona (Arizona Criminal Justice Commission, 1991) utilized law enforcement reports and crime data to determine the extent of their gang problems; and studies of specific cities (Spergel, 1983; Curry and Spergel, 1988, 1992; Klein et al., 1991; Maxson et. al, 1985) depended heavily on law enforcement statistics in their analyses of gang problems. These studies demonstrate that, perhaps because of the generally conservative nature of law enforcement and criminal justice statistics (Spergel, 1995), they may be the most useful and accessible resource for determining the prevalence and location of criminal youth gangs and groups and the seriousness of their activities.

Conspicuously absent from the body of research is information on the location and seriousness of youth gang and group activities in North Carolina. Only scant research information that addresses collective youth crime in the State is available (see North Carolina Governor's Crime Commission, 1992); most information has largely consisted of anecdotal descriptions or media reports, primarily focusing on the State's largest metropolitan areas and municipalities. The lack of information on youth gangs and groups in the State may lead one to believe that there is not a problem or that the problem is not very serious. A more likely scenario is that the problem is either not reported or is underreported by officials. Moreover, suburban and rural gangs and groups may not be as visible when compared to those collectives found in the inner-city, perhaps because the metropolitan media pay less attention to them (Johnstone, 1981). The indications of a collective youth crime problem are not always obvious nor clear, and where reliable data are absent, any determination of where the problems exist becomes even more difficult.

There is a great deal of diversity in the perceptions of the collective youth crime problem, as the previous definitional analysis demonstrated, but by utilizing the consensual or standardized definitions developed in the previous chapter, it becomes possible not only to determine the nature of the problem with greater consistency, but also the locations of these youth collectives. The conceptual framework established thus far provides an opportunity to present, at the very minimum, information on law-violating youth groups in North Carolina from the practitioner's perspective. The analysis in this chapter is primarily concerned with the perceived scope of the problem, not just the presence of law-violating youth groups. The complexity of designating the activities of youth collectives as *problematic* must not be underestimated, since the classification of localities relied greatly upon the perceptions of respondents and the use of aggregate crime statistics provided by the North Carolina State Bureau of Investigation. Furthermore, as Miller (1982) discovered, the presence of youth gangs or groups in a community does not necessarily mean there is a collective youth crime problem, so any attempt to ascertain the seriousness of the problem must take into account the level of their criminality. This was evident, for instance, in a large number of responses from school officials; despite the presence of youth collectives in many of the schools surveyed, most activities involved disruptive behavior within classrooms, overt displays of disrespect for authority, and minor vandalism and fighting.

A second concern involved the constraints inherent in the methods and procedures utilized to gather the information for the study. There may be many other cities and rural communities, those with populations below 5,000, that are presently experiencing, or at some time in the past may have experienced, law-violating youth group problems. Collecting data from cities below 5,000 would have required a prohibitive amount of resources — time, effort, and expenses — and would most likely have yielded very little useful data. As discovered in this study, few organizations routinely and systematically collected information on law-violating youth groups, especially nongang collectives. However, it was also discovered that, in general terms, the more serious the crime problem, the greater the likelihood that useful data and information on collective youth crime was available. More often than not, the localities that provided the most useful information were the larger towns and cities, since they were also the ones that had the more serious youth crime problems.

It must be re-emphasized that the assessment of the nature and seriousness of law-violating youth groups and their presence throughout the State is not based on objective or quantifiable information, such as statistical data on the criminal activities of youth gangs or other data that tracks prevalence figures. The responses and estimates provided by the respondents were the only sources of information available for this analysis; in light of this constraint, the reader must be made aware that the figures provided herein may not be truly valid estimates of the actual problem, but represent the perceptions of individuals whose perspectives of the problem may be unique.

B. Distribution of Localities

An important consideration for identifying particular locations of law-violating youth groups was the *unit of locality*. Needle and Stapleton (1983) and Curry et al. (1994) focused their research on selected cities, with the primary goal of examining police responses and procedures for dealing with youth gangs. Spergel et al. (1990) and Miller's (1982) studies were significantly broader in respect to both the organizational diversity of respondents and the geographic units of analysis. The latter two studies—which included a wider range of professional orientations such as law enforcement, community service organizations, prosecutors, and corrections—expanded the units of locality to counties, metropolitan areas, cities, towns, unincorporated areas, city districts, regions, and judicial districts.

The present study also utilized a broader conception of locality, since the exploratory nature of the research, coupled with the goal and objective of broad geographic coverage, required this approach. Locality, therefore, is an inclusive term referring to all of the various types of geographical units (Miller, 1982). The localities defined for this study were cities, towns, counties, judicial districts, and sites (corrections). The use of broader geographical units was important because organizations that have limited jurisdictions (e.g. city and town police) could not adequately and reliably address the scope and nature of collective youth crime problems beyond defined boundaries. However, city organizations were critical to this study because the large majority of youth gang and group crime occurred in municipal and metropolitan localities.

The data for this study was collected during the 1994 calendar year. Specifying the period of research when examining law-violating youth groups, especially youth gangs, is important because the characteristics and seriousness of the problem may show considerable variation over time, particularly with respect to location, numbers, and criminal activity patterns (Miller, 1982). Studies and assessments have reported sharp increases and decreases in youth gang and group activities in many cities over relatively short periods of time (Miller, 1982; Spergel 1990; Spergel et al., 1990). Therefore, only an extended study of collective youth crime could reasonably determine any historical variations in the scope and nature of the problem.

C. Location of Law-Violating Youth Group Problems

Research studies on youth gangs and groups have generally indicated that the problem has been, at least in the past, confined to relatively large urban centers and other metropolitan areas. Even though large-scale research initiatives (e.g. Miller, 1982; Needle and Stapleton, 1983; Spergel et al., 1990) have consistently discovered very high prevalence rates of law-violating youth groups in large cities, evidence was also presented that indicated a growing presence of youth gangs and groups in smaller cities, towns, and municipalities around the country, particularly those with populations below 100,000. The data from the national-level research projects further confirmed that there were strong positive correlations between the populations found in urban areas and the scope and nature of the local collective youth crime problem: the larger the city, the more pronounced and serious the collective youth crime problem. The findings from the present study also indicated similar correlations, but more significantly, it found that, based on self-reports by informants, there were youth gang and group problems in very small towns and cities (populations less than 30,000 in cities and less than 70,000 in counties) throughout the State. If the self-reports and perceptions of respondents were in any way accurate, this would represent a growing and troublesome phenomenon. Klein's (1995) findings of the proliferation of youth gangs around the country in the past ten to fifteen years—in particular noting the graphical data on North Carolina—demonstrates a growth rate that, if it continues on the present course, will likely see many more cities both large and small succumb to gang and other group problems.

The summary data in Table 4.1 illustrates the response rate for each respondent organizational category, including those respondents who were uncertain as to the nature of their problem, and those who indicated that they did not have a problem. The data are based on the self-reported problem (Appendix, Section II). Respondents were provided the opportunity to make an assessment of their problem based on their own experiences, perceptions, and definitions. Respondents reporting youth gangs or youth groups (only) were nearly equally represented in regard to total numbers,[1] but when examining the problem classification separately there were a few differences. Individuals from the Corrections category reported the highest proportion of locations with youth gang problems, followed by Juvenile Services, Sheriff and Police Departments, and Schools; for respondents reporting youth groups, the ordering was somewhat different. A significant number of respondents reported that they had neither youth gang nor group problems, with respondents from the School category representing the highest proportion and Corrections the lowest.

Table 4.1
Survey Response Summary (Self-Report)

Category	Youth Gangs	Youth Groups	Not Sure	No Problem
Police (N=59)	13 (22.0)	15 (25.4)	4 (6.8)	27 (45.8)
Sheriff (N=62)	15 (24.2)	8 (12.9)	4 (6.4)	35 (56.5)
Schools (N=86)	9 (10.4)	13 (15.1)	14 (16.3)	50 (58.1)
Juv. Serv (N=32)	8 (25.0)	11 (34.4)	4 (12.5)	9 (28.1)
Corrections (N=11)	6 (54.5)	1 (9.1)	0	4 (36.4)
Unknown (N=7)	0	7 (100.0)	0	0
Totals (N=257)	51 (19.8)	55 (21.4)	26 (10.1)	125 (48.6)

Because the analysis of definitions and the concepts conveyed by respondents produced a variety of ways in which the problem could be framed, it was necessary to identify and extract the most commonly used components and develop a consensual definition to better measure and validate the prevalence and location of youth gangs and groups across North Carolina. The diversity of definitions made the task of identifying gang and group problem localities particularly difficult, since what may be perceived as youth gangs in one city, may not be considered gang in another. To address this validity concern, respondents (N=125)—those who had earlier self-reported in the survey questionnaire that their localities were experiencing youth gangs (19.8 percent) or groups (21.4 percent), or if they were uncertain of the nature of the problem (10.1 percent)—were interviewed.

More specifically, all 125 respondents were given the consensual definition of youth gang and gang-related incident (see earlier chapter) and asked whether they agreed or disagreed that the characteristics of their problem and the methods for designating gang-related incidents comport

---

1. If respondents identified both youth gangs and youth groups in their jurisdictions, the responses were listed in the youth gang category for analytical purposes.

to or are consistent with the definitions. The objective was to determine the proportion of respondents who, for example, self-reported youth gang problems and agreed that their problem fit the consensual definition of gangs. If the proportion of respondents is high—e.g. those who self-reported gang problems and confirmed that their problem was consistent with the consensual definition of youth gangs—then there may be room to argue that those localities were most likely experiencing gang problems, at least within the parameters established by the consensual definition. Conversely, if respondents self-reported gang problems, but disagreed with the consensual definition, then the validity and reliability of their assertions become more questionable. The perceptions of the youth gang problem in the latter hypothetical situation were likely framed in quite different terms, which may not adhere to the fundamental concepts found in the consensual definition and the concepts emphasized in the research literature.

For those respondents who perceived and self-reported youth groups as their problem, or were uncertain if they had youth gang or group problems, this exercise was equally important. If these respondents self-reported group problems in the initial survey or were uncertain, but later confirmed during the interview that their problem was reflected in the consensual definition of youth gangs, then their localities may have had gang problems. Because the definition of criminal or delinquent youth group is overly general and nebulous, and a group-related incident need only involve multiple offenders, requiring no other discernible factors like those found in gang-related incidents, it was impractical to similarly develop and use consensual definitions as they pertain to youth groups. In essence, then, the priority was not only to determine the localities that had youth gang problems using a standardized definitional framework, but to differentiate the gang problem localities from those that were more likely experiencing group problems. There may be some disagreement in using a standardized youth gang definition that emphasizes criminality to ascertain the scope of the problem—particularly among academics, social agency professionals, and other researchers outside the criminal justice community who favor pluralistic definitions that de-emphasize criminal activities—but it was the only practical measure that could be taken to assess with consistency the nature of the problem across a large region. It must be emphasized that the consensual definition of youth gang is a composite, or amalgamation, of the key ideas and concepts conveyed by practitioners who deal with the problem in their professional capacities; likewise, the consensual definition of gang-related incident is based on the key methods practitioners used to identify these incidents.

The information in Table 4.2 illustrates the results of the definitional validity check. The top figures in each cell reflect the number of respondents who self-reported the nature of the problem—youth gang, youth group, or not sure. The bottom figures reflect the number and proportion of respondents who confirmed that their problem could be defined in terms of the consensual youth gang definition. For example, in looking at the police category, there were 15 respondents who self-reported *youth group* problems, but there were two respondents who later confirmed that the consensual definition of youth gangs reflected the nature of their problem. Therefore, it is possible that these two respondents misidentified or were uncertain how to define youth gangs. More importantly, what may have been perceived as a youth group problem, may in actuality be a youth gang problem. Fortunately, in the vast majority of cases (94.6 percent), the same respondent who completed the written surveys were also available for the subsequent interviews, otherwise the validity check would have been questionable.

Table 4.2
Proportion of Respondents Whose Problem is Reflected
by the Consensual Definition of Youth Gang
(Based on Earlier Self-Reports)

Category	Youth Gangs	Youth Groups	Not Sure
Police (N=32)	13	15	4
	12 (92.0)	2 (13.3)	1 (25.0)
Sheriff (N=27)	15	8	4
	12 (80.0)	1 (12.5)	1 (25.0)
Schools (N=36)	9	13	14
	5 (56.0)	1 (7.6)	2 (14.2)
Juv. Serv. (N=23)	8	11	4
	7 (88.0)	2 (18.0)	1 (25.0)
Corrections (N=7)	6	1	0
	6 (100.0)	0	0
Totals (N=125)	51	48	26
	42 (82.4)	6 (12.5)	5 (19.2)

In analyzing the aggregate statistics at the bottom of the table, there was a relatively large proportion (82.4 percent) of respondents who self-reported youth gang problems and agreed that the nature of their problem, or its characteristics, was reflected in the concepts and parameters established in the consensual definition of youth gangs. However, there were nine respondents (17.6 percent) in the same category who did not concur that the definition characterized their problems, which calls into question their earlier self-reported assessments. In the youth group category, six (12.5 percent) of the respondents could characterize their problem in terms of the youth gang definition framework, which possibly indicates a more serious problem than previously thought. Lastly, five respondents (19.2 percent) in the Not Sure category also agreed that their problems closely adhered to the parameters of the consensual definition of youth gangs, demonstrating that these respondents appeared to have a better idea of the nature and characteristics of their problem when presented with more objective criteria.

The response pattern for each of the respective respondent categories was not altogether very surprising. Respondents who were from the Corrections category and self-reported youth gang problems all agreed that the consensual gang definition characterized the problems within their institutional settings. Once again, these respondents seemed to employ and adhere to standardized methods or techniques for defining gangs and other security threat groups. Generally speaking, there was relatively strong concurrence across all respondent categories who self-reported youth gang problems, with the exception of school respondents who had the lowest concurrence scores (56.0 percent). Within the community context, respondents from police agencies attained the highest scores (92.0 percent), which buttresses the reliability of these respondents designating a particular city as one that may have been or currently is experiencing gang problems. In other words, since law enforcement officials broadly concurred that the consensual gang definition characterized what they also self-reported as youth gang problems, then there may be reason to believe that their assessments across the State were relatively consistent. Conversely, in the cities where the only respondents were school officials, there may be reason to doubt the consistency of their self-reports. Moreover, even though there was a small proportion of respondents (12.5 percent) from the youth group category who agreed that their problem could be characterized by the consensual gang definition, the youth gang problem may be more widespread than what was previously reported. As a precautionary note, since there was a 15 month time period between the completion of the initial written questionnaire (August 1994) and the telephonic interviews (November 1995)(definitional validity checks), there is the possibility that the characteristics and nature of the problem could actually have changed.

The listing in Table 4.3 is a compilation of the localities where respondents self-reported the nature of their problems—the 58 cities, 95 counties, 32 judicial districts, and 11 correctional institutions represented by respondents were categorized accordingly. However, when the results of the analysis of the consensual gang definition were considered—e.g. placing greater reliance on the perceptions of those respondents who agreed that their problems were consistent with the parameters established in the consensual definition of youth gang—the number of locations demonstrated slight variation. Within the youth gang category, no asterisk denotes those localities whose respondent—for those localities where there was only one—self-reported gang problems, but during the interview did not agree with the consensual gang definition, regardless of professional orientation. If there were two respondents (law enforcement and school officials) from a particular city and county, and the law enforcement respondent did not agree with the definition of gangs, the location also did not receive an asterisk. As noted earlier, the 92.0 and 80.0 percent definitional concurrence rates among respondents from police agencies and sheriff's departments, respectively, may provide greater credence and reliability when it comes to their assessments of the problem, whereas school respondents (city and county system officials), with their low concurrence rates, may be less reliable. If respondents from a particular professional category, in this case school officials, cannot generally agree with the youth gang definition established for this study, then it becomes difficult to ascertain, with any degree of confidence, whether the gang phenomenon they have characterized in one city is consistent, in terms of general characteristics, with those self-reported in others. For the Youth Group and Not Sure categories, an asterisk denotes those localities whose respondent(s), regardless of their professional orientation, self-reported youth group problems but later concurred that the gang definition also reflected the characteristics of their problem.

Table 4.3
Type of Problem by Area (Self-Reported)
(City, County, District, Correctional Facilities)

A. *Youth Gangs*

Cities: n=18   %N=31.0

Brevard	Havelock*	Morganton*
Charlotte*	Kannapolis*	Mt. Airy
Durham*	Kinston*	Raleigh*
Elizabeth City	Lenoir	Southern Pines*
Fayetteville*	Lexington*	Waynesville*
Greensboro*	Lumberton*	Asheville*

Counties: n=15   %N=15.7

Buncombe*	Forsyth*	Mecklenburg*
Caldwell*	Guilford*	New Hanover*
Cumberland*	Hertford*	Pasquotank
Durham*	Hoke*	Perquimas
Edgecombe	Lenoir*	Wake*

Judicial Districts: n=8   %N=25.0

4*, 6B*, 11, 20*, 21, 27A*, 28*, 30*

Correctional Facilities: n=6   N%=54.5
        Sandhills Youth Center*

Blanch Youth Center*
Wake Regional Juvenile Detention Facility*
Morrison Youth Center*
Juvenile Evaluation Center*
Stonewall Jackson School*

B. *Youth Groups*

Cities: n=18   %N=31.0
   Albermarle   Goldsboro*   Mathews   Snowhill
   Boone   Graham   Moorehead City* Wilson
   Burlington   Henderson   Oxford   Winston-Salem
   Carrboro   Hendersonville   Roanoke Rapids
   Clinton   Hickory   Salisbury

Counties: n=23   %N=24.2
   Alamance   Duplin   Pender   Union
   Alexander   Gates   Pitt   Vance
   Avery   Harnet   Rockingham   Washington
   Brunswick   Iredell   Stanly   Wilkes
   Catawba   Northampton*   Transylvania   Yadkin
   Chatham   Onslow   Tyrell

Judicial Districts: n=11   %N=34.4
      10*, 13*, 15B, 18, 19B, 22, 23, 24, 25, 26, 29

Correctional Facilities: n=1   %N=10.0
      C.A. Dillon School

C. Not Sure

Cities: n=8   %N=13.7
   Asheboro   Kings Mt.   Shelby   Thomasville
   Chapel-Hill*   Mt. Holly   Smithfield   Williamston

Counties: n=13   %N=7.3
      Burke   McDowell   Warren
      Carteret   Montgomery   Wayne
      Gaston   Person   Wilson*
      Haywood*   Rowan
      Lee   Sampson*

Judicial Districts: n=4   %N=12.5
      3B, 16A, 19C*, 27B

---

* Denotes those locations where respondents concurred during interviews that the consensual definition of youth gang reflected the characteristics of their problem.

As Table 4.3 demonstrates, the number of cities whose respondent(s) self-reported youth gang problems was 18 (31.0 percent of the city sample), but when considering the number of respondents who concurred that their problem could be defined in terms of the consensual gang definition, the number drops down to 14. For counties, the number drops from 15 to 12, and the number of judicial districts drops from 8 to 7. The analysis of the youth group category actually notes a number of cities and counties that may have had youth gang problems, based on the fact that respondents in these locations agreed that their problem could be characterized within the parameters of the gang definition. Finally, in the Not Sure category, there were five (20.0 percent) locations that might have been experiencing youth gang problems, according to the consensual definitional analysis; if true, this would indicate an even wider prevalence of youth gang problems across the State.

Cities and counties were also divided into population categories (Table 4.4) to illustrate and compare the variation of collective youth crime problems across the State. The five largest counties and four of the five largest cities had respondents who self-reported youth gang problems in the survey questionnaire. Not surprising, youth group problems were self-reported in all cities and counties found within the largest population categories. However, the generally held assumption — that there is a direct relationship between collective youth crime problems and city size — was not confirmed by the data generated in this study. According to the t-tests, there was a strong relationship ($p < 0.01$) between city and county size and the proportion of localities classified (self-reported) as having youth gang and group problems for the largest population categories (greater than 50,000 for cities, and 100,000 for counties), yet there were no statistically significant relationships (e.g. $p < 0.05$) discovered among the smaller population categories (50,000 and below for cities and 100,000 and below for counties).

Table 4.4
Law-Violating Youth Group Problems by City and County Size
(Self-reported)

Size of Locality	Problem Classification				
Cities	N	Youth Gangs	%N	Youth Groups	%N
5,000 - 10,000	38	4	10.5	4	10.5
10,000 - 20,000	30	5	16.7	7	23.3
20,001 - 30,000	6	3	50.0	3	50.0
30,001 - 40,000	3	0	0.0	1	33.0
40,001 - 50,000	4	0	0.0	2	50.0

50,001 - 100,000	4	2	50.0	1	25.0
> 100,000	5	4	8	0.0	00.0
totals:	90	18	20.0	18	20.0
Counties					
<10,000	8	0	0.0	2	25.0
10,000 - 40,000	41	4	9.8	9	22.0
40,001 - 70,000	21	2	9.6	4	19.0
70,001 - 100,000	13	1	7.8	4	30.8
100,001 - 200,000	12	3	25.0	4	25.0
> 200,000	5	5	100.0	0	0.0
totals:	100	15.0	23.0		

The absence of any definitive relationship may be due to the disproportionate representation of localities in the smaller population categories. For example, cities classified in the two smallest population categories, those with populations between 5,000 and 20,000, represented 75.6 percent (N=68) of all cities in the sample universe. More significantly, these cities constituted 55.6 percent (N=20) of all cities classified as having youth gang or group problems. In terms of aggregate numbers for cities, there was an identical reporting of youth gang problems (20.0 percent) compared to those cities where respondents reported only youth group problems (20.0 percent). There was also a disproportionate representation of counties classified as having youth gang and group problems within the two smallest population categories (39.5 percent). However, t-test results in this analysis did not indicate any significant statistical relationships between locality population and the reporting of youth gangs or groups. The wider reporting of youth groups, at least in counties, confirms many previous assertions that "most of those who offend with others are not members of large or structured groups...rather, most delinquent offenses are generally committed by two or three individuals who are loosely associated with one another" (Reiss and Farrington, 1991, p. 361). The stronger representation of cities identified as experiencing youth gang problems is not easily explained; perhaps the assessment is accurate, but considering the lack of statistical data on collective youth crime, this anomaly could be due to methodological constraints inherent in this study, or even the misidentification or mislabeling of the problem by some of the respondents.

Table 4.5
Judicial Districts Reporting Law-Violating Youth Group Problems
(Total Number of Districts Reporting: N=32)

Judicial District	Population	Youth Gangs	Youth Groups
24	98,624		X
6B	119,225	X	
23	121,680		X
13	129,238		X
19B	129,892		X
15B	132,610		X
30	143,094	X	
29	148,190		X
28	174,821	X	
27A	175,093	X	
11	190,502	X	
4	246,544	X	
20	262,972	X	
25	264,865		X
21	265,878	X	
22	275,011		X
18	347,420		X
10	423,380		X
26	511,433		X
Totals:		8	11

However, there was also a relatively equal representation of youth gangs and groups reported across judicial districts by juvenile court counselors (Table 4.5). Out of the 32 Judicial Districts in North Carolina, court counselors reported youth gang problems in eight districts (25.0 percent) and youth group problems in eleven districts (34.4 percent). The majority of districts classified as experiencing youth gang problems had populations —the sum of all county populations found within a particular judicial district—between 170,000 and 263,000. The pattern was significantly different for districts experiencing *only* youth group problems. Six (54.5 percent) districts had populations below 150,000, while the other five districts had populations exceeding 260,000. There was a moderate relationship between districts reportedly having youth gang problems and the population size of the districts, but when examining districts that were experiencing youth group problems, no discernible relationship between these variables was discovered. Youth gang problems were more prevalent in districts with populations in excess of 170,000, whereas youth group problems were disproportionately represented in districts with populations under 170,000.

In the correctional setting, youth gangs were reported as the predominant security problem, posing disciplinary problems for the institutional staff and displaying aggressive, predatory behavior against fellow inmates. In addressing the implication of gangs formed in prison, Spergel (1990, p. 26) noted that "prison and street gangs are interrelated...prison gangs are [often] outgrowths of street gangs, but there is evidence that gangs formed in prison may also immigrate to the streets." Camp and Camp's (1985) study on prison gangs similarly discovered that a large majority of gangs in prisons had ties to gangs in the street. The extortion, intimidation, drug-trafficking, assaults and other assorted felonious activities that gang members demonstrate in the prison environment may very well become problems within the community once the gang members are released. Out of the eleven correctional sites (youth correctional institutions, training schools, detention facilities, and evaluation centers) that were included in this study, respondents in six (54.5 percent) facilities reported youth gang problems and one reported experiencing only youth group problems.

Table 4.6 provides a brief description of the key characteristics that differentiate one site from another, as well as the nature of the problem. This table is significant because it demonstrates that the youth gang and group problems were not confined to large institutions, where, as previous studies have concluded, the influence and prevalence of law-violating youth groups was the greatest (Camp and Camp, 1985). It is also important to note that these sites have diverse age ranges and security levels, which may, to some extent, influence the scope and seriousness of group activities within the respective facilities. However, the more serious problems were generally reported in the institutions with the larger youth populations (e.g. greater than 130), those with higher security levels (e.g. closed, medium), and those with the most serious offender classifications (e.g. felons versus delinquent). Within the facilities where youth gang problems were reported, the criminal activity of gang members also demonstrated a remarkably uniform pattern: there was evidence that the seriousness of criminal activities became progressively more serious as the age range of the facility increased.

Table 4.6
Facility Descriptions for Correctional Institutions (N=11)

Name	Security Level	Type	Age	Problem	Popula-tion
Blanch Youth Center	Closed (Max.)	Felons	>20	Gangs	132
Sandhills Youth Center	Minimum	Felons/Misd.	<18	Gangs	225
Morrison Youth Center	Medium	Felons	18-21	Gangs	400
Juvenile Eval. Center	Minimum	Delinquents	>17	Gangs	182
Stonewall Jackson Sch.	Medium	Felons/Misd.	<16	Gangs	160
Wake Regional	Closed (Max.)	Felons/Misd.	>17	Gangs	18
C.A. Dillon School	Minimum	Delinquent	<19	Groups	92
Juvenile Service Center	Minimum	Delinquent	<17	None	10
Dobbs School	Minimum	Delinquent	<19	None	151
Cumberland Regional	Minimum	Delinquent	<17	None	25
Wilkes Regional	Minimum	Delinquent	<18	None	30

One final, but important note regarding the method of classifying localities in the aforementioned sections. All analyses were based on dichotomous problem classifications: a locality was classified as having either youth gang or youth group problem, or neither. Had the previous analyses considered localities that had both types of collective youth problems, the proportion of localities with youth group problems would have been higher. With the exception of two cities, one county, and two judicial districts, all localities whose respondents reported youth gang problems also reported the presence of less serious youth groups. This finding generally support Thrasher's (1936) hypothesis regarding the evolution of youth groups into youth gangs, and Klein's (1995) notion of a "tipping point" whereby groups become more committed to criminal activities, accept intergroup rivalries, and begin a process of self-actualization as gang members through dress, demeanor, and vocabulary. Spergel (1990, p. 181) similarly argues that "delinquent groups in some cities can be converted or organized into gangs and that youth gangs in turn are changing into criminal organizations of various kinds." The group dynamics and the "group to gang" evolutionary processes are influenced by a number of factors, such as entrepreneurial drug-trafficking opportunities, the socialization of criminal youths into gangs while incarcerated, and general criminal opportunities within the community. There is strong support, in previous literature and in the present research findings, that the presence of youth groups is antecedent to more serious collective youth formations.

D. Seriousness of Law-Violating Youth Group Crime Problems

Providing a reasonable estimate of the scope and nature of youth gang and group activities poses a number of challenges. Official crime statistics, such the Uniform Crime Reports compiled by the North Carolina State Bureau of Investigation, do not provide estimates on the number and types of crimes attributable to youth collectives, but do provide the number of recorded offenses within various age categories. These statistics were useful in the present study because they at least served as a barometer that "permit[ed] one to determine, both qualitatively and quantitatively, the intensity of [crime] and its change over time" (Sellin and Wolfgang, 1969, p. 4). Moreover, from the micro-analytical perspective, the available official statistics provided a baseline to estimate the proportion of crime respondents attributed to youth gang and group involvement. The estimates provided by respondents, therefore, became the critical link that enabled the assessment of how serious youth gang and group problems may have been in particular localities.

Since a primary criterion for ascertaining seriousness should logically entail criminal activity (Sellin and Wolfgang, 1969; Miller, 1982; Sanders, 1994), criminal justice organization estimates, particularly police and sheriff's departments, may be the most reliable sources. But in an effort to ascertain the validity and reliability of respondent estimates of index crimes attributed to youth gangs and groups, an analysis very similar to the previous one on youth gang definitions was conducted. There is no conclusive way to determine the accuracy of respondent estimates, since gang and group-related arrest and conviction data were not routinely compiled by respondent organizations, nor were similar data even made available for research purposes. Yet by asking respondents whether they agreed with the consensual definition of gang-related incident that was developed in the previous chapter, it became possible to determine, to some extent, the reliability of respondent estimates. In particular, the analysis identifies the respondent categories that may provide the most meaningful and reliable indication of the scope and seriousness of youth gang activities. If a large proportion of respondents from a specific category agreed with the consensual definition of gang-related incident — whether they self-reported gang or group problems, or were unsure — their estimates may be considered the most reliable. But whether respondents ardently followed these criteria when reporting and recording incidents may be another story entirely.

If there is greater agreement among respondents in one category compared to the others, then it would appear appropriate to rely more heavily on the index crime estimates from the one respondent category for reliability and consistency reasons; if the proportion of respondents who agreed with the consensual definition is high for all categories, so goes the argument, all of the estimates may be worthy of consideration; but, on the other hand, if there were very little agreement on the consensual definition across all of the respondent categories, then it would be arguably wise to question the reliability of the estimates. Fortunately, the latter scenario did not occur. The respondents who self-reported youth group problems were also presented the opportunity to agree or disagree with the consensual definition of gang-related incident. If a large proportion of respondents (generally and within each respondent category) from the youth group category agreed with the definition, it could be interpreted that these respondents were most likely able to identify a gang-related incident if it occurred, and also to discern the differences between gang and group-related incidents. Logically, if these respondents were in fact aware of the criteria necessary to designate an incident as gang-related, and an incident occurred that did not meet the criteria, but did involve multiple offenders, the incident hopefully would have been designated as a group, not gang-related incident. For those respondents who were unsure how to classify the nature of the problem in their communities, there was evidence that some of these respondents were aware, to some extent, of the criteria for designating an incident as gang-related.

Table 4.7 demonstrates that there was a modest proportion of respondents (75.0 percent) who had self-reported youth gang problems and also concurred with the consensual definition of gang-related incident. The proportion of concurring respondents from the Corrections category (100.0 percent) had the highest scores overall, and police agency respondents (92.0 percent) had the highest scores within the community context. The other two criminal justice organizations — sheriff's departments (80.0 percent) and juvenile services (75.0 percent) — also attained reasonable, but lower, consensus scores. It is particularly important to note that school respondents achieved very low scores, especially for those respondents who self-reported youth gang problems. This last finding makes their estimates of index offenses highly questionable, since school officials across the State do not appear to have a clear understanding of what factors and criteria are essential for identifying gang-related incidents and activities. Therefore, in light of the findings presented thus far, the most reliable and reasonably valid estimates for determining the seriousness of the youth gang problem (based on index crime estimates) at the city and town level may be those of police agency respondents, while respondents from sheriff's departments may be the most reliable sources of index crime estimates at the county level.

Table 4.7
Proportion of Respondents Who Agree with the
Criteria for Designating Gang-Related Incidents

Category	Youth Gangs	Youth Groups	Not Sure
Police (N=32)	13	15	4
	12 (92.0)	12 (80.0)	1 (25.0)
Sheriff (N=27)	15	8	4
	12 (80.0)	6 (75.0)	2 (50.0)
Schools (N=36)	9	13	14
	3 (33.0)	6 (46.0)	2 (14.2)
Juv. Serv. (N=23)	8	11	4
	5 (63.0)	7 (63.6)	1 (25.0)
Corrections (N=7)	6	1	0
	6 (100.0)	1 (100.0)	0
Totals (N=125)	51	48	26
	38 (75.0)	32 (68.0)	6 (23.0)

Another validity issue, and one that provides further support for rely-ing on law enforcement index crime estimates, concerned what to do when multiple respondents from the same locality provided estimates of index crimes. There was no way of knowing whether some of the crime esti-mates provided by one respondent were included or excluded from the estimates of another. In other words, if two respondents from the same city estimated that the proportion of assaults attributed to youth gangs was ten percent, are they referring to the same incidents, some common por-tion, or are the incidents totally exclusive of one another? The implication is that, if the estimates are exclusive of one another, the problem may be much more serious. Because there was no way to make this determina-tion, due to the lack of verifiable data, it was necessary to use undupli-cated responses—utilizing the responses from the most reliable sources —to acquire a more conservative estimate and simultaneously preclude the chances of exaggeration. In this case the most reliable sources came from law enforcement respondents: city police and county sheriff depart-ment officials. The strong definitional concurrence of gang-related inci-dent by these two respondent categories signifies that the criteria appears to be used across many jurisdictions with the greatest consistency. More-over, in a typical county jurisdiction, the police have the responsibility of collecting and investigating incidents within city limits and municipalities; while crime that occurs beyond city limits, in rural communities, or in unincorporated municipalities, falls within the investigative responsibili-ties of county sheriff departments. Because of this fact, there is a strong probability that the index offense estimates provided by these two respondent categories are based on separate and exclusive experiences. Those estimates provided by respondents from correctional institutions are also treated as exclusive estimates, since the incidents that they attribute to youth gangs or groups refer to those committed within the institutional environment.

Classifying localities proved to be a very complicated process, since the definition of seriousness has many subjective meanings, depending on the types of crimes committed, the frequency of their occurrence, and the proportion of crimes in certain categories compared to others. Earlier studies (Sellin and Wolfgang, 1964, 1969; Cohen, 1969) made significant advances in measuring the seriousness of youth crime, including youth gangs and groups, but the indices utilized in these studies and the factors that were measured required data that were not available in the present study. The seriousness index (Table 4.8) designed for this analysis was based on the Standard Classification of Offenses established by the Federal Bureau of Investigation and the index weight placed on those crimes by the Punishment Chart for North Carolina (Rubin, 1992). To determine the seriousness of collective youth crime in different localities, the eight most serious crimes (homicide, rape, robbery, aggravated assault, burglary, larceny, motor-vehicle theft, and arson), which comprise the Part I or Index Crimes found in the North Carolina Uniform Crime Reports, were used in the index. These crimes come to the attention of criminal justice organizations with the greatest regularity and signify the offenses that are perceived as the crime problem (Conklin, 1992). The index crimes could also be broadly classified as offenses against the person and property, with offenses against the person comprising the most serious offense grouping. The classification of different localities was far from systematic due to the crude methods and procedures employed, therefore any interpretation of data must be made cautiously.

Table 4.8
Seriousness Index for Offenses and Locality Classification

Offense Category	Specific Offenses	Index Classification
Crimes against the Person	Homicide and Aggravated Assault	Very Serious
	Rape and Robbery	Serious
Crimes against Property	Burglary, Arson, Larceny, and Motor-vehicle theft	Moderately Serious
Miscellaneous Crimes	Vandalism, Simple Assault, Petty Larceny, Minor Drug Violations, Disorderly Conduct, Statutory Offenses	Least Serious

Unlike Miller's (1982) study that required respondents to rate the seriousness of youth gang and group problems on a scale, the procedures and indices used in the present analysis provided for greater objectivity; the estimates of index crimes attributed to youth gangs and groups (Appendix, Section III), albeit subjective in nature, were scaled according to the overall youth crime rates for the same index offenses. This method negated some of the subjectivity in defining the seriousness of various activities, since the professional orientation of respondents (e.g. police and sheriff officials at the city and county-level), size of respondents' localities, and other factors may have had a significant influence on their perceptions of the scope and nature of the problem. For example, police in small towns may have considered group intimidation, vandalism, and larceny serious problems, whereas police officials in a larger metropolitan locality may have perceived the same activities as more of a nuisance than a threat to safety. By asking respondents to estimate the proportion of index offenses attributed to youth gangs and groups, rather than the seriousness of activities, scaling the seriousness of the problem became more standardized across jurisdictions and localities. Miller (1982) also discovered that some respondents had a tendency to compare the seriousness of contemporary problems with those of the past, thereby confounding the seriousness of the current problem. The technique and scaling procedure used in the present analysis eliminated this potential problem by eliciting estimates for specific crimes over the previous year; however, a separate question was included to determine if respondents had experienced problems in the past.

Referring back to the seriousness index, offenses were classified into the four broad categories: *very serious, serious, moderately serious,* and *least serious.* Offenses committed against the person received the highest categorical classification of very serious and serious; all property crimes were classified as moderately serious, and the lowest classification, least serious, constituted the miscellaneous misdemeanor crimes committed against both person and property. The last category of offenses did not receive proportional estimates by respondents because of the frequency and prevalence of these activities and the difficulty in making even a reasonable estimate. The formulas discussed below were derived from the law enforcement strategic planning guides developed by the North Carolina Justice Academy for long-term crime prevention forecasting and resource allocation. Because official crime statistics pertaining to youth collectives were nonexistent, this method provided the only practical way to broadly assess the seriousness of the problem from an offense perspective. In order for a locality (city or county) to receive a *very serious* classification, law enforcement respondents must have attributed at least 20 percent of either homicide or aggravated assault offenses to youth gangs or groups, or the cumulative total of both crimes must have been equal to

or greater than 25 percent; any proportion less received a *serious* classification. The same criteria also applied to the serious classification, except
the primary offenses in this case were rape and robbery; again, lower estimates received the next lower classification. For a *moderately serious*
classification, at least 20 percent of any primary offense within this category (burglary, larceny, motor-vehicle theft, and arson) must have been
attributed to youth gangs or groups, or a cumulative total equal to or
greater than 25 percent using a combination of two to four offenses. The
least serious classification was assigned to localities that reportedly experienced relatively minor collective youth crime problems; however, some
of the respondents in these localities did report criminal offenses from
the more serious categories, but the proportion of reported index offenses failed to meet the criteria of the other classifications. In fact, most of
the respondents in the localities classified as *least serious* reported less
than two percent for any single index offense and less than five percent for
any combination of offenses. It is important to note that the seriousness
classifications refer to the percentage of offenses law enforcement and
correctional respondents attributed to youth gangs and groups, and not
the actual number of offenses members from these collectives may have
committed.

Table 4.9 illustrates the problem seriousness classification of cities, counties, judicial districts, and correctional sites for youth gangs and groups.
There were only a few localities, specifically counties and judicial districts,
where respondent estimates were not provided for this analysis. Generally, in localities where respondents reported youth gang problems, when
compared to those localities where youth group problems were reported,
there was a disproportionate representation of *serious* and *very serious*
classifications. Of all the localities where sufficient data were available,
61.7 percent of the localities where youth gang problems were reported
received classifications in the two most serious categories, but only 26.1 percent of the localities where youth group problems were reported were classified into these same categories. This finding was not only consistent with
the previous research that suggested youth gangs were more violent than
nongang youth collectives (Klein and Meyerhoff, 1967; Cohen, 1969;
Maxson et al., 1985; Spergel, 1990), but may demonstrate that the youth
gang problem in North Carolina may be more serious and widespread
than previous research has indicated (e.g. Miller, 1982; Spergel et al., 1990;
Curry et al., 1993; Curry, 1994; Klein, 1995). However, no relationship
was discovered between locality population and seriousness rating, which
questions the widely held assumption that youth gang and group activities were more serious in highly populated areas. Localities that fell between
the most populated and least populated categories did not display any
clear pattern with regard to seriousness classification.

Table 4.9
Problem Seriousness of Localities

1. *Localities Reporting Youth Gangs*	Index Rating
A. Cities	
Charlotte, Durham, Elizabeth City, Lenoir, Lumberton	Very Serious
Asheville, Fayetteville, Havelock, Raleigh, Southern Pines	Serious
Morganton, Greensboro	Moderately Serious
Brevard, Kannapolis, Kinston, Lexington, Mt. Airy, Waynesville	Least Serious
B. Counties	
Hoke, Caldwell, Mecklenburg	Very Serious
Buncombe, Cumberland, Forsyth, New Hanover, Pasquotank, Wake	Serious
Durham, Guilford, Lenoir	Moderately Serious
Edgecombe, Hertford, Perquimas	Least Serious
C. Judicial Districts	
4, 6B, 21	Very Serious
27A	Serious
11	Moderately Serious
20, 28, 30	Least Serious
D. Correctional Sites	
Morrison Youth Center, Juvenile Evaluation Center, Blanch Youth Center	Very Serious
Sandhills Youth Center, Stonewall Jackson School, Wake Regional	Serious

2. *Localities Reporting Youth Groups*	Index Rating
A. Cities	
Henderson, Carrboro	Very Serious

Goldsboro, Moorehead City, Winston-Salem	Moderately Serious
Albermarle, Boone, Burlington, Clinton, Graham, Hendersonville, Hickory, Mathews, Oxford, Roanoke-Rapids, Salisbury, Snowhill, Wilson	Least Serious
B. Counties	
Wilkes	Very Serious
Ashe, Caldwell, Pitt, Union, Tyrrell	Serious
Alamance, Harnet, Pender, Yadkin	Moderately Serious
Alexander, Avery, Chatham, Duplin, Iredell, Onslow, Transylvania, Vance	Least Serious
C. Judicial Districts	
19B	Very Serious
22, 24, 13	Serious
15B, 23, 25	Moderately Serious
10, 29	Least Serious
D. Correctional Sites	
C.A. Dillon School	Moderately Serious

A major assumption in the large body of research on group offending is that youth gangs and groups represent two separable aggregates, identifiable by distinct patterns of behavior (Cohen, 1969). Curry and Spergel (1988) similarly concluded that youth gangs and groups engage in a similar range of minor and serious crime, but gang crime is significantly more violent because it is committed "within a framework of communal values in respect and mutual support, conflict relations with other gangs, and a tradition of turf, colors, signs, and symbols" (p.382). If these aforementioned premises are valid—that youth gangs and groups are distinct aggregates that display variations in offense patterns—it is plausible that by analyzing the aggregate offense data provided by respondents, certain parameters specifying the boundaries of these collectives may become more apparent. A general hypothesis was formulated for this particular analysis: Because youth gangs, more so than youth groups, commit offenses that are more aggressive in nature, a greater proportion of violent offenses should be attributed to gangs; moreover, since youth groups are often perceived as less violent in nature, group activity should be characterized by a greater proportion of property offenses (Cohen, 1969).

Table 4.10
Mean Proportion of Index Crimes Attributed to
Youth Gangs and Youth Groups
(N=Respondents)

Offense	Youth Gangs (N=51)	Youth Groups (N=55)	(t)
Homicide	0.87	3.82	ns
Rape	1.53	1.57	ns
Robbery	10.06	3.30	**
Aggravated Assault	22.03	9.72	**
Burglary	8.56	5.42	ns
Larceny	15.23	11.60	ns
Vehicle Theft	7.87	4.06	ns
Arson	4.12	0.69	ns
Means (All Offenses)	8.78	5.02	ns

$p \leq 0.05^*$ $p \leq 0.01^{**}$ $p \leq 0.001^{***}$ ns=not significant

The summary data (Table 4.10) illustrate the aggregate means of estimated index offenses attributed to youth gangs and groups by respondents. With the exception of homicide, the proportion of all index offenses attributed to youth gangs was generally higher than for youth groups. In particular, the proportion of violent offenses attributed to youth gangs, when compared to youth groups, was not significantly different for the crimes of homicide and rape, but there was a significant statistical variation for the crimes of robbery and aggravated assault. For all index offenses, robbery and aggravated assault together accounted for the highest difference (19.1 percent) between youth gangs and groups. The data further indicate that youth groups, when comparing all offenses attributed to these collectives, were disproportionately involved in larceny, whereas youth gangs were disproportionately involved in aggravated assaults. Generally, respondents from the law enforcement category attributed more serious crime to both youth gangs and groups when compared to the respondents in the other categories, especially when compared to school respondents. Because the offenses of robbery and aggravated assault accounted for almost one-third of all index offenses combined for youth gangs, there is reason to support the argument that conflict and violence are the very identities that attract individuals to gangs (Sanders, 1994) and that violence reestablishes the *respect* and *honor* sought within the gang context (Jankowski, 1991).

Within respective collective classifications, very little variation was discovered between the proportion of total crime committed against the person and property; in other words, when comparing the crimes that constitute these two broad offense rubrics, both youth gangs and groups committed a relatively equal proportion of crimes against the person and property.

The data, however, clearly indicated that respondents attributed a greater proportion of crime in both offense rubrics to youth gangs, which supports the hypothesis that gangs are more violent and demonstrate greater criminal propensities than youth groups. However, Curry and Spergel (1988) assert that youth gangs and groups are not necessarily exclusive of one another, but represent distinct social phenomena that can be analytically separated. It may be inferred from the previous analysis that youth gang and group activity do in fact demonstrate variant forms of behavior, possibly evolving from distinct etiological foundations. Yet, some of the theoretical distinctions between youth gangs and groups that were addressed in previous research were not readily discovered in the present data. Even though there was a strong perception among respondents that youth gangs were more actively involved in violent criminal behavior, gang involvement in property crimes was also estimated to be quite high.

In sum, the central purpose of this analysis was to determine, in a broad perspective, the perceived level of criminal participation in index crimes by youth gangs and groups and any differences in the levels of participation for each offense category. Without more refined and specific types of data —such as member age, sex, and ethnicity—it will remain difficult to measure the variations that are essential to prevention and intervention programming. Research designs for an analysis of this nature "should be constructed that separate, first, various subcultural delinquent events from each other, and, second, individual delinquent behavior within and outside the context of the gang, particularly [if] the offender is employed as the unit of analysis" (Cohen, 1969, p. 135). This analysis was not conducted to reject or affirm previous theoretical propositions pertaining to collective criminal behavior; the lack of vital data made this action unjustifiable and inappropriate. However, even though specific, verifiable data were not available, the findings—based on the perceptions of informants—did provide a sufficient amount of new information from which a more informed examination of the scope and nature of the problem could be conducted.

E. Conclusion

Determining the scope and nature of youth gang and group activities and their locations throughout North Carolina, especially where statistical data and more comprehensive information were sparse, was a very challenging endeavor. The information provided by respondents indicated that youth collectives were more ubiquitous and that the crimes they committed were more serious than has been documented in the research literature. Based on the definitional criteria discussed in the previous chapter and the perceptions of the problem provided by respondents, two general classifications—Youth Gang and Youth Group—were used to classify 100 different localities. 18 (31.0 percent) cities, 15 (15.0 percent) counties, eight (25.0 percent) judicial districts, and six (54.5 percent) youth correctional facilities were classified as experiencing youth gang problems. Whereas 18 (31.0 percent) cities, 23 (24.2 percent) counties, 11 (34.4 percent) judicial districts, and one (10.0 percent) youth correctional facility were classified as experiencing youth group problems only. The classification Not Sure was utilized for localities (N=26) where respondents were uncertain about the nature of their collective youth crime problem and where definitions and corroborating information were not sufficient enough to confidently classify these localities. Localities classified as having youth gang problems, with the exception of five, were also experiencing problems with youth groups, but for the purpose of this analysis, classifications were treated dichotomously.

After analyzing the seriousness of the problem, those localities classified as having youth gang problems, vice youth group problems, experienced much more serious criminal activity in general terms. This finding was also supported by the examination and comparison of the mean proportion of index offenses attributed to youth gangs and groups. Youth gangs demonstrated the greatest propensity for violent offenses, particularly robbery and aggravated assault, but were generally perceived as more active in all index offenses when compared to youth groups. While youth gangs and youth groups disproportionately committed one or two types of crimes, there were no significant statistical variations found between the proportion of offenses committed against the person and property within each respective collective.

Finally, while it can be generally stated that localities found within the largest population category tended to have more severe problems with both youth gangs and groups, the pattern was less predictable for the other population categories. In addition to the numerous large metropolitan areas and counties that were experiencing serious collective youth crime problems, there were also many smaller towns and cities throughout the State that were experiencing similar problems. In a small number of cases, the smaller localities had more serious problems than many larger, more populated areas. Even though the data indicate that youth gangs presently pose the more serious crime problem, the proliferation of other law-violating youth groups "should be granted increased recognition with respect to both research and policy" (Miller, 1982, p. 49).

5

Youth Gang and Group Characteristics

A. Introduction

The analysis in the previous chapter provided information on the broad scope and nature of youth gang and group activities throughout the State. The present chapter provides a much more detailed examination of particular characteristics or parameters (e.g. socio-demographic, structural) of youth gangs and groups; moreover, this chapter addresses whether these characteristics are in any way related to each other. As Spergel et al. (1990) discovered in their research, strong statistical correlations of key characteristics may suggest that the number of distinct underlying dimensions may be fewer than the number of variables used in defining the scope and nature of the problem.

The factors that are important for extending knowledge of the collective youth crime problem are addressed in four sections. The first section, *Size of the Youth Gang and Group Problem*, provides estimates of the number of youth gang and group members and the estimated number of collectives for each locality. The high concentration of youth collectives in urban areas may influence the seriousness of the crime problem in particular cities (e.g. Miller, 1982; Curry and Spergel, 1988; and Hagedorn, 1988), but the recent trends of gangs and groups forming in suburbs, and especially the growth of these collectives in small towns and rural areas (Spergel et al., 1990; Zevitz and Takata, 1992; Zevitz, 1993) have made it necessary to evaluate the perceived scope of collective youth crime problems outside the urban setting.

The second section, *Socio-demographic Characteristics of Youth Gangs and Groups*, examines the relationship between two key socio-demographic factors: race and age. Youth gang and group problems involve predominantly Hispanic and black teenagers at the national level, but in North Carolina, problems primarily involve white and black youth in their late teenage years, which reflects the racial characteristics of the State. The roles race and age play in the scope and nature of the collective youth crime problem is highly complex according to recent research (Miller, 1982; Spergel et al., 1990). Spergel (1990) asserts that gang activities vary by race and ethnicity, but these variations may also be a function of acculturation, access to criminal opportunities, and community stability factors; furthermore, recent research on criminal careers (Cohen, 1986; Farrington, 1986) discovered variations in criminal career patterns as individuals age. An understanding of how age and race interrelate in the group context may provide promising information for prevention and intervention programming.

The third section, *Youth Gang and Group Criminality: Influencing Factors*, extends the analysis of the relationship between age and race by incorporating the variables of adult involvement in activities and a number of key measures that indicate the level of criminality. According to Spergel (1990), the average age of individuals involved in gang activities has become progressively older over the past ten years; this phenomenon may be due to the changing structure of the economy and loss of unskilled employment opportunities, or perhaps an aging of the youth population. However, to what extent the involvement of older youth and young adults in gang and group activities increases the scope and seriousness of activities is not altogether clear.

The final section, *Youth Gang and Group Patterns: Interrelationship of Structural and Behavioral Characteristics*, provides an analysis of the relationships between a wide variety of structural and behavioral features. Two important characteristics that are examined include the relationship of youth gangs and groups to adult criminal groups and the presence of non-local youth gangs and groups. There has been a growing concern within the criminal justice system that youth collectives have become more sophisticated in many of their criminal pursuits. Much of this perception is due to a greater adult involvement in activities and the growing drug-trafficking problem. The extent to which gangs and groups are affiliated with adult criminal enterprises has received scant attention in the research literature, so it is therefore important to address this relationship in the present study. The presence of youth gangs and groups whose members reside in nearby cities or towns is also an important feature in need of examination, since the presence of non-indigenous collectives may indicate efforts to expand activities or establish territory for illicit purposes, particularly "by recruiting or converting existing street groups, often in different neighborhoods or cities, to sell, store, or aid in the marketing of drugs" (Spergel, 1990, p. 210).

The correlational statistical procedures utilized in this chapter attempt to interrelate youth gang and group characteristics using important dimensions. This analysis is important for a number of reasons: it provides more specific information regarding variations between the complex structures of gangs and groups; and it provides the necessary information to understand better the organizational responses to the problem and the prevention and intervention strategies employed (Chapter 7).

B. Size of the Youth Gang and Group Problem

The most current national-level survey of youth gangs (Curry, 1994) revealed a statistically significant growth in youth gangs since the initial assessment projects (Spergel et al., 1990; Spergel and Curry, 1990b) commenced in 1987. Even though these studies were based on official records, the national estimate of the number of gangs increased from 1,439 to 4,881 between 1987 and 1992, and during the same period the estimated total gang membership increased from 120,636 to 249,324. This variation, according to Curry's et al.'s (1994) preliminary estimates, constituted a 239.2 percent increase in the number of gangs and a 106.7 percent increase in gang membership. More significant for this study, however, is that the recent assessment of local law enforcement records indicated that approximately 60 percent of all U.S. cities with populations between 25,000 and 150,000 reported gang crime problems in 1994. With respect to North Carolina, Curry et al. (1994) and Curry (1994) only indicated gang or gang-like problems in Charlotte, Raleigh, and Durham. However, because these studies relied only on law enforcement reports in relatively large cities (populations greater than 100,000), no assessments were available for the vast majority of North Carolina cities that fell below 100,000. In essence, beyond the perceptions and estimates provided by respondents in this research project, very little knowledge exists that provides some basis for determining if the youth gang and group problem in North Carolina has grown or proliferated in recent years.

The notion of gang migration — defined broadly as the dispersion of gangs from one city to another for temporary or long-term visits (e.g. Maxson, 1993; Maxson and Klein, 1993) — has received considerable attention in the research arena (see also Avery, 1988; Flannery, 1989; Martin, 1992; Hanson, 1990; Harney and Moses, 1992). However, there is mixed evidence of whether youth gangs and other criminally oriented youth groups are systematically expanding their organizations for criminal entrepreneurial purposes, such as the trafficking of narcotics and other controlled substances. Yet, other direct and indirect reasons for migration, according to Maxson (1993), may pertain to law enforcement crackdowns in the community or city, pressure from rival gangs (e.g. violence and intimidation), drug market saturation (low profits and strong competition), and economic and social pressures levied on individuals and families. Reiner (1992) and Spergel (1990) support the hypothesis that street gang migration is driven predominantly by pressures on families who relocate to other cities and states because of perceived or actual economic or lifestyle opportunities. Juveniles committed to the gang lifestyle, through what Skolnick (1993) terms "symbolic association," may continue their gang activity in the new surroundings, often adopting the same names, colors, and traditions of the former gang. "Loose ties may have been retained with the old gang, occasionally enhanced by return visits, but the primary orientation [is] toward the activity and people in the new environment" (Maxson, 1993, p. 5).

An interim report (Maxson and Klein, 1993) found that gang migration, involving both temporary and long-term visits, was widespread throughout the United States. The report did not attempt to explain this phenomenon, but identified more than 700 cities and towns — 200 of which were in the South — that have experienced some gang migration. The preliminary findings of this study should be viewed with caution since the conclusions relied on respondent perceptions, not official records. The impact of youth gang migration may be difficult to discern, especially since we cannot fully comprehend the dynamics and complexity of this activity. Determining the attraction of destination cities, the motivations for migration, the link between "drug" and street gangs, the ethnic variations in migration, the spatial patterns of migration, and if migration involves individuals or collectives, all have important intervention and prevention implications (Maxson, 1993). But "[t]he major concern is the corruption of indigenous community youth by outsiders, especially criminally sophisticated, big city gangsters as portrayed by the national media" (p. 3).

Estimates of Youth Gang and Group Populations. The estimates provided in this section once again rely heavily on the information provided by respondents from the two law enforcement groupings: city police agencies and county sheriff's departments. The strong consensual scores of youth gang and gang-related incident definitions established their general reliability for making further assessments. Spergel et al. (1990) also asserted that law enforcement estimates of youth gang populations are often viewed as more reliable, conservative, and have the greatest credence since these organizations have the primary responsibilities for collecting and maintaining information for crime prevention purposes. To recapitulate the previous findings in the present study, 92 percent of the police respondents and 80 percent of the sheriff's department respondents who self-reported youth gang problems, also agreed that the consensual definition of youth gangs characterized the problems they had been experiencing. And outside the community context, 100 percent of the corrections respondents similarly agreed. Moreover, where *youth group* problems were self-reported, few of the respondents from these categories confirmed that their problem could be characterized in terms of the consensual youth gang definition, which likely indicates that these areas were not experiencing youth gang problems. Therefore, it can be argued that the estimates provided by respondents from these three categories (police agencies, sheriff's departments, and corrections) may be the most reliable, in the sense that their estimates were most likely based on consistently used definitional parameters and key gang-defining characteristics.

Furthermore, to avoid the duplication of population estimates and to increase their reliability, law enforcement respondents served as the primary sources of information in those locations where law enforcement and school officials both made estimates. However, estimates provided by school respondents were also considered and listed if they were the only respondent from their respective jurisdictions. The population estimates provided by juvenile court counselors were excluded because of the overlap in respondent jurisdictions: each judicial district—each containing one juvenile court counselor agency—not only consists of one or more counties, which overlap with sheriff's departments jurisdictions, but also contains many cities and towns, which are under the jurisdiction of police agencies. A similar problem arose in the previous chapter regarding how to unravel the index crime estimates provided by multiple respondents in the same jurisdiction. On one hand, it is highly probable that, because of the overlap in respondent jurisdictions, some of the same youth gang and group members were likely considered in each respondent's estimates. There also exists a strong possibility that the population estimates provided by multiple respondents from a particular locality or jurisdiction were exclusive from one another to some unknown degree, which lends support to the argument that the actual gang and group member populations across the State were larger. Since there was no way to be absolutely certain of either argument, nor the extent of the duplicitousness in the estimates, it was again necessary to rely on one respondent per locality or jurisdiction, and as it has been discussed, law enforcement respondents were considered the most reliable sources of these estimates. The population estimates may be substantially lower than the actual or true number—given that not all respondent estimates in each locality were considered and that some estimates were not even available for many *group* localities—so the listed estimates should be considered conservative in nature.

The population estimates (in parenthesis) for youth gang and group members and the estimated number of gangs and groups (in brackets) are listed for each of the localities where the data were available, otherwise the population estimates and number of gangs and groups are annotated as *unknown* (Table 5.1). All respondents were asked the following question in the survey questionnaire (Appendix, Section III):

> *How many individuals would you estimate are in youth groups or youth gangs in your community or jurisdiction?*

Following the survey, selected respondents—those who self-reported gang or group problems—were also interviewed by telephone and asked to estimate how many youth gangs and groups there were in their respective jurisdictions, and how many members belonged to each of these collectives. Based on the methods and criteria discussed above, there were an estimated 2,772 youth gang members across 39 localities, which included eighteen cities, fifteen counties, and six correctional institutions. The average size youth gang for all localities was 17.1 members, while the average size was 16.1 members in cities, 19.4 in counties, and 15.6 in correctional institutions. These figures are based on self-reported youth gang member estimates and the estimates of the number of youth gangs in each particular locality. Those localities whose respondents could not make both estimates (N=8)—these were county and corrections respondents—were not included in these calculations; therefore, the general figures may have been skewed to some extent.

Table 5.1
Member and Collective Estimates (Self-Reported)
(City, County, and Correctional Facilities)

A. *Youth Gang Members/Gangs* (Total Member Estimate 2772; Gangs 127)

City (N=18) Estimates: Members 1262; Gangs 76 (Reported)

Brevard (100) [4]	Havelock* (20) [2]	Morganton* (50) [3]
Charlotte* (150) [6]	Kannapolis* (50) [3]	Mt. Airy (20) [3]
Durham* (125) [6]	Kinston* (75) [4]	Raleigh* (82) [8]
Eliz. City (90) [4]	Lenoir (30) [3]	Southern Pines* (15) [2]
Fayetteville* (75) [4]	Lexington* (20) [2]	Waynesville* (75) [4]
Greensboro* (80) [4]	Lumberton* (125) [10]	Asheville* (80) [4]

County (N=15) Estimates: Members 1180; Gangs 38 (Reported)

Buncombe* (45) [unk]	Forsyth* (100) [unk]	Mecklenburg* (150) [unk]
Caldwell* (150) [6]	Guilford* (100) [5]	New Hanover* (60) [unk]
Cumberland* (90) [unk]	Hertford* (35) [2]	Pasquotank (25) [2]
Durham* (100) [4]	Hoke* (75) [4]	Perquimas (50) [3]
Edgecombe (35) [2]	Lenoir* (40) [4]	Wake* (125) [6]

Correctional Facility (N=6) Estimates: Members 330; Gangs 13 (Reported)

Sandhills Youth Center* (75) [4]
Blanch Youth Center* (20) [2]
Wake Regional Juvenile Detention Facility* (40) [unk]

Morrison Youth Center* (125) [7]
Juvenile Evaluation Center* (40) [unk]
Stonewall Jackson School* (30) [unk]

B. *Youth Group Members/Groups* (Total Member Estimate 1450; Groups 84)

City (N=18) Estimate: Members 350; Groups 45 (Reported)

Albermarle. (unk)	Graham (70) [6]	Oxford (10) [2]
Boone (unk)	Henderson (unk)	Roanoke Rapids (20) [4]
Burlington (50) [5]	Hendersonvl (unk)	Salisbury (unk)
Carrboro (30) [5]	Hickory (35) [4]	Snwhill (20) [3]
Clinton (50) [7]	Mathews (15) [2]	Wilson (unk)
Goldsbr* (10) [2]	Moorehd City* (15) [2]	Win-Sal (25) [3]

County (N=23) Estimate: Members 1080; Groups 39 (Reported)

Alamance (15) [3]	Harnet (200) [unk]	Transylvania (unk)
Alexander (10) [2]	Iredell (50) [5]	Tyrell (unk)
Avery (200) [unk]	Northmptn* (unk)	Union(200) [unk]
Brunswick (40) [6]	Onslow (50) [unk]	Vance (unk)
Catawba (10) [2]	Pender (10) [2]	Washingt(50)[7]
Chatham (unk)	Pitt (20) [4]	Wilkes (unk)
Duplin (50) [unk]	Rockingham (unk)	Yadkin (100) [unk]
Gates (25) [3]	Stanly (50) [5]	

Correctional Facility (N=1) Estimate: Members 20 (Reported)

C.A. Dillon School (20) [unk]

---

* Denotes those locations where respondents concurred during interviews that the consensual definition of youth gang reflected the characteristics of their problem.

The four cities with the largest youth gang member estimates (Brevard, Charlotte, Durham, and Lumberton) disproportionately represented 39.6 percent of the total estimate for the city subsample. Charlotte and Durham are two of North Carolina's largest metropolitan areas, whereas Brevard and Lumberton are relatively small cities. With the exception of Lumberton, these cities also had the largest average size gangs, ranging from 21 to 25 members. According to respondent estimates, the other two cities whose gangs averaged at least twenty members were Greensboro and Asheville. According to t-test results, there were no statistically significant relationships discovered between the general populations of cities and the gang member population estimates provided by respondents. However, the four largest cities (Charlotte, Raleigh, Durham, and Greensboro) did have slightly larger sized youth gangs when compared to the other cities in the subsample, though the relationship did not reach any level of significance.

The findings for the county subsample were similar in a number of respects. Out of the fifteen counties where estimates were available, the two counties with the largest gang member estimates (Mecklenburg and Caldwell) disproportionately represented 25.4 percent of the total gang member estimate for the county subsample. And by examining the five largest counties by general population (Mecklenburg, Forsyth, Guilford, Durham, and Cumberland), the gang member estimates for these counties represented almost half (45.8 percent) of the total estimates for the counties, even though these same counties represented only one-third of the county subsample. Caldwell and Durham County, with the largest reported youth gang member populations (150 and 100, respectively), also had the largest average sized gangs at 25 members. However, this analysis excluded Mecklenburg and Forsyth Counties—whose estimated gang member populations were 150 and 100, respectively—because the estimated number of youth gangs was not reported or was unknown. Unlike the city analysis, a t-test demonstrated a statistically significant relationship ($p < 0.05$) between general population of the counties and the respondent estimates of the gang member populations and the average size of the youth gangs. In general, the larger the county population, the greater the probability that the youth gang member population and average size of the gangs will be larger, at least based on the respondent estimates. Lastly, within the correctional setting, there were six institutions whose respondents reported an estimated 330 youth gang members, with the Morrison Youth Center representing 37.9 percent of the total estimate. In the correctional institutions, respondents from the Sandhills Youth Center and the Morrison Youth Institution reported that youth gangs averaged approximately 18 members in size, with the latter institution having the largest number of reported youth gangs (seven).

There were an estimated 1450 youth group members reported across eighteen cities, twenty-three counties, and one correctional institution, with the average size youth group just over seven members (7.1) for all localities. However, it is important to note that there were thirteen localities (six cities and seven counties) where group member estimates were not even provided by any of the respondents. There were also six localities (all counties) where member estimates were provided, but the estimated number of groups in the locality were not. Therefore, the total group member estimate and those estimates for each of the respective city and county subsamples were most likely substantially larger than reported here. The nonresponse was largely a problem confined to the smallest cities and counties, but there was no way to know the effect that the nonresponse had on the overall group member projections short of extrapolation. Based on the group member estimation patterns discovered in similarly sized cities and counties, the group member populations would likely fall somewhere in the range of 15 to 30 individuals in cities and towns, and in the range of 20 to 50 individuals in counties. Therefore, the total group member estimates for cities and towns could potentially increase anywhere from 90 to 180 more youth (or more), and for counties the increase could involve 140 to 350 or more youth. Based on these extrapolation figures, the total youth group member population could fall anywhere in the range of 1680 to 1980 individuals, a potential increase of 14 to 27 percent above the reported estimates. It is also important to reiterate that the reported estimates were based on localities that were experiencing only youth group problems and do not take into account the youth groups that were most likely present in the cities and counties where respondents self-reported youth gang problems. There were no statistically significant correlations between city and county general populations and the group member estimates provided by respondents, but because of the modest number of localities where estimates were not available, there is the possibility that the correlation results were skewed. One final reminder, and a key point that threatens the validity of both the youth gang and group member estimates, is that the estimates for each locality were provided by only one respondent to negate the possibility of duplication. Thus, by excluding multiple respondents in both cities and counties — as well as juvenile court counselors whose jurisdictions overlap many of the law enforcement and school system jurisdictions — the estimates listed may be very conservative; in fact, they may moderately or substantially underestimate the actual conditions.

The important aspect of this analysis is not the aggregate gang and group member estimates — since counting members and the gangs and groups to which they belong is too often fraught with imprecision due to definitional problems, unsystematic intelligence gathering and recording methods, or other organizational idiosyncrasies — but simply to identify, and place within some perspective, the localities that appear to have higher concentrations of members and collectives. As Spergel et al. (1990. p. 33) notes, "all of the perceptions, particularly by type of respondent category or area have their own distinctive reality that frames the problem and provides a basis for dealing with it, whether effectively or not." The diversity of the definitions provided in an earlier chapter clearly demonstrated this point; even though there was reasonable explanatory power and consensus provided by the definitions of youth gangs and groups, there may still be other factors (e.g. professional orientation, past experiences) that affect perceptions. Consequently, these unknown underlying constructs invariably affect the extent to which the estimates can legitimately be aggregated (Miller, 1982; Spergel et al., 1990; Spergel, 1990). This analysis should facilitate the opportunity to explore, in a more thorough and systematic manner, the areas that have comparatively large and disproportionately represented youth gang and group member populations.

C. Socio-Demographic Characteristics of Youth Gangs and Groups

The national-level studies (Miller, 1982; Needle and Stapleton, 1983; Spergel et al., 1990; Curry et al., 1994), as well as much of the research literature (e.g. Moore, 1978, 1985; Hagedorn, 1988; Fagan, 1989; Jankowski, 1991; Horowitz, 1983; Spergel, 1990), indicate that black and Hispanic youth constitute the vast majority of individuals involved in both youth gangs and groups throughout the country. But as Spergel (1990) posits, even though race and ethnicity are significant factors in the development of gang and group problems, the precise role of these factors is very complex. The common finding that youth gangs and groups are disproportionately located in lower-class minority communities is further complicated by such characteristics as social instability, poverty, unemployment, and social isolation (Cartwright and Howard, 1966; Moore, 1978, 1985; Hagedorn, 1988; Spergel, 1990, 1995; Jankowski, 1991). The degree of social disorganization — i.e. the existence of several of the previously mentioned factors — influences gang and group delinquency through indirect means: it influences social and economic opportunities within the community; conventional social bonding; the frequency, duration, and intensity of exposure to delinquent peers; and the types of collectives that are more or less prevalent in the neighborhood or community (Shaw and McKay, 1942; see also Bursik and Grasmick, 1993).

Earlier studies (Spergel, 1964; Cartwright and Howard, 1966; Cohen, 1969; Klein, 1971) have demonstrated that gang and group delinquency could not solely be predicted based on socioeconomic factors, and more recent research on criminal patterns of gang members (Curry and Spergel, 1988; Skolnick et al., 1988, 1993; Spergel et al., 1990; Chin, 1990) indicates that race may in fact be a significant influence relative to involvement in certain types of crimes, particularly drug-related activities and the level of turf-related violence. Even though the relationship between youth collectives, criminal activity, and race is complex, the increasing involvement of gang and group members (from all races) in drug-trafficking activities has effectively begun to transform earlier conceptions of group behavior: traditional turf and neighborhood oriented youth gangs and groups are evolving into collectives whose activities have begun to center more and more on drug distribution and profits.

Recent attention has been given to the effect of age on the criminal pattern of individuals involved in youth collectives, both gang and nongang in nature. Research on age, offense patterns, and co-offending (Reiss, 1986, 1988; Reiss and Farrington, 1991) found that violent offenses had the lowest rates of co-offending and were most likely committed by older youth and young adults (17 years and older), but the relationship between co-offending and property offenses was independent of age. Knowledge of the age-crime curve of particular offenses, especially if the offenses involved co-offending, has significant prevention and intervention implications (Blumstein et al., 1985, 1988; Cohen, 1986; Farrington, 1990, 1992). Spergel (1990, p. 219) succinctly concluded that "if the middle or early adolescent period accounts for most gang violence and serious gang crime, one set of theories and policies strategies may be appropriate. If [collective crime and violence occurs in] the late adolescent and young adult period, an entirely different set of explanatory theories and policy interventions may be called for." The present study design, and the lack of necessary data on co-offending within the gang and group setting, preclude the opportunity to investigate these patterns longitudinally; however, at the general level the data do provide important insights regarding the relationship between age and criminal propensities.

1. Age Characteristics

Research has broadly estimated that the typical age range of youth gang members is between eight and twenty-two years, with a mean age of approximately eighteen to nineteen years (Miller, 1982; Horowitz, 1983; Spergel, 1986; Bobrowski, 1988; Spergel, 1990). A number of studies discovered that the most violent gang offenders were disproportionately in their late teens to early twenties (Torres, 1980; Maxson et al., 1985; Spergel, 1983), which refutes the widely held assumption that gang violence is most often perpetrated by young teenagers and adolescents; moreover, the median age of gang members may also vary based on race and ethnicity (e.g. Chin, 1990; Horowitz, 1983), their locations in different cities (e.g. Hagedorn, 1988; Collins, 1979), and the sophistication of their activities. For example, in the Los Angeles greater metropolitan area, Maxson et al.(1985) discovered that the median age for gang homicide offenders was 19 to 20 years old, and in Chicago, Spergel (1986) found that the largest proportion of gang homicide offenders fell between the ages of 17 and 18. Chin's (1990) research on Asian gangs indicated that the median age for members was 19, with an age range from the early teens to almost 40 years old. Though there have been a number of studies that have reported gang membership starting at very early ages (e.g. 8 to 9 years of age) and continuing well into adulthood (e.g. 30s), the median age of membership was generally reported to be between 17 and 19 years of age (see Collins, 1979; Miller, 1982; Horowitz, 1983; Spergel, 1986; Bobrowski, 1988).

The data in the present study also support these findings. Respondents were specifically asked to estimate the age range of gang and group offenders within their respective jurisdictions (Appendix, Section III, Questions 12a and 12b). It should be emphasized that the age estimates are for *offenders* — i.e. gang and group members who most likely came to the attention of authorities due to a criminal violation or some type of behavioral infraction — and not the estimated age for members in general. Based on the available estimates, the average reported age of youth gang and youth group offenders was 18 and 17.2, respectively, with the largest proportion of offenders from both types of collectives (95.3 percent) falling within the age range of 13 and 25 years. There was a larger proportion of youth group offenders falling within the 13 to 15 age range when compared to youth gang member age estimates (14.3 versus 8.6 percent), but, conversely, there was a larger proportion of youth gang offenders who fell within the older age range of 18 to 20 years of age (41.2 versus 33.6 percent). There were no data provided in regard to age specific offense patterns, but respondents generally reported during interviews that certain activities, namely violent criminal offenses and drug trafficking activities, were more often perpetrated by individuals in their late teens and early twenties, regardless of whether they belonged to gangs or groups. Because there was a lack of official data addressing the age-offense patterns of gang and group criminal activities, only correlations based on respondent estimates of these two variables (age and index offenses attributed to these collectives) could be conducted. The correlations and the variations between these two collectives will be explored in greater detail in forthcoming discussions.

To gather some idea of the effect and influence age has on general crime patterns, it is useful to examine a recent study. Blumstein's (1995) research on the age specific homicide and assault rates for 1992 provides evidence of the relationship between age and violent crime, and also indicates an alarming trend. The study found that the peak age for homicides and assaults in 1992 was eighteen years of age, compared to 1985 when the peak age for each offense was twenty-four and eighteen, respectively. The extent to which these offenses were attributable to collective youth criminal activities is open for speculation, but the peak age of eighteen in 1992 includes two troubling developments: first, the per capita homicide rate from 1985 to 1992 more than doubled, with stranger-on-stranger homicides accounting for 34 percent of the total for offenders eighteen years and younger; and second, the number of offenses involving the use of guns by and against young people increased from the mid-1980s, from 62 to 83 percent. The broad implication is that as younger individuals become more involved in violent offenses, it becomes critically important to know whether these violent and criminal youth are acting with others or alone. The younger the age of onset of serious criminal behavior, the greater the likelihood of a continuous and more serious criminal career (see Farrington, 1992). Moreover, the earlier youth become involved in youth gangs and other deviant and criminal group networks, the greater the likelihood that more serious criminal patterns will also ensue. However, co-offending relationships do not necessarily persist for a great length of time, and appear to be largely influenced by the age of offenders (Farrington, 1990; Reiss and Farrington, 1991). Thus, as gang and group offenders age, they may be less likely to commit offenses with others, even though the group processes may have been instrumental in instigating the criminal activities in the first place.

The age range of offenders (whether they belong to youth gangs or groups) may be fundamental to developing appropriate strategies to reduce the criminal activities. The implication of not considering the age range of offenders could be profound: efforts that target youth gang and group criminal activities—when in actuality these criminal activities may have been performed by older youth acting alone—may have little effect on reducing or preventing the offending; conversely, if the criminal activity is perpetrated by younger individuals (e.g. 14-16 years of age), targeting the group may be more effective than targeting each individual separately.

2. Cultural and Racial Characteristics

The youth gang problem today is dominated by inner-city, lower class males in their mid to late teens from predominantly Hispanic and black ethnic groups. Miller (1982) discovered that Hispanics (44.4 %) and blacks (42.9 %) constituted the majority of gangs in nine of the largest American cities, with white and Asian gangs making up the remaining 13 percent. Spergel et al. (1990), who surveyed 45 cities compared to 26 in Miller's study, found that black gang members most often came to the attention of survey respondents. However, Spergel's study made two distinctions: relatively more blacks came to the attention of law enforcement, whereas Hispanic and white gangs more often came to the attention of non-law enforcement agencies, such as youth intervention agencies. Both surveys discovered that race and ethnic composition vary between cities and regions and have differing impacts on gang development and the nature of the activity. However, neither study considered the possibility that variations in youth gang and group activities may reflect the population of youth in cities surveyed.

Table 5.2
Gang Race and Ethnic Classification

Rubric	Variations
Hispanic	Mexican American, Puerto Rican, Cuban, Central and South American
Black	African American, Jamaican
Asian	Korean, Chinese, Japanese, Vietnamese, Thai, Laotian, Cambodian, Hmong, Taiwanese, Pacific Islander
White	European descent

Furthermore, there may be quite distinct variables that influence gang involvement and delinquency between ethnic groups. In a limited study focusing on Chicago, Curry and Spergel (1993) discovered that intrapersonal variables, such as self-esteem and educational frustration, had a greater influence on Hispanic youths joining gangs, whereas social and interpersonal variables, such as exposure to gang members at school and home (relatives), had a greater influence on African-American youths. This highlights the importance of understanding the dynamics of ethnic variables in designing prevention and intervention approaches. Gang race can be broadly classified into four rubrics (Table 5.2), each containing an array of ethnic variations. There have been studies that found diversity in certain gangs; however, most evidence indicates that gangs are racially homogeneous. The racial and ethnic composition of gangs most often mirrors the communities from which individual members are drawn.

Hispanic Gangs. Hispanic gangs, predominantly Mexican American, have existed since the turn of the century and constitute some of the oldest established gangs in the United States. These gangs are best characterized as highly territorial, where identity with and sense of barrio has been refined, and codes of conduct and tradition established over generations (Jackson and McBride, 1985; Vigil, 1990). Unlike Thrasher's Hispanic gangs, contemporary gangs persist and often span several generations, which strengthens the social fabric of the barrio subculture (Moore, 1978; Vigil, 1988). As Spergel (1991a) concluded, these gangs possess a cohesiveness and extended kinship structure similar to the larger Hispanic culture from which they evolved. This link is not prevalent in other gangs. Age graded cohorts, or klikas, remain very important to members throughout the lifetime of the gang, since the individuals remain in the same klika from the time they enter until the time they leave the gang, which could last well into the adult years (Moore, 1978). This tradition increases cohesiveness and loyalty among members of the same klika as they grow older.

However, duration of gang affiliation depends on a variety of factors, such as motivation to join the gang initially, its cohesiveness, and the personal and social circumstances that influence the transition out of the gang.

More important is the pattern of crime and violence committed by Hispanic gangs. In Los Angeles, where the majority of gang membership is Hispanic, Reiner (1992) found that Hispanic gang violence in a single year (1989-1990) increased by 96 percent within the county's jurisdiction. Reiner attributes this rise in violence to three factors: rapid growth in the Hispanic population, rapid growth in Hispanic immigration, and a shift of anti-gang resources away from Hispanic neighborhoods to predominantly black ones. Throughout the 1980s, Hispanic gangs committed on average 60 percent of all gang-related homicides in Chicago, compared to 30 percent committed by black gangs. The statistical significance lies in the fact that Chicago's population is 40 percent black and only 14 percent Hispanic. Gang homicides in Los Angeles in the mid-1980s, conversely, were disproportionately committed by black gangs (Spergel, 1984; Curry and Spergel, 1988). Spergel (1984) noted that the disparity is most likely due to the Chicago Police Department's more restrictive definition of gang-related offenses. The definition requires gang affiliation of both victim and offender and a gang-related motivation. Los Angeles, by contrast, utilizes a broader definition that requires gang affiliation of either the victim or the offender, with little emphasis on motive.

The existence and especially the persistence of Hispanic gangs, particularly Mexican American, is difficult to explain. Vigil (1988) introduced the concept of "multiple marginality" which stresses the structural and ecological influences that adversely affect the acculturation of the Hispanic subculture. Marginality caused by discrimination, poverty, cultural factors, and social instability strongly influences gang formation and perpetuation. Population acculturation becomes problematic where there is community instability and where the subcultural population finds difficulty in modifying necessary social institutions (Spergel, 1984). Finally, because adolescent bravado and acts of masculinity are deeply rooted in cultural norms, gang membership and associated criminality, especially violence, may be tolerated to some degree by the community. Horowitz (1987, p. 443) discovered that "while few parents would acknowledge that they think it is important or good for their son to be a gang member or want him to be constantly fighting, most would see violence—and, occasionally, deadly violence—as a proper and justifiable response to offenses against family honor." Because of the complexity of socio-cultural factors found within Hispanic communities, many cities have found it quite difficult to design and implement effective intervention and prevention strategies.

Black Gangs. There have also been many studies on the growth and development of African-American gangs through the years (see Thrasher, 1936; Short and Strodtbeck, 1965; Spergel, 1984; Hagedorn, 1988; and

Huff, 1989). Like Hispanic gangs, African-American gangs evolve predominantly in lower class, inner-city communities. However, recent research has begun to focus on the emergence and activities of black gangs in smaller cities and towns. Evidence indicates that, at least in Chicago, the most economically dependent areas that are highly segregated and predominantly black, also account for the highest gang delinquency rates (Spergel, 1984). Vigil's (1988) concept of multiple marginality does not readily explain the existence of African-American gangs, yet there is reason to believe that the notion of a black underclass, where individuals are permanently excluded from participating in mainstream economic and social opportunities, provides similar ecological and social influences for gang development (see also Moore, 1985, 1989; Huff, 1989).

Hagedorn (1988) studied this "black underclass" phenomenon in a city (Milwaukee) where there has been a notable decline in low wage occupations and change in prevailing economic conditions in minority neighborhoods. The study links economic conditions (primarily unemployment) with the formation of gangs — a contentious issue in contemporary criminological research. Severe unemployment conditions, as Hagedorn posits, also increase the likelihood that individuals will remain in the gang longer because of greater opportunities, albeit illicit. Unlike Hispanic gangs, African-American gangs in this study do not develop or maintain as strong an identity for their particular neighborhoods, but may instead become alienated. It was pointed out that school desegregation, with forced busing from surrounding communities, was the primary cause for not developing a loyalty towards the neighborhood. The "underclass" theory has been examined in a significant body of research, but it is the notion of economic isolation of inner-city ethnic groups, especially blacks, which has provided a new angle for analysis. Underclass theory, assert Curry and Spergel (1993), offers promise in explaining African-American gang socialization processes because "African-Americans appear closer to the bottom of the socioeconomic ladder. [Furthermore] institutional racism and the more pervasive alienated status ... more than poverty per se could possibly explain the more encompassing gang influence on African-American youth" (p. 276). Whether the problem is "multiple marginality", an underclass dilemma, or a multiplicity of complex socioeconomic factors, three points can be made based on the available research that focuses on African-American gangs: first, gangs in black communities represent a survival strategy, which has had the effect of supplanting the family and other social institutions as the primary reference group; second, African-American gangs are concentrated in lower economic, inner-city communities where a female is often the head of the household; and third, African American gangs are most often more homogeneous than gangs of other ethnic backgrounds (Johnstone, 1981; Spergel, 1984).

Asian Gangs. Asian gangs, according to Spergel (1991a), make up only a fraction of reported gangs, but have become twice as numerous as white gangs over the past few years. Most Asian gangs are located primarily in large coastal cities (e.g. New York, Los Angeles, Seattle) where there are proportionately large Asian immigrant populations. These gain-oriented gangs, however, have slowly begun to proliferate around the country. The formation and perpetuation of Asian gangs can be traced to similar socio-ecological influences found in other ethnic gang formations, especially Hispanic gangs. Because many Asian gang members are recent immigrants, acculturation problems and diminishment or breakdown of traditional values greatly influence the propensity for delinquency. Exacerbating this problem is the continuous influx of new immigrants with teenage children who quickly become socially and economically alienated. Perceived and actual blocked opportunities (Cloward and Ohlin, 1960) due to discrimination or other factors beyond individual control (e.g. language barriers), have an especially influential impact on Asian youths who seek opportunities available through gangs.

With only few exceptions, most Asian gangs have an identifiable organizational structure which facilitates the execution of more organized criminal activities, such as gambling, extortion, and drug trafficking (Chin, 1990). These groups are difficult to detect since they do not behave as typical or traditional street gangs, in the sense of identifying with particular neighborhoods, the use of colors or symbols, or protecting turf from encroachment by other gangs. Protecting "turf" most often involves the protection of a particular illicit enterprise—a business rather than a traditional interest. Adding to the difficulty of policing Asian gangs is their high degree of mobility and complexity of organizational structure. Equally problematic is the fact that these gangs are often closely linked to adult gangs and organized crime triads, which may partly explain the high median age (18-28) and high proportion of homicides when compared to other gangs (Jackson and McBride, 1985; Chin, 1990; Spergel, 1991a). Even though Asian gang structure and activity may vary between ethnic variations, research has consistently found that the gangs are well organized, motivated by economic gain, and in most cases do not adhere to traditional street gang orthodoxies.

White Gangs. Finally, white gangs comprise the smallest proportion of youth gangs in most recent assessments (Miller, 1982; Spergel, 1990, 1991a; Spergel et al., 1990; Reiner, 1992). The most common classifications are Motorcycle gangs and Skinheads, though there are gangs such as "Stoners," "Satanics," and "Punks" that make up only a small fraction of white gang membership. Actually, classifying the latter grouping as gangs may be a misnomer, since they more closely resemble near-groups characterized by Yablonsky (1962). The lack of structure, cohesiveness, and unstable membership places them closer to social groups than delinquent gangs. These groups often come from middle-class families and participate in activities out of the need for companionship and because of a "general rebellion against adults and conventional society" (Covey et al., 1992, p.64), but rarely partake in delinquency as the primary activity of the group. However, the more structured White gangs (Motorcycle gangs and Skinheads) are involved in illicit activities in varying degrees, with drug trafficking, theft and vandalism most common in Motorcycle gangs, and racial, anti-semitic violence prevalent among Skinheads. These gangs tend to be well structured, older in age than most youth gangs, and adhere to elaborate rituals, dress codes, and unique values. But because these gangs are small in number, they have yet to become a major law enforcement or public policy concern at the national level (Spergel, 1990).

In order to acquire the necessary information regarding the racial characteristics of youth gang and group members who came to the attention of respondents, the following question was posed (Appendix, Section III):

> Of the youth group or youth gang members who came to your attention in recent years, what percent were White, Black, Hispanic, Asian, or Other?

If the youth gang or group members could not be classified into one of these four categories, respondents had the opportunity to specify the particular race or ethnicity. According to the data in Table 5.3, the majority of members who came to the attention of respondents were classified as black, which included African-American, Jamaican, and other Caribbean and African natives. The second largest racial representation constituted white individuals. Members were least represented in the Hispanic category, which included Mexican-American, Cuban, and South American ancestry, and the Asian category, which included any individual with Asian and Pacific Islander ancestry.

Table 5.3
Mean Percentage of Members Based on Race

Race	Youth Gangs Mean	Youth Groups Mean
White	24.3	25.8
Black	66.1	62.6
Hispanic	1.6	1.6
Asian	1.7	3.2

These racial groups were equally represented in both youth gangs and youth groups. Where youth gangs were reported, there was a slightly higher mean percent of members classified as black when compared to the members in youth groups. Based on the available estimates, black youth gang and group members were disproportionately represented relative to the general population of the State. According to the most recent census data on North Carolina (1990), blacks represented 22.0 percent of youth between the ages of 15-25 and whites constituted 75.5 percent, but the estimated percentage of youth gang and group members who were black was over twice that found for white members. The population distribution for Asians and Hispanics in the State was significantly small, representing less than three percent of the total population; therefore, it was not surprising that the estimated percentage of youth gang and group members classified into these two racial groups was similarly small. Among respondent categories, officials from correctional institutions (71.4 percent) reported that the majority of known youth gang members were black; similarly, law enforcement officials reported that the large majority of youth gang members coming to their attention were also black (76.5 percent). But for court counselor and school respondents, the percentages were modestly lower, 62.5 and 55.6 percent, respectively. The pattern for youth groups was similar, though the percentages were slightly lower.

One possible explanation for these variations may be due to the fact that many court counselor and school respondent jurisdictions consisted of counties with relatively large rural white populations, thereby increasing the probability that more white youth gangs and groups would be found. The disproportionate number of blacks found in correctional institutions across the State most likely had a significant influence on youth gang and group membership demographics in the correctional setting. But why black youth gang and group members came to the attention of law enforcement officials at significantly higher rates than members of other racial groups, particularly members of white youth collectives, needs some explanation. The reasons may be two-fold: first, due to routine law enforcement patrol patterns—i.e. more frequent patrols in high-crime minority neighborhoods (where youth gangs and groups are often found)—the probability of apprehension may increase; and second, the more serious nature of crime committed by black youth gangs and its members often leads to focused targeting by law enforcement organizations.

Compared to the national youth gang and group studies (Miller, 1982; Spergel et al., 1990; Curry et al., 1994), the estimated percentage of youth gang and group members who were classified as white was relatively large, and the estimated percentage of members classified as Hispanic was quite small. Miller (1982) estimated that in the nine largest American cities, 44.4 percent of the gang members were Hispanic, 42.9 percent were black, 9 percent were white, and 4 percent were Asian. Spergel et al.'s (1990) estimates for 45 cities and 11 sites were 46 to 53 percent black, 28 to 30 percent Hispanic, and only 1 to 3 percent were white or Asian. The effect of race on the criminality and structure of youth gangs and groups will be addressed shortly, but it is interesting to note that most respondents who reported the presence of white youth gangs and groups classified them in very traditional terms (e.g. territorial, colors, symbols) rather than the more radical characterizations—e.g. stoners, freaks, satanic worshipers, skinheads, punkers—commonly found in the research literature. Perhaps the more traditional aspects of belonging to a gang or group (e.g. belonging, status, protection) have attracted more white youth into joining these collectives.

D. Youth Gang and Group Criminality: Influencing Factors

Knowledge of the relationship between age, race, adult involvement, and the level of criminality has significant prevention and intervention implications. The reality of resource constraints, particularly those faced by law enforcement organizations, mandates the need for information that could aid in the targeting of at-risk individuals. This section searches for the nexus between the above socio-demographic factors and measures of criminality, with the intention of gaining a greater understanding of their potentially influencing effect on one another. The four key measures of criminality—proportion of index offenses attributed to youth gangs and groups, the estimated percentage of members with prior criminal records, drug distribution as a primary activity, and the importation of drugs into the community—serve as the primary variables in this analysis. Underlying this general discussion are two themes: the effect that group processes may have on the potential criminality of members of a group or on the collective as a whole; and the connection, if any, between violence committed by youth gangs and groups and drug trafficking activities.

In addition to the effect of socio-demographic factors on criminal patterns, what influence do other individuals within the group have on these same criminal patterns? How does the structure of the youth gang, as opposed to youth groups, differentially influence behavioral patterns and activities, particularly if these patterns are criminal in nature? It is widely agreed that gang members engage in more delinquent and criminal activity than other nongang delinquents, but not necessarily easy to explain. As Thornberry et al. (1993, p.56) concluded, "although we know that gang members are involved in more delinquency and drug use than nongang members, we know surprisingly little about whether gangs attract adolescents who are already highly delinquent or whether they create highly delinquent adolescents as part of the gang process." As mentioned earlier, within the gang structure there are small, loosely-knit subgroups (cliques) of individuals who are largely responsible for the bulk of the gang's delinquency, and who greatly influence the scope and nature of activities (Klein, 1968a; Hagedorn, 1988; Spergel, 1990; Taylor, 1990). It is thought that these smaller, more cohesive groupings stimulate the pattern of activity and the behavior of other members.

However, the general level of participation within the gang structure —transient versus stable membership—may not necessarily have a significant impact on the actual level of delinquency while participating in gang activities. Thornberry et al. (1993) discovered that transient members—those who participated in the gang for less than a year—had similar levels of delinquent behavior compared to the more stable members who remained in the gang for at least two consecutive years. The most interesting finding in the study, which also has serious theoretical implications, was that the transient members demonstrated a much lower mean delinquency level before they joined and after they left the gang. This finding best supports the study's *social facilitation* model,[1] which states that by joining a gang "normative structure and group processes of the gang are likely to bring about high rates of delinquency," (p. 58) and that "gang members are intrinsically no different than nongang members. Rather, group processes of the gang and the normative support it provides for delinquent behavior generate a context in which such behavior flourishes " (p. 79). Thus, there is something unique about the structure and group processes of gangs, when compared to youth groups, that makes these collectives a greater concern.

Cohesiveness plays a critical role in all aspects of group development, but is a particularly important dimension in the youth gang context, since it may determine the quality of group interaction and serve as the principal mechanism for criminal behavior. Gang criminality and cohesiveness, though tenuously related, appears to have a positive correlation, since opportunities for deviance are learned and reinforced through mutual association with other members (Sutherland and Cressey, 1978) and engaging in delinquency leads to increases in associations with delinquent peers (Thornberry et al., 1994). Longitudinal research outcomes with great consistency reveal peer relations as the most important, proximal contributor to gang delinquency (Cartwright et al., 1975). There is also reason to suspect that cohesiveness and criminality reciprocally influence one another, though the causal direction of this relationship is debatable. Lucore (1975) found that a circular, dependent relationship exists where criminal behavior increases with more contact among gang members, and cohesiveness increases with more involvement in criminality. Criminal behav-

---

1. Contrast this model with the selection model, which posits that gangs recruit members from adolescents who are already delinquent, or have a high propensity for delinquency; and the enhancement model, where gangs recruit delinquent adolescents and the gang process encourages delinquency (Thornberry et al., 1993, pp.58-59).

ior, according to this reasoning, could occur to strengthen cohesion during times of disorganization or when confronted by external threats, such as rival gangs and strong law enforcement tactics. In contrast, Klein and Crawford (1967) assert that group cohesion is antecedent to criminal behavior. It is the external sources of cohesion—poverty and social disorganization, for example—that continually throw gang members together, forcing the kinds of interaction that increase the likelihood of delinquency. Klein (1971) later found that criminal behavior and cohesiveness were more interactive, albeit the most influential direction was still from cohesion to criminality.

Other research (Yablonsky, 1962; Short and Strodtbeck, 1965) found that situational determinants of gang leaders' behavior ultimately determine the degree of group dynamics (normative definitions), communication patterns, and level of cohesion; status threats to leaders, in particular, represent a process that, when operated within the framework of gang norms and values, often involves violence and delinquency. This "chicken before the egg" argument regarding cohesion and group criminality, and the extent to which status striving affects the whole process, has confounded many researchers and led to much disagreement. Research nevertheless suggests that, despite the causal directions, "group processes revolving around such dimensions as status, solidarity, and cohesion are likely to increase the level of delinquency for gang members," (Thornberry et. al., 1993, p. 59) . This is perhaps true even if gangs are simultaneously cohesive and loosely knit, stable and unstable in the same setting (Spergel, 1991). Cohesiveness, therefore, remains a powerful characteristic of group development and a powerful influence on the nature of gang interaction. The patterns of gang structure, organization, and activity, the degree of group cohesion, and the flux and function of gang members vary considerably and are heavily influenced by member age, race, and extent of adult involvement in group activities. The general hypothesis is that older youth and young adults are better able to stimulate and create criminal opportunities within the community context, thereby influencing group processes and illicit activities. The correlations in the following two sections—which demonstrate, to some degree, the acceptability of this hypothesis—were based on responses to questions addressed earlier (e.g. racial characteristics of members, estimates of index offenses) and the following new questions (Appendix, Section III):

What percentage of youth gang or group-related incidents or cases coming to your organizations attention involved adults and juveniles?

What percentage of youth group or youth gang offenders who came to your organization's attention in 1993 had prior police records?

Is drug distribution one of the purposes of existence? (for youth gangs or groups)

Are youth gang or group members involved in the importation of drugs from outside your jurisdiction?

1. Age and Criminality

Respondents estimated that most of their cases involved members with prior criminal records (66.7 percent where gangs were reported and 52.1 percent where groups were reported), and that drug distribution was a primary activity for both gangs (68.6 percent) and groups (52.0 percent). The importation of drugs from outside the community was also cited by a modest majority of respondents, particularly where gangs were reported (64.7 percent). Law enforcement respondents, in particular, cited that the vast majority of their gang-related cases involved drug-related activities (72.5 percent) and older members (16 years and older) with felony records (64.7 percent); whereas group-related activities more often involved first-time offenders, or offenders with less serious criminal records. Respondents from the court counselor category reported that drug-related incidents were more common among gang-related cases when compared to group cases (75.0 versus 54.5 percent, respectively); the majority of these respondents (62.5 percent reporting gangs, 54.5 percent reporting groups) also reported that many of their gang and group member probationers had prior criminal histories. Drug-related activity (both street-level distribution and importation) among gang and group members was perceived as less prevalent and serious by school system officials; however, most school officials were unable to comment, with any degree of certainty, on the prior criminal histories of known youth gang and group members. Not surprisingly, drug-related activity involving youth gangs and other groups was cited as a very common problem by officials (85.7 percent) within the correctional setting, regardless of the institution's age range; the majority of correctional officials (71.4 percent) also reported that individuals who were members of both gangs and groups had prior criminal histories.

Perhaps the age of members involved in youth gangs and groups had a significant, and variable effect on the pattern of reporting. Because these descriptive statistics do not provide any information regarding the important effect or influence age may have on the levels of criminality (drug-related activities and index offenses in general), a number of correlations were conducted. The data in Table 5.4 illustrate the results of the correlations conducted on the four key measures of criminality and the estimated percent of incidents attributed to adults (16 years and older). The correlations indicate a number of significant relationships for both youth gangs and groups. For youth gangs, there were significant positive correlations ($p < 0.05$) between the percent of incidents attributed to adults, index offenses attributed to gangs, percent of members with prior criminal records, and drug distribution; there was one highly significant positive correlation (p< 0.01) between the estimated percentage of incidents attributed to adults and drug importation.

Table 5.4
Pearson Correlations between Measures of Criminality and
the Estimated Percent of Incidents Attributed to Adults

	Index Offenses	% Prior Record	Drug Distribution	Drug Import
Youth Gangs (N=51)				
% Incidents Adults	.342*	.267*	.313*	.396**
Youth Groups (N=55)				
% Incidents Adults	.057*	.028	.217*	.186

p≤0.05* p≤0.01** p≤0.001***

In the youth group category, there were only two significant positive correlations (p< 0.05) involving adult members: percentage of index offenses attributed to groups and involvement in drug distribution activities. The correlations in this table support the hypothesis that where the percentage of incidents attributed to adults is substantial, whether they are involved in youth gang or group activities, the criminal activities of the collectives to which the older members belong may be more serious in nature. In order to further examine the criminal patterns of youth gang and group members based on the adult age criterion, correlations between the estimated percent of incidents attributed to adults and each of the eight index offenses were conducted (Table 5.5). The strongest statistical correlations were once again found in the youth gang category: two of the most serious index offenses (robbery and aggravated assault) and one property offense (larceny) achieved positive statistical significance at the 0.01 level. Two other offenses, motor vehicle theft and arson, were negatively significant at the 0.05 level, which may indicate that these offenses are more commonly perpetrated by individuals under 16 years of age. A similar, albeit less significant, statistical pattern can be found within the youth group category: the more serious offenses of robbery and aggravated assault may have been perpetrated with greater frequency by adult group members, whereas property-related offenses may be more prevalent among the younger members.

Table 5.5
Pearson Correlations between Index Offenses and Estimated Percent
of Incidents Attributed to Adults

	Homicide	Rape	Robbery	Agg. Assault	Burglary	Larceny	MV Theft	Arson
Youth Gangs (N=51)								
% Incidents Adults	.162	.077	.293**	.373**	-.079	.338**	-.224*	-.241*
Youth Groups (N=55)								
% Incidents Adults	.108	.064	.270*	.3 60*	.130	-.083	-.326*	-.222*

p≤0.05* p≤0.01** p≤0.001***

The data in Tables 5.4 and 5.5 demonstrate that the more serious index offenses were strongly associated with older youth and young adults, rather than youth in their early and mid-teens, thus strengthening the hypothesis noted above. The negative statistical pattern of adult involvement in the property offenses of arson and motor vehicle theft inferentially and partially supports the general research on age and offense seriousness (e.g. Blumstein et al., 1988; Farrington, 1992) and the specific research on youth gang and group criminal patterns (e.g. Spergel, 1990; Sanders, 1994; Thornberry et al., 1993, 1994).

2. Race and Criminality

The second key dimension for understanding the nature of the youth gang and group problem was the relationship between race and level of criminality. Implicit in this relationship is the notion that race and ethnicity differentially influence involvement in certain types of criminal activities. Spergel (1990) suggests that the ratios of personal to property crime for white and Hispanic gangs were much smaller than those found among black gangs. Other studies on drug trafficking (Skolnick et al., 1988; Chin, 1990) discovered that crack cocaine was the drug of choice for black gangs, methamphetamines, PCP, and marijuana were commonly distributed by white and Hispanic gangs, and heroin was reported as the primary drug in the Asian gang drug business.

Table 5.6
Pearson Correlations between Race (% of Members)
and Measures of Criminality

	Drug Distribution	Drug Import	Index Offenses	Prior Record
Youth Gangs (N=51)				
% White	.118	-.131	.027	-.122
% Black	.344*	.226*	.124	.336*
% Hispanic	.165	.085	.109	.090
% Asian	.012	.038	.098	.055
Youth Groups (N=55)				
% White	.373*	-.241*	.029	-.278**
% Black	.290*	.333*	.050	.350**
% Hispanic	.064	.085	-.056	-.022
% Asian	.008	.103	.027	.014

p≤0.05* p≤0.01** p≤0.001***

The data presented in Table 5.6 illustrate the correlations between the estimated percentage of members who could be classified into one of the four race categories and the four variables that provide some indication of criminality: 1) involvement in drug distribution activities as a primary purpose; 2) involvement in drug importation activities; 3) proportion of index offenses attributed to gangs or groups; and 4) the percentage of members with prior criminal records. There were a number of statistically significant correlations between the percent of members classified as white and black who belonged to youth gangs and groups, but none were discovered in the analysis of members who were classified as Hispanic and Asian. For youth gangs and groups, the distribution of drugs as a primary activity and drug importation were significantly related (p< 0.05) to the estimated percent of members classified as black; moreover, there were strong positive correlations between the percent of members classified as black and the percent of individuals with prior criminal records. There was a significant positive correlation between drug distribution and the percent of group members classified as white, but the correlation for drug importation was significantly negative. The percent of individuals with prior criminal records was also significantly correlated (p< 0.01) with the percent of members classified as white within the youth group category; however, this correlation was negative.

In interpreting these findings, the statistically significant positive correlations between the percentage of members estimated to be in black youth gangs and groups and the measures of criminality appear to indicate more active, and potentially more serious, involvement in criminal activities, particularly drug-related activities beyond street-level dealing (e.g. Spergel et al., 1990). The correlations also demonstrate that black youth collectives may have been much more active in drug-related activities than the other three racial groups, but since these correlations are based on respondent perceptions and estimates, there is no way of knowing the true conditions. It was also interesting to discover that, even though white youth groups appeared to be actively involved in street-level drug dealing, there was still a negative relationship between the estimated percentage of white youth group members and prior criminal records. Perhaps the high profile of black youth gangs and groups leads to more arrests, or quite possibly the involvement in drug importation activities required a more intense and systematic response from law enforcement organization within the community. Though the interpretations are largely inferential, the correlations possibly illustrate differences between the major racial groups.

E. Youth Gang and Group Patterns: Interrelationship of Structural and Behavioral Characteristics

This final section attempts to identify the relationship patterns of other behavioral and structural characteristics that were also important, such as the relationship between the measures of criminality and structural features (e.g. size of collective, affiliation with adult criminal groups). Many behavioral and structural patterns have not been adequately addressed in the research. Therefore, the examination of how these characteristics were interrelated may result in a better understanding of contemporary youth gang and groups, thereby increasing the potential for developing more effective prevention and intervention policies and programs (e.g. Spergel et al., 1990). This analysis was once again concerned with the primary measures of criminality, but the particular interest was whether key structural variables — estimated number of members, average size of collectives, local versus non-local collectives, and the affiliation with adult criminal organizations — were in any way related to four selected measures of criminality (percent of index offenses attributed to youth collectives, involvement in drug distribution, involvement in drug importation, and the percentage of members with prior criminal records). In addition to the information derived from the questions listed in the previous sections, the data obtained from the questions below were important for this particular analysis (Appendix, Section III).

*Have you ever had youth group or gang activity originate from out-
side your community?*

*Are there youth groups or gangs present which appear to be affiliat-
ed with or used by adult criminal organizations for illicit purposes,
or for any other reason that would concern your organization?*

As a precursor to the analysis of the correlations, it is important to
briefly note the variations in respondents' perceptions to the above two
questions. Law enforcement officials widely reported (74.5 percent)
that the majority of their youth gang and group problems originated
outside their respective communities or jurisdictions. The problem of
mobile gangs and groups does not appear to be a significant problem
according to school officials (only 22.7 percent reported such a problem),
at least for those respondents who could even address the issue. Yet the
perception among court counselors (68.4 percent) is similar to that of
law enforcement officials, in that youth gangs and groups, particularly youth gangs, are often from communities outside their jurisdiction.
Another issue that concerned the majority of respondents, especially
those from the largest six cities, five counties, and four judicial districts
across the State, was that youth gangs and groups were somehow affiliated with or heavily influenced by adult criminal organizations. This
was a major concern of law enforcement respondents (72.5 percent),
particularly those who reported youth gang problems. It was also a
concern of court counselor (63.2 percent) and correctional respondents
(71.4 percent). The least concern was found among school officials
(18.2 percent). Why are the issues just discussed a concern? Are certain
measures of criminality somehow related to adult criminal group affiliation, or by the nonlocal characteristic of youth gangs and groups, or
perhaps by other structural characteristics? To unravel these questions,
the analysis now turns to the results of the correlations performed on
selected variables.

Table 5.7
Pearson Correlations between Structural Characteristics
and Measures of Criminality

Measures of Criminality	Est. # of Members	Average Size	Nonlocal	Affil. w/Adult Crim. Groups
Youth Gangs (N=51)				
% Index Offenses	.386*	.099-	.104	.116
Drug Dist.	.395*-	.107	.309*	.069
Drug Import	-.114	.036	.426*	.330*
% Prior Record	.129	.104	.296*	.334*
Youth Groups (N=55)				
% Index Offenses	.156	.019	-.106	-.109
Drug Dist.	.106	.012	.410*	.212
Drug Import	.070	-.103	-.101	.258*
% Prior Record	.133	.219	.329*	.307*

$p \leq 0.05$* $p \leq 0.01$** $p \leq 0.001$***

The results of the correlations, which are depicted in Table 5.7, demonstrate that there were a number of statistically significant correlations for both youth gangs and groups. For youth gangs, the estimated number of members was strongly related to the percentage of index offenses attributed to these collectives. As expected, the larger the youth gang member population in a particular community, the greater the likelihood that a large percentage of index offenses will be attributed to gang members. A similar relationship was also discovered with drug distribution as a primary activity. The size of the youth gang member population had a statistically significant positive relationship to the involvement in drug distribution activities. There were also strong correlations between the importation of drugs and youth gang affiliation with adult criminal organizations, and between nonlocal gangs and both types of drug-related activities. These findings may indicate that drug-related activities were primarily attributed to youth gangs from other communities, where affiliations with adult criminal organizations most likely facilitated the acquisition of drugs and collusion of activities. These correlations are supported by recent studies (Skolnick et al., 1988, 1993; Skolnick, 1993; Maxson et al., 1993) that assert that youth gang movement into communities is most likely the result of seeking areas where drug dealing profits may be substantially greater and the risk of apprehension considerably lower.

Finally, the percent of youth gang members with prior criminal records was strongly correlated with the nonlocal variable and affiliation with adult criminal groups. Perhaps there is a strong nexus, though not evident in these correlations, between drug importation activities, affiliation with adult criminal groups, and the percent of youth gang members having prior criminal records. It seems quite plausible that drug-related activity and affiliating with adult criminal groups may be significant attractions for individuals who already have experience in criminal activities. Furthermore, it also appears that much of the drug-related activity and the percent of members with prior criminal records are largely a nonlocal gang phenomena. There were fewer statistically significant correlations for youth groups; however, the data again revealed a strong relationship between drug distribution and nonindigenous youth groups. Furthermore, the strong correlation between affiliation with adult criminal groups and drug importation is possible evidence that youth groups were also becoming more organized and gain-oriented in their activities. It is reasonable to argue that groups from outside the community may also attempt to establish new drug territories or markets for the purposes of greater profits and safety. And according to the significant correlations between prior criminal record and the nonlocal group variable, many of the group members who reside in other towns or communities are also likely to have prior criminal records. Similar to the youth gang analysis, there was a strong association between prior record and the affiliation with adult criminal groups. The lack of other significant correlations for youth groups is indicative that the estimated number of members in the community and the average size of the collectives had little effect on the perceived levels of crime, specifically index offenses and drug-related activities. For both youth gangs and groups, the affiliation with adult criminal organizations did not influence, to any great extent, the proportion of index offenses or drug distribution activities attributed to these collectives. Similarly, nonindigenous youth gangs and groups were not significantly involved in index offenses within the local community where they may appear, but were actively involved in drug-related activities. Apparently, youth gangs and groups from other communities were more gain-oriented, avoiding the criminal activities that may draw attention from the local authorities and citizenry. However, members in these nonlocal collectives were also likely to have prior criminal records, but the scope and nature of the previous criminal activities could not be determined.

Table 5.8
Point Biserial Correlations between Nonindigenous Factor
and Selected Characteristics

	Estimate # Members	Avg. Size	% White	% Black	% Hispanic	% Asian
Youth Gangs (N=51)						
Nonlocal	.367*	.356**-	.071	.339*	-.101	-.026
Youth Groups (N=55)						
Nonlocal	.236*	.227*	-.095	-.042	-.012	-.011

p≤0.05* p≤0.01** p≤0.001***

Since nonindigenous youth gangs and groups were significantly involved in drug-related activities, an additional correlation was conducted to determine if race was a factor or feature of these collectives. The correlations (Table 5.8) demonstrate that the relationship between the percent of members classified into one of the four race categories and the nonlocal characteristic of the youth collective was strongest for black youth gangs. In other words, respondents perceived that the most likely racial composition of nonindigenous youth gangs was black, and that it was black youth gangs who typically traveled from other communities to commit offenses. No other significant correlations were discovered between the other racial classifications of members and the nonlocal characteristic for either type of collective. Youth gangs and groups comprised of members who were not from the local community was also significantly related to the average size of the collectives and the estimated number of members. Spergel (1990) discovered similar findings for youth gangs and concluded that there was a greater possibility that gangs belonged to a larger network or alliance across neighborhoods as the number of non-local gang members and gangs increased. The study also posited that there was a epidemiological characteristic about gangs and gang members: as membership multiplies gangs geographically disperse, and as membership decreases, gangs become more consolidated within certain boundaries.

Table 5.9
Point Biserial Correlations between Affiliation with Adult Criminal Groups
and Selected Characteristics

	Youth Gangs (N=51)				
	Est. # Members	%White	%Black	%Hisp.	%Asian
Affil. w/Adult Criminal Groups	-.121	.169	.395**	.086	.018
		%Members Adults		%Index Offenses	Prior Record
Affil. w/Adult Criminal Groups		.222*		.227*	.265*

	Youth Groups (N=55)				
	Est. # Members	%White	%Black	%Hisp.	%Asian
Affil. w/Adult Criminal Groups	-.133	.056	.137	.048	.039
		%Members Adults		%Index Offenses	Prior Record
Affil. w/Adult Criminal Groups		.124		.109	.180*

p≤0.05* p≤0.01** p≤0.001***

Finally, Table 5.9 examines the relationship between youth gang and
group involvement in adult criminal groups or organizations and a number of socio-demographic factors and measures of criminality. There was
a highly significant relationship between black youth gangs and involvement
with adult criminal groups, but there were no other significant findings
discovered among the other races in both collective categories. Involvement with adult criminal groups also had an effect on the proportion of
index offenses attributed to youth gangs and the percentage of gang members who had prior criminal records. This last finding possibly indicates that
youth gangs may become more criminally active—commit crime with
greater frequency and seriousness—after becoming affiliated with adult
criminals. The data further demonstrate that adult gang members may
have had closer connections to adult criminal groups than juvenile members; however, this does not imply that adult gang members were necessarily involved in organized criminal activities, but merely points out a
potential influence on criminal propensities.

F. Conclusion

There were an estimated 2,772 youth gang members and 1,450 youth group members reported across different jurisdictions and localities in North Carolina (representing approximately one percent of the youth population between the ages of 15 and 24), with a disproportionate number of members from both types of collectives concentrated in a small number of localities. The average size youth gang across 39 localities approached 18 members, while for youth groups the average size across 42 localities was approximately seven. Respondents also reported that the vast majority (approximately 75 to 85 percent) of both youth gangs and groups ranged in size from three to twenty members. The largest proportion (approximately 65 percent) of gang and group members who came to the attention of authorities were black, followed by whites who comprised 25 percent of all members; Asian and Hispanic members comprised only a fraction (less than five percent) of the total estimate. Even though the age of gang and group members ranged from the early teens to the late twenties, the largest proportion fell within the mid-teenage years (16-18), with a median age of 18 for gang members and 17 for group members.

An important objective of this research was to determine the perceived scope and seriousness of activities and the factors that may have influenced the criminality of youth collectives. The analysis presented in the four sections of this chapter identified patterns that may have influenced the scope and nature of the youth gang and group problem. The primary objective was to determine if certain variables—structural and behavioral—were in any way interrelated and to what extent they influenced the patterns that emerged. Variables that were examined using univariate and multivariate statistical procedures could be classified into three categories: socio-demographic characteristics (age and race); criminal propensity (percent of index offenses attributed to collectives, percent of members having prior criminal records, drug distribution as a primary activity, and involvement in drug importation); and structural factors (estimated number of members, average size of collectives, presence of nonindigenous collectives, and affiliation with adult criminal organizations).

Respondents estimated that almost half of all youth gang and group incidents involved adults, individuals who were 16 years and older. Within youth groups, the proportion of incidents attributed to adult members was strongly associated with the estimated number of index offenses and the percentage of members who had prior criminal records; the relationship between incidents involving adults and drug-related activities was highly significant for both youth gangs and groups. These findings support the research that has demonstrated that there is a greater propensity for criminality among older members of youth gangs and groups (Torres, 1980; Miller, 1982; Horowitz, 1983; Maxson et al., 1985; Bobrowski, 1988; Hagedorn, 1988). There was also a strong perception that youth gangs and groups were actively involved in or affiliated with adult criminal organizations, but according to the correlations, individuals who affiliated with adult criminal groups were most likely adult gang members. Affiliation with adult criminal organizations most likely increases the probability of involvement in drug importation activities for both youth gangs and groups. However, determining the causal direction—whether the affiliation increases criminal propensities or simply attracts individuals who already have criminal records—was not possible using the available data (see Hirschi, 1969; Sutherland and Cressey, 1978; Thornberry et al., 1993, 1994). This association, regardless of the limited evidence and data, has led to the perception and fears that gangs were becoming more active as organized drug enterprises, and that the incipient violence was somehow intrinsically associated with this illicit business activity. The use and sale of drugs by gang members was not a prominent theme in earlier research; even though drug dealing did occur, drug use and abuse were often not tolerated by core members and had very low legitimacy as normative behavior (Short and Strodtbeck, 1965). Recent research by Maxson et al. (1993) found that gangs participated substantially in cocaine sales, but were not dominant in large scale cocaine distribution.

The data indicated that the severity of the problem was strongly associated with levels of drug distribution and importation, rather than index offenses. However, there was very little evidence connecting drug-related activities with more serious index offenses, namely homicide and aggravated assault. A substantial rise in the violent juvenile crime rate—particularly an increase in reported violent crime attributed to gangs—and a greater availability of cocaine were concomitant in the mid-1980s, yet contemporary research on gangs is unable to conclusively ascertain a clear interdependent or causal relationship between gangs, drugs, and violence (Spergel, 1990). This is despite the credible body of research demonstrating that gang members commit a disproportionate number of offenses when compared to their nongang counterparts (Klein and Maxson, 1989; Spergel, 1990), that there are variables that distinguish gang crimes, particularly homicide, from nongang incidents (Maxson et al., 1985), and that there is strong consensus that the prevalence of drug use and dealing is greater among gang than nongang adolescent populations (Moore, 1978; Dolan and Finney, 1984; Spergel, 1984; Fagan et al., 1986).

Klein et al. (1991) examined the relationship between violence and crack dealing among African American gangs in Los Angeles and discovered that there were few reported violent incidents associated with arrests for drug trafficking. It appears that gang involvement in drug dealing is no more likely to include higher quantities or a greater likelihood of firearm presence than nongang drug dealing (Maxson et al., 1993). Furthermore, even though gang homicides were more likely to reveal drug involvement than nongang homicides, the motive for the homicides had little to do with drugs. Violence among both African American and Hispanic gangs occurred, as Fagan (1989) also discovered, independent of drug possession and trafficking. The homicides which occurred, according to these studies, most likely involved traditional gang motives—such as defending neighborhood turf or honor, or perhaps to acquire or maintain status within the gang. Reiner (1992, p. 87) succinctly concluded that "illicit drugs tend to breed violence in all settings, but they do not seem to have an especially severe impact on gangs" and furthermore, "gang homicides are much less likely to be motivated by drugs than are nongang homicides."

Spergel (1990) noted that the relation between gangs, drugs, and violence appears to be variable. Attributing to the diversity of views are factors such as: city size, which affects opportunities; the socialization process of gangs and their organization (traditional versus nontraditional); and the nature of the local drug market, which operates under supply and demand forces. Contrary to Skolnick's theory, the majority of gang literature concludes that traditional gang structures are not "directly functional to drug use, selling, and associated enterprises, which requires different kinds of organization, communication, and distribution" (Spergel, 1990, p. 197). While drug distribution in the present study was characteristic of both white and black youth gangs and groups, the importation of illicit substances into the community was most characteristic of black youth gangs and groups who were not from the local community. This phenomenon, if true, is not easy to explain. Skolnick's (1993) "cultural resource" theory stresses that the cultural and structural organization of gangs, rather than market or law enforcement pressures, best explain the dynamics of gang migration and drug distribution. Yet, the study findings contradict established research on group processes (particularly Short and Strodtbeck, 1965; Klein, 1971; and Fagan, 1989) by positing that "cultural" (street) gangs, which are rooted in traditional gang values, rather than "instrumental" (drug or entrepreneurial) gangs, best facilitate venturing into new markets and territories. The notion of migratory gang patterns and drug distribution are more likely than not dependent upon family movement and social connections, rather than a well-organized enterprise. As Maxson (1993, p. 5) concludes, "[i]t is advisable to approach the issue of collective and organized migration for drug distribution objectives with skepticism, a skepticism wrought from descriptions of gang structure, organization, and activity produced by gang researchers over several decades."

It cannot be over-emphasized that the findings in this chapter are tentative at best, since drawing conclusions about individual activity from aggregate data is often problematic. The complexities of the relationship between criminal activities, structural factors, and demographic influences not only make it difficult to distinguish traditional, turf-oriented youth gangs from those gangs that are nontraditional (gain-oriented), but it is also becoming increasingly difficult to distinguish gangs from other criminally oriented groups. But regardless of the collective structure, as adult involvement in gangs and groups increases, there is a greater propensity that drug distribution and importation activities will also increase. As Spergel et al.(1990, p. 52) concluded, "it is likely that the availability of drug trafficking opportunities has influenced the development of a serious [collective youth] problem more than the presence of youth [collectives] has influenced the creation of the general crime problem."

6

Perceived Causes of Collective Youth Crime

A. Introduction

Explaining and understanding the formation and perpetuation of youth gangs and youth groups has been stimulated by many theoretical perspectives since the classical works of Thrasher (1936), Park (1936), Burgess (1928), and Shaw and McKay (1942). Contemporary theoretical developments have become more comprehensive in nature than the classical works and theories developed between the 1930s and 1960s. Theoretical developments have also been influenced by methodological and theoretical advancements through the years; these advancements, consequently, have influenced the integration of concepts into a broader framework that accounts for social structural conditions, social institutional processes, and social psychological influences. The diversity of theoretical viewpoints is evidence that there are many possible propositions that may explain why youths join and participate in collective youth criminal activities. Each theory, integrated or not, attempts to sort out the potentially related or unrelated factors that may provide the greatest insight into the formation, evolution, and persistence of deviant and criminal youth collectives.

The purpose of this chapter is not to develop any new theoretical insight into the causes of collective youth crime, since that is beyond the scope and design of this study. The discussion centers on two key areas: it first elaborates on the theoretical perspectives (causes and conditions) that have remained dominant in the literature on youth gangs and groups; and secondly, it presents information on what respondents in the present study perceived to be the primary causes of the problem and how they ranked those causes. An analysis of perceived causes and the underlying theoretical constructs was important because it established some foundation for the systematic examination of what strategies organizations employed to address the youth gang and group crime problem.

Before intervention and prevention strategies can be effectively designed and implemented, whether in a particular organization or across the community, it is necessary to have some idea as to what factors may be causing the problem before actions can be taken to ameliorate it. As Spergel et al. (1990, p. 80) assert, "organizations at first respond to social problems, including gang crime, in terms of traditional organizational mission, specific disciplinary approaches, and contemporary fashions...ideas of cause or justification for the strategies of action taken usually come as afterthoughts, in part to justify methods of action already selected. A systematic causal analysis does not often precede a course of agency action." Therefore, in order to address this concern, an analysis was performed to determine the conditions or factors, albeit based on respondents' perceptions, that may contribute to the emergence or persistence of gang or group problems in communities throughout North Carolina. This action may later prove beneficial for developing State-level policy and programs, since planning and executing community and organizational levels of action should be based on the actual or perceived problem causation and theoretical foundations (see Spergel, 1995; Miller, 1990).

B. Theoretical Perspectives

Thrasher's study of the gang and Shaw and McKay's demonstration of the extent to which juvenile crime is a group activity gave full recognition to the importance of the group process variables and their important influence on delinquency. Contemporary research since the 1960s has been marked with many different perspectives; the many different viewpoints can be attributed to the changes in the social behavior of gangs, as well as methodological and theoretical shortcomings (Gilbert, 1986). Recent theoretical developments have begun integrating broad, comprehensive concepts that take into account underlying social structural factors and social institutional processes, as well as social psychological factors. Developing a theory on gangs, according to Covey et al. (1992), not only requires a multi-level explanation that takes into account community, organizational, small group, and individual level influences, but must also consider the different *career* aspects of gang activity (e.g. formation, persistence, and disintegration) and reconcile divergent studies of gangs over time and across cultures.

Why collective youth crime problems, particularly youth gang, develop and persist in one community and not another, has led many theorists to conclude that the problem is most directly produced by a defectiveness in local social institutions and their fragmented relationships with each other. These local social institutions—e.g. families, schools, church—are heavily influenced by external environmental factors, such as movements in the population, general social and economic conditions, the unemployment situation, the lack of community resources, and ineffective social policies produced by the government (Spergel, 1995). The two broad approaches that emerged to address the interrelationship of social institutions within the wider social structural environment are the theories of social disorganization and social ecology.

The Chicago school of sociology's (Thrasher, 1936; Shaw and McKay, 1942) theory of social disorganization offers one of the first attempts at explaining gang delinquency through the integration of the three explanatory levels—social structural, social institutional, and social psychological. Social disorganization, in the broadest sense, refers to the dysfunctional condition of the normative and value systems within the community, where social and organizational relationships lack the integration that is necessary to keep dominant cultural values in check—in other words, weak social institutions inhibit the community's social support and control mechanisms. "The youth gang arises under circumstances in which the social. . .needs of its members have not been adequately satisfied by local community institutional capacities and arrangements. Vulnerable youths find each other and create, or join already established, peer groups to meet their needs" (Spergel, 1995, p. 153).

Ecological theory posits that there is a strong interrelationship between the community's social institutions, surrounding material conditions, and population characteristics that, because of limited resources and opportunities, create conflict (Bursik and Grasmick, 1993). Underlying these two theoretical perspectives is the premise that environmental conditions affect how individuals adapt and interact with others in their community over time. The method of adaptation largely depends on the extent to which the following conditions are present: poverty, unemployment, weakness in social institutions, unavailability of legitimate resources, and social disorder. "The presence of these ecological forces, and more specifically the interaction of factors of social disorganization and lack of legitimate [resources] and/or availability of alternate illegitimate resources, may largely account for the development of deviant gang subcultural phenomena in certain communities and institutional contexts" (Spergel, 1995, p. 112). The distinctiveness of a community's collective youth crime problem largely depends on such factors as demographic and racial/ethnic variation, cultural tradition, socioeconomic conditions, opportunity structure, and the extent the community is socially and culturally isolated from mainstream society.

In an effort to relate social structural conditions and cultural variables (external factors), Wilson (1991) posits in his "underclass" thesis that there are groups within society that have few legitimate employment opportunities and poor job information networks, which "not only give rise to weak labor force attachment but also raise the likelihood that people will turn to illegal or deviant activities for income" (p. 472). This broad theoretical perspective does not specifically address the development of youth gangs and other deviant groups within particular communities, but does indicate some of the *conditions* that give rise to criminal activity. These conditions or factors include the racial concentration of urban poverty, urban migration, age structures, distribution of jobs and income, social isolation, lack of neighborhood resources, and restricted social mobility. However, these variables appear to only provide a general framework for understanding why crime occurs in predominantly lower class environments.

In essence, poverty is central to Wilson's thesis. There may be a direct relationship between the availability of resources, economic opportunities, and the development of the underclass in certain communities, but these general conditions have been widely viewed as factors that contribute to the crime problem in general. Only a few researchers have applied the "underclass" theory specifically to explain the formation and perpetuation of youth gangs. Taylor (1990) asserts that many traditional gangs evolve into gain-oriented gangs because of severely limited economic and social opportunities, where youth are "trapped" in a perpetual underclass state. Hagedorn (1988) concludes that in cities or neighborhoods where low wage occupations and economic conditions are bleak (e.g. minority neighborhoods), there is a greater likelihood that youth will remain in gangs because of social and economic opportunities. Though Hagedorn posits that gangs typically form where underclass conditions are present, he later argued that the "underclass" theory was also insufficient because it did not take into account or address issues such as community social control, citizen mobilization, and the influence of poorly developed social institutions (Hagedorn, 1991). One other researcher (Vigil, 1988) utilized poverty, segmented labor markets, and lower class culture to develop the concept of "multiple marginality," which stresses that structural factors influence the acculturation of Hispanic youth. The problem of social instability caused by the difficulty of adapting to or modifying important social institutions appears at the heart of the this concept. The "marginality complex...prevents many youths from attaining their version of the American dream via the traditional pathways of education and hard work. Unable to adopt the dominant culture, they turn to gangs as a means of acquisition without assimilation" (Vigil and Yun, 1990, p. 147). Socioeconomic factors and conditions that lead to the marginalization of individuals or groups within society are important interrelated variables that contribute to our understanding of deviance. However, these variables may be related indirectly to the problems that contribute to social disorganization and the group processes that emerge in socially disorganized communities.

The social disorganization and ecological perspectives, having received considerable attention in recent literature (see Cartwright and Howard, 1966; Cohen, 1969; Sampson, 1986; Stark, 1987; Felson, 1987; Curry and Spergel, 1988; Bursik and Grasmick, 1993), is evidence that community characteristics play a very important part in explaining collective youth crime. The Chicago school perspective, therefore, is credited for having established a broad framework from which a significant body of theoretical research has emerged. The social disorganization and ecological perspectives describe the social conditions that may give rise to collective youth crime: individuals join gangs because of the needs and desires not fulfilled by conventional social institutions (e.g. families, schools, and church) within the community. These two macrosocial perspectives, however, also provide the framework for four theoretical approaches that address, more specifically, the processes or conditions that may contribute or lead to youth involvement in gangs and other criminally-oriented groups. Inherent in the first two theoretical approaches (*strain* and *subcultural* theories) is the notion that macrosocial factors create conditions that lead to strain, where youth are forced to seek alternative means to achieve status in the community; the third approach (*social learning* theory) addresses the social processes and factors that give rise to criminal behavior and offers some insight into how youth collectives may influence activities; the fourth and final approach (*social control* theory) offers a different perspective compared to the others, in that the problem of deviance, and indirectly, youth involvement in delinquent gangs and groups, is due to inadequate socialization processes and control mechanisms.

1. Strain Theory

Merton (1938) formulated what became known as the first strain theory, expanding upon and revising Durkheim's (1933) theory of anomie. In refining Durkheim's general premise that strain occurs where there is a breakdown in society's regulation of goals, Merton asserted that strain occurs because: one, there is simply a "breakdown in the relationship between goals and legitimate access to them"; and two, opportunities to realize aspirations are further constrained by social class (Cloward and Ohlin, 1960, p. 83). The severity of strain, therefore, depends on where in the social structure the individual originates. Merton developed a conceptual scheme that identified possible adaptations (conformity, innovation, ritualism, retreatism, and rebellion) where disjunctures exist between cultural goals and the institutional means to achieve those goals. The adaptation most likely to result in delinquent or criminal behavior was *innovation*, where societal goals are maintained but normative constraints on individual means are rejected. The modes of adaptation constitute a typology of the responses to strain, but do not provide an explanation as to why individuals choose one adaptation over another nor the influence of social processes.

While Merton and Durkheim established the general concepts of anomie and strain, Cloward and Ohlin (1960) were able to apply strain theory specifically to gang delinquency, but expanded their hypothesis by integrating strain theory with the social ecological approach (Shaw and McKay, 1942) and elements of differential association (Sutherland and Cressey, 1978). According to Cloward and Ohlin, each individual occupies a position in both legitimate and illegitimate opportunity structures, but these opportunities are not equally distributed in each community or neighborhood. An underlying assumption is that lower-class youths, who face adjustment problems, blame their failure to achieve success (financial and material) on prescribed societal rules; ensuing alienation and strain encourages youths to enter delinquent subcultures where normative rules are redefined and deviant behavior is legitimized.

Figure 6.1
Gang Delinquency Model: Cloward and Ohlin
(source: Regoli and Hewitt, 1994, p. 169)

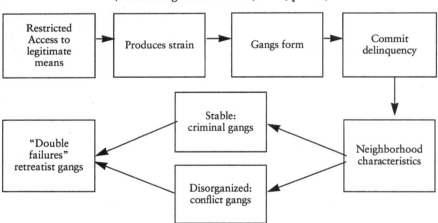

This perspective also allows us to examine "how the relative availability of illegitimate opportunities affects the resolution of adjustment problems leading to deviant behavior" (Williams and McShane, 1993, p. 135). Cloward and Ohlin not only asserted that subcultures[1] emerge in order

---

1. Classified by the authors as *criminal*, where juveniles become integrated in adult criminal networks; *conflict*, where legitimate and illegitimate opportunities are limited

to adapt to the availability or non-availability of opportunities in particular communities—which supports the concept that certain deviant values and skills can only be learned in certain neighborhoods—but they
also asserted that individuals require support in the performance of their
roles within the deviant subculture. "Variable age-role and conventional
criminal networks based on available opportunities apparently contribute
to the development of different crime and youth gang patterns in the different neighborhoods" (Spergel, 1995, p.147). By integrating social ecological, strain, and learning theories, Cloward and Ohlin explain why
gangs and subcultural delinquency may exist in particular communities, how
illegitimate opportunity structures affect the modes of adaptation within
the social structure, and finally, why different gangs may engage in certain types of illegal behavior.

The strain theories developed by Durkheim, Merton, and Cloward and
Ohlin have received criticism for their primary focus on the relationship
between goals and perceived access to means. In an earlier study, Cohen
(1955) asserts that much gang delinquency is initiated for thrill and excitement, even where legitimate opportunities are perceived as available. Furthermore, the underlying concept of blocked opportunities in the strain
theories has the greatest credence when attempting to explain gang delinquency in economically deprived communities, but may require modification where gang involvement exists in more economically viable neighborhoods. Short and Strodtbeck (1965), on the other hand, found support
for blocked opportunities since the "relative absence of middle-class achievement opportunities and concerns [in lower-class communities] leaves a
vacuum" (p.272) that becomes occupied by gratification-seeking gang subcultures. Strain theory is further buttressed indirectly in Covey et al. (1992)
who assert that neighborhoods experiencing high crime rates have significant influence on the form of local markets for illegal goods and services;
in other words, neighborhood characteristics affect the extent and nature
of criminal activity through the availability of illegitimate opportunities
(see also Spergel, 1964).

2. Subcultural Theory

Cohen's (1955) theory of subcultural formation adopted the perspective that
working class juveniles, who experience difficulty in adjusting or adapting
to normative behavior defined by the middle-class value system, respond

---

and social disorganization is prevalent; and *retreatist*, where individuals have failed at
both legitimate and illegitimate opportunities.

by joining gangs. The delinquent subculture emerges because youths are denied status in respectable society because they have failed to meet the criteria defined by the dominant value system. The problem often begins when lower-class youths enter schools, where performance criteria are evaluated according to a middle-class measuring rod. The initial failure in school produces strain and frustration.

Similar to Cloward and Ohlin's ideas, youths who are unable to solve status frustration problems seek others; the job of problem-solving is adopted as a group solution. As the tentative solutions spread to more youths over time, subcultures form as the numbers increase. By breaking the norms of the dominant value system through the defiance of authority, the new "reference group" develops and institutionalizes its own deviant value system—defined by Cohen as reaction-formation—that persists as long as the needs of its members are fulfilled. As pointed out earlier, the delinquent acts perpetrated center on excitement, with little or no regard for utilitarian gains. The search for excitement often involves what Cohen characterizes as malicious, negativistic, and hedonistic behavior. These characteristics provide an alternative status system within the subcultural group context which justifies the hostility and aggression against status frustration sources (Cohen and Short, 1958). However, these behavior characteristics, coupled with the conspicuous defiance of authority, may also illustrate an overconformity to criminal norms in order to win acceptance from more sophisticated gang members or acculturated criminals. "Non-utilitarian" behavior, which initially may appear random or purposeless, may actually assist in securing access to gain-oriented criminal roles (Cloward and Ohlin, 1960).

Figure 6.2
Gang Delinquency Model: Cohen
(source: Regoli and Hewitt, 1994, p. 167)

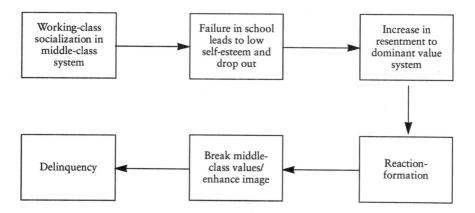

Cohen's theory has received considerable support, especially in the description of delinquent behavior most common among Hispanic gangs. Hispanic gangs place positive value on *locura*, or craziness, which is often illustrated through irrational acts of violence, elements of machismo (sexual prowess, fighting), and general partying (Moore, 1978; Horowitz, 1987). Conversely, low value is placed on scholastic achievement and success through diligence and hard work. The Cholo subculture, at least, replaces traditional cultural values with a value system that permits youth to attain status within newly defined boundaries. Other research (Short and Strodtbeck, 1965) has found little support for the "reaction-formation" hypothesis, stressing that group processes that lead to delinquency involve issues more complex than the reinforcement and collective manifestation of negative attitudes instigated by status frustration. A youth is not unaware of or unsympathetic toward middle-class values, "but his own situation within the group, his need for membership and status, successfully isolate him and make him open to group pressures in which gang norms, such as sexual prowess and toughness, or alternatively coolness, lead to situational involvements which require delinquency" (Hood and Sparks, 1977, p. 612). Kitsuse and Dietrick (1959) and Sykes and Matza (1957) also question the central thesis that delinquent youths could be strongly and fundamentally ambivalent about their status in the middle class system. In response to Sykes and Matza's critique, Cohen and Short (1958, p. 21) retort:

> The formation of a subculture is itself probably the most universal and powerful of techniques of neutralization, for nothing is so effective in allaying doubts and providing moral reassurance against a gnawing superego as the repeated, emphatic, and articulate support and approval of other persons.

Because Cohen posits the concept that delinquent behavior emerges where there is a failure in status attainment, it is also reasonable to classify subcultural theory under the strain rubric. The strain implicit in subcultural theory is critical for explaining the *emergence* and *persistence* of delinquent subcultures, rather than providing a framework for explaining gang delinquency in general.

Miller (1958) offers another dimension to the subcultural perspective by introducing a lower class gang delinquency theory. The theory assumes that there is a distinct lower class culture where behavioral norms are characterized by a set of focal concerns or "areas or issues which command widespread and persistent attention and a high degree of emotional involvement" (p. 7). The focal concerns (trouble, toughness, smartness, excitement, fate, and autonomy) are unique to the milieu of the lower class structural and social environment. Contrary to Cloward and Ohlin and Cohen,

Miller posits that gang delinquency involves a positive effort to achieve status, conditions, and qualities valued within immediate reference group norms, which in this case is the lower class. Even though delinquent activities may be perceived as nonconforming and in violation of middle class values, the activity is not viewed as rebellious or rejective in nature.

Figure 6.3
Gang Delinquency Model: Miller
(source: Regoli and Hewitt, 1994, p. 155)

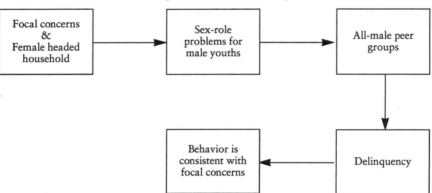

Gang delinquency in the lower class culture is strongly tied to the values, attitudes, and patterns designed to support and maintain basic features of life within lower class communities. According to Miller (1958, p. 7), motivational support from the commission of delinquency "derives from a positive effort to achieve what is valued within [lower class] tradition," rather than from a "delinquent subculture" that may arise through conflict with middle class culture. Delinquent groups emerge as a response to growing up in a female headed household, where the control and authority of a woman stirs resentment in traditional masculine norms. To compensate for this family structure, lower class youths attempt to create an artificial social environment where values and standards are transmitted within the company of other males. Maintaining and enforcing values and standards, identified in focal concerns, leads to activity and behavior that is within the expectations of lower class culture, but is defined as delinquent by middle class norms (Regoli and Hewitt, 1994). Similarly, in a study on delinquency and middle-class goals, Spiller (1965, p. 466) discovered that "lower-class gang members are motivated more by attempts to achieve standards and measure up to the qualities valued within their own subculture milieu than by efforts to achieve culturally distant or ill-understood values."

Miller's lower class theory can be challenged on a number of grounds. Cloward and Ohlin (1960, p. 70) found that lower class focal concerns may not differ significantly from middle class concerns to a point where conformity to these values and standards "automatically" leads to delinquency. It may also be unrealistic to assume that lower class gang delinquents are not effected by middle class values, since there is a significant likelihood of exposure to middle class images through the media (Regoli and Hewitt, 1994). The significant participation of gang members in lucrative drug trafficking activities, as discussed earlier, is highly indicative of the preoccupation to acquire wealth and material goods. Short and Strodtbeck's (1965, p. 76) interpretations also note that lower class gang members endorse middle class prescriptive norms and values (success themes) uniformly.

Furthermore, Miller theorized that where there is a disjuncture between lower class aspirations and the means to achieve those goals, different patterns of proneness to delinquency emerge.[2] This appears to contradict, or at least complicate, the hypothesis that relative isolation exists between lower and middle class cultural systems. Because Miller focuses exclusively on delinquent acts, rather than examining the dynamics of group processes and influences on delinquency, the greatest inadequacy lies in the failure to account for the origins of delinquent norms. Within the theoretical framework of the subcultural theories discussed, the assertion that lower class values and normative definitions differ from those found in the middle class system may be a fundamental weakness. The difference between the value systems may be more the manner in which values are expressed, rather than two disparate systems. Universal goals of success are consistent across social and demographic boundaries, but the means to achieve goals (legitimate and illegitimate) may receive differing degrees of support (e.g. Short and Strodtbeck, 1965; Cloward and Ohlin, 1960)

Yablonsky (1962) adopted a significantly different view of gangs, and one that utilizes a unique conception of the "delinquent subculture." Similar to previous delinquent subculture theorists, Yablonsky also asserts that gangs emerge in socially disorganized, lower class communities, where violent behavior manifests from norms that promote aggressive responses. However, Yablonsky presents a "middle-range" theory that describes gangs as near-groups,[3] where loosely organized collectives of youths encour-

---

2. These were identified as: *"stable" lower class*, which consists of youth who do not aspire to higher status or who have no realistic possibility of achieving desired aspirations; *aspiring but conflicted lower class*, which represents those for whom family or other community influences have produced a desire to elevate their status, but cultural pressures inhibit aspirations; and *successful aspiring lower class*, which represents the group that has both the will and capacity to elevate status.

3. These gangs are located on a continuum of properties which fully define well-organized groups at one end of the spectrum and disorganized mobs and crowds at the other end.

age the development of the conflict or violent gang in order to meet the needs of individual members (see also Cartwright et al., 1975). According to Yablonsky (1962, p. 7):

> Today's violent gang is characterized by flux. It lacks features of an organized group, having neither a definite number of members, specific membership roles, a consensus of expected norms, nor a leader who supplies logical directions for action. It is a mobile collectivity that forms around violence in a spontaneous fashion, moving into action — often on the spur of the evening's boredom — in search of kicks .

Yablonsky offers a number of antecedent factors (e.g. decline of social control, extensive adult-adolescent divisions) that encourage gang formation, but focuses more on individual character traits to explain what he calls the impulsive and sociopathic nature of violent gang members and leaders. Violent gangs "originate in order to adjust to individual emotional problems, for reasons of self-protection and defense, for channeling aggression, in response to prejudice, because of the peculiar motivations of disturbed leaders or because of a combination of these factors mixed with special external conditions produced by enemy gangs" (p. 93). Why violence is the central activity is not easily explained, but Kennedy and Baron (1993, p. 91) offer an enlightening summary of the subculture of violence perspective:

> Violent behavior stems from the adherence to norms that define violence as a necessary response to actions that are derogatory to the self. Individuals adhering to these norms are likely to perceive situations as insulting, and are more willing to use violence as a response. The subcultural norms are backed up with social rewards and punishments: Individuals who abide by the norms are admired and respected by other members of the subculture, and those who do not conform are ridiculed, criticized, and/or expelled.

Yablonsky's near-groups, characterized as collectives of psychologically disturbed individuals who "manifest paranoid delusions of persecution and grandeur" legitimize the wider range of violent, abnormal behavior within the group context; thus, "the group pattern of violent expression appears to be a more acceptable and legitimate social form for acting out pathology than is individual behavior" (1962, p. 194). The near-group concept has received direct support in recent research on small city youth gangs (Zevitz and Takata, 1992; Zevitz, 1993). However, a number of studies (Short and Strodtbeck, 1965; Kornhauser, 1978; Hagan, 1985) question whether violence is an integral component in the gang process and if violent norms can even be transmitted through the group process. Support for a conflict and violence-oriented subculture — where gaining status and displaying courage through physical combat are important aspects of the gang process, but not necessarily the sole purpose — can be found in numerous studies (Cohen, 1955, 1965; Cohen and Short 1958; Cloward and Ohlin 1960; Miller,1958; Horowitz and Schwartz, 1974). Other research contradicts Yablonsky's assertion that gangs, especially violent ones, generally lack cohesion and have diffuse role definitions (Hagedorn, 1988; Vigil, 1988; Horowitz, 1990).

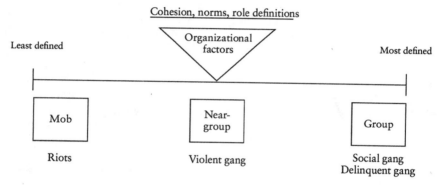

Figure 6.4
Gang Delinquency Model: Yablonsky
(source: Hood and Sparks ,1977, p. 606)

The disagreement in gang characterization possibly reflects the different types of gangs studied by different researchers in a diversity of settings. Furthermore, because the focus of Yablonsky's research was on individual factors in his theoretical constructs, intervention at the microsocial level raises many important policy implications if the theory proves valid. Even though violent gangs may lack cohesion outside the core members, pathological behavior and cohesiveness may increase in response to external pressures, such as well-intentioned intervention programming.

3. Social Learning Theories

Social learning theory posits that all behavior is a result of a conditioning process that varies with the environment and consists of a system of rewards and punishments for certain behavior. According to Goldstein (1991, p. 55), social learning theory is "a combined situational, cognitive, and physiological orientation to the acquisition of behavior," but more significantly, direct application can be made to explain the process involved in instigating and maintaining anti-social and aggressive behavior. In the delinquent group and gang setting, evaluative definitions are placed on behavior in the form of discriminative stimuli, whereby individuals engage in activity that receives positive reinforcement and refrain from activity that is negatively reinforced (Williams and McShane, 1993). The maintenance or external reinforcement of deviant definitions, which becomes somewhat more complex in explaining subcultural group and gang aggression, emphasizes the importance of vicarious interaction through three modeling influences: familial, substructural, and symbolic. This particular learning process involves the acquisition of aggressive behavior through direct observation, whether it is through physically and verbally abusive parents, aggressive and violent peers, or the violent images portrayed in the media (Goldstein, 1991).

Sutherland and Cressey (1978) found that criminal behavior is learned largely through the symbolic interaction of intimate groups that have incorporated criminal values. These groups provide the social opportunities to learn criminal patterns and definitions contrary to legal norms, in addition to acquiring necessary criminal skills and techniques. Whether individuals adopt criminal or noncriminal patterns is dependent upon the frequency, duration, priority, and intensity of the particular group association. The individual who receives greater exposure to conforming, law-abiding peer group patterns is less likely to become delinquent than the individual who associates with a group that actively participates in and provides reinforcement for law-violating definitions. Sutherland and Cressey's (1978) concept of differential-association, therefore, is dependent upon the exposure to definitions favorable or unfavorable to the violation of law.

A reformulation of differential-association theory, conducted by Burgess and Akers (1966), incorporated social learning theory's focus on the importance of external reinforcement with Sutherland's nine propositions. Their addition of "nonsocial factors" (e.g. money, drugs, material gains) as reinforcing behavior acknowledges that, in addition to the group process postulated in differential-association, the environment may also support deviant behavior through positive and negative reinforcements (principles of operant conditioning). Esbensen and Huizinga (1993) similarly concluded that individual characteristics are not solely responsible for higher levels of involvement in street crime. There are likely reinforcing effects that manifest in the gang environment, which in turn contribute to the criminal behavior of gang members. Behavior that has more frequent and higher probability of reinforcement, whether it is social or not, will recur in situations to which the behavior can be applied. More succinctly, "the specific class of behavior learned and the frequency of its occurrence are a function of the effective and available reinforcers and the deviant or nondeviant direction of the norms, rules, and definitions that in the past have accompanied the reinforcement" (Goldstein, 1991, p. 61).

There have been a number of studies where the findings were contrary to the theoretical constructs found in differential-association and differential-association reinforcement. Short and Strodtbeck (1965) found that associating with delinquent peers had a separate independent effect on delinquency and had little to do with definitions favorable and unfavorable to the violation of the law. Hirschi (1969) contends that crime is a natural motivation and occurs before peer groups form any associations. Sutherland's and Akers' focus on group processes in reinforcing and learning deviant values and behavior excludes individual predisposing factors — such as temperament and disposition, conditionability, and potential for socialization — which may affect the level and the scope of participation in certain activities and, in the broader perspective, the nature of the group activities. Even though the theories are very general, the central premise — that delinquent behavior is learned — remains valid as evidence of its incorporation into a number of competing integrated theories (Feldman, 1977; Hagan and Jones, 1983; Wilson and Hernstein, 1985).

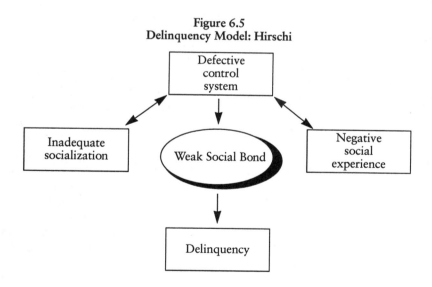

Figure 6.5
Delinquency Model: Hirschi

4. Social Control Theory

Social control theory approaches the causes of delinquency from quite a different perspective than the strain, subcultural, and learning theories discussed earlier. The central argument focuses on two key assumptions: first, individuals are socialized into values deemed important by society (e.g. law-abiding); second, everyone has the predisposition to commit delinquent acts. The underlying implication is that individuals who are not properly socialized—more specifically, taught not to offend—will have a greater propensity for deviancy. The deviance, therefore, occurs because of a breakdown or weakness in the socialization process.

The central construct of social control theory lies in the highly conceptual social bond (Hirschi, 1969, Reckless, 1961). The social bond is effected by both external controls or containments (e.g. family and institutional reinforcement) and individual internal controls or containments (e.g. moral values, strong self-concept, goal oriented). Reckless (1961) asserts that the external controls serve as a buffer in the individual's immediate social world, regulating normative behavior by simultaneously directing the individual towards legitimate societal expectations and away from deviant tendencies and influences. More specifically, the social bond depends on: the strength of the attachment to other people (particularly parents), which affects the bounds of acceptable and unacceptable behavior; commitment to organized society, where individuals are committed to conventional goals; involvement in conventional activities, which affects the opportunity to commit deviant acts; and belief in a common value system (Hirschi, 1969). A strong social bond, according to control theory, will reduce the likelihood of delinquency.

In the deviant youth group and gang context, the attachment to peers is an important component that influences the scope and nature of delinquent activity and the quality of group interaction (Vigil, 1988; Horowitz, 1983; Goldstein, 1991). Sutherland and Cressey (1978) also posit that close relationships between deviant peers increase delinquency. The central contention of control theory in this regard is that the effect of delinquent peers on deviancy is also contingent upon the level of attachment to parents. In other words, "delinquent friends will have a greater impact on delinquent involvement when parental support is weak than when it is strong" (Poole and Regoli, 1979, p. 188-189). Thus, inept parenting, according to a recent examination of control theory, promotes the antisocial characteristics that lead to associations with delinquent peers, and in turn to increased involvement in delinquency (Gottfredson and Hirschi, 1990).

Attachment to peers may best explain the dynamics of the emergence and persistence of gangs (Vigil, 1988), but remains weak in explaining the direct effect of delinquency. Other studies (Patterson and Yoerger, 1993; Simons et al., 1994), in offering a compromise between control and peer influence models, have suggested that peer influence is a more significant factor in explaining youth delinquency in middle-adolescence, but control theory best explains delinquency during early adolescence. Even Hirschi concedes "there are group processes important in the causation of delinquency whose automatic operation cannot be predicted from the characteristics of persons" (1969, p. 230). Thornberry et al. (1994) introduced an interactional theory to reconcile the divergent causal argument between the learning and social control perspectives. The study found that:

> The issue should not be posed as a question of whether associations with delinquent peers causes delinquency, or whether adolescents, once having committed delinquent behavior, seek out and associate with others who engage in similar behaviors. Choosing either of these models leads to a perspective that is only half right (p. 75).

Commitment to conventional activities (ambition), according to the concept of social bonding, makes individuals less likely to commit delinquent acts, since the negative consequences of delinquency (e.g. punishment) may be perceived as an inhibitor to achieving legitimate goals. The strain theorists (Merton, Cohen, Cloward and Ohlin), conversely, found that ambition leads to delinquency. Belief in a common value system was supported by Short and Strodtbeck (1965) who discovered that gang members positively support conventional goals, such as acquiring a job and performing well in school. With the exception of Miller (1958), research generally supports the common value system argument, but addresses the motivation for deviance under differing models. Control theory, in regard to the belief element in the bonding process, explains the occurrence of delinquency "as a variation in the extent to which people believe they should obey the rules of society ... the less the person believes he should obey the rules, the more likely he is to violate them" (Hirschi, 1969, p. 30). Moreover, *delinquent* beliefs have been found to increase delinquent peer group associations and delinquency involvement, but the strength of this causal direction is not yet clear (Thornberry et al., 1994).

Control theory (Reckless, 1961; Hirschi, 1969) and its variation, neutralization theory (Sykes and Matza, 1957), have received a significant amount of support in the literature, especially where elements have been incorporated into broader theoretical perspectives (see Kornhauser, 1978;

Hagan, 1985; Cohen and Land, 1987; Warren, 1983; Short, 1989; and Thornberry et al., 1994). However, gang delinquency is not specifically addressed by control theory because associating with deviant or criminal peers is a result of involvement in illegal activities, not the cause. Nevertheless, elements of control theory are evident in Vigil (1988) and Moore (1978) which found that regular and peripheral gang members could be characterized and differentiated based on the level of their family's stress; stress due to financial or relationship hardships, for example, may loosen social control resulting in youths spending an inordinate amount of time on the streets. Elements of social control theory, when integrated with other theoretical perspectives, such as differential association theory, is not only useful for understanding the dynamics that lead to the formation of youth gangs and other criminally-oriented youth groups in the community, but also the behavior that manifests and perpetuates in the group environment.

In this focused discussion of delinquency theory as it relates to group delinquency, it should not come as a surprise that no single theory offers a complete and satisfactory explanation. However, theories from a number of competing perspectives—strain, subcultural, social learning, and social control—provide important elements and concepts that, when collectively integrated into one model, may provide more plausible explanations for why youths become involved in gangs. For example, socially disorganized communities (characterized by factors such as weak social institutions, poverty, and single-headed households) may have an adverse effect on a youth's bond to important social institutions (e.g. family, school, church); the loss of adequate social control provided by the family and schools (due to weaker bonds) may increase a youth's exposure to gangs in the community and increase his or her susceptibility to deviant social learning processes. Research has established that joining gangs and participating in criminal activities is influenced by three different explanatory levels: individual, social institutional, and social structural. Socially disorganized communities provide the necessary conditions for gang formation, but the decision to participate is influenced by social institutional attachments and group processes within the community. To further complicate any complete explanation, there may also be unique reasons at the social-psychological level that encourage individuals to participate in collective delinquent activities. It may be that, because of the many possible theoretical propositions surrounding youth gangs and other group formations, addressing collective youth crime problems may involve quite unrelated reasons for their formation, evolution, membership and organizational structure, and involvement in illicit activities.

C. Perceived Causes of Collective Youth Crime

The remaining discussion in this chapter focuses on what respondents in this study perceived to be the primary causes of the collective youth crime problem and how these causes were ranked relative to one another. Analyzing the perceived causes of the collective youth crime problem has two specific advantages in this study: first, it will put in perspective the theoretical developments discussed up to this point — e.g. the extent that theory and the perceptions of practitioners coincide; and second, and more importantly, it will aid in determining if there is any relationship between perceived causes and the implementation of particular prevention and intervention strategies discussed in the next chapter. In regard to the second point, knowing what the perceived causes of the collective youth crime problem are may assist in determining if the strategies employed by respondent organizations in the community are appropriate for mitigating the conditions that may lead to youth gang and group problems.

In order to gather information related to the cause of the problem, respondents were provided the opportunity to identify and rank what they perceived as the five most important causes or conditions that contribute to the collective youth crime problem in their respective communities. The analysis of responses was based on the following survey question (Appendix, Section VI):

> *What do you think are the five most important causes of the youth group or youth gang problem in your community? Please rank...*

The responses from all respondents (N=257), and not just those who were experiencing youth gang and group problems, were content analyzed into the three broad causal categories discussed in the research (Shaw and McKay, 1942; Cohen, 1969; Felson, 1987; Curry and Spergel, 1988; Spergel, 1990; Wilson, 1991; Bursik and Grasmick, 1993; Spergel, 1995). The first causal category pertained to macro-system or social-structural conditions, such as poverty, unemployment, lack of opportunities, and lack of community services and programs. The second category, referred to as meso-level or social institutional problems, includes conditions such as dysfunctional family life, poor education and failure in school, and the lack of positive role models in the family and community. The third and last category involved micro-level or social psychological problems; those problems that are found at the individual level, such as drug and alcohol abuse, low self-esteem, peer pressure, and the need for acceptance. Since one of the objectives was to provide information that would be potentially useful for planning and policy development at the State-level, a more generalized and aggregated analysis was conducted. There may have been variations in perceived contributing factors and conditions across different communities—such as variations in poverty levels, economic problems, unemployment, and family disorder—but most problems in communities involve a combination of all of these factors.

Table 6.1 illustrates the results of the content analysis conducted on the 257 responses in the survey. The data from respondents who were experiencing youth gangs and groups were aggregated because there were no significant differences in the patterns of causal explanation among respondents who had experienced either type of collective. This finding precluded the need to make a comparative analysis based on the nature of the collective youth crime problem. Furthermore, to reduce excessive detail and to maintain an analytically viable sample size, responses from each of the organizational categories (e.g. law enforcement, court counselor agencies, schools, and correction institutions) were similarly aggregated. The results combine respondents from all organizational categories regardless of whether the problem involved youth gangs, youth groups, or neither.

Table 6.1
Perceived Causes of Collective Youth Crime Problems (N=257)

Causes	Number of Times Cited	Frequency
A. Macro-Level (Social Structural)	197	76.7
Lack of Opportunities	69	26.8
Poverty	64	24.9
Criminal Opportunities	25	9.7
Lack of Service/Programs	22	8.6
Unemployment	17	6.6
B. Meso-Level (Social Institutional)	162	63.0
Dysfunctional Families	100	38.9
Poor Education	39	15.2
Lack of Role Models	23	8.9
C. Micro-Level (Social Psychological)	164	63.8
Need for Acceptance	48	18.7
Drug/Alcohol Abuse	47	18.7
Peer Pressure	39	15.2
Low Self-Esteem	30	11.7

According to the ordering of perceived causes in Table 6.1, 76.7 percent of the respondents perceived that social structural problems were the primary cause of youth gang and group problems, in particular, the lack of legitimate, worthwhile opportunities (such as recreation and employment) and poverty. These two factors, when combined, were cited by 51.7 percent of all respondents as one of the five causes of the problem. The vast majority of respondents cited at least three different causal factors or conditions that may contribute to the collective youth crime problem. This table reflects the total number of times each of the causal factors was cited by all respondents in the survey. Research that focused on macro-level conditions (Cohen, 1955; Cloward and Ohlin, 1960; Short and Strodtbeck, 1965; Vigil, 1988; and Hagedorn, 1988) suggests that blocked economic and social opportunities increase the probability of membership in deviant youth collectives. Underlying macro-level conditions is the strain produced by the lack of access to legitimate opportunities, which could be due to factors such as educational deficiency, racism, and access to the labor market. Youth must search for an available medium that will help then adapt to the stress and strain in their communities; this medium may involve membership in youth gangs and groups. The impact of blocked opportunities may have a more salient and direct impact on older youths and young adults, especially when there is a lack of access to worthwhile employment opportunities. For juveniles, however, the lack of social opportunities — which may indirectly affect conventional bonding and potentially increase exposure to youth gang and group members — most likely serves as the more critical influence on joining and remaining in gangs and groups.

The second and third levels — social institutional and social psychological factors — were almost equally represented in perceived causes. For all three causal levels, and especially the social institutional level, dysfunctional family relationships were thought to contribute most significantly to youth involvement in gangs and groups. According to research tradition, delinquent behavior, including the participation in deviant youth collectives, primarily occurs where there are defects in family relationships, poor parental character, and ineffective child rearing (Hirschi, 1969; Rutter and Giller, 1983; Gottfredson and Hirschi, 1990; Sampson and Laub, 1993). However, Horowitz (1983) asserted that a dysfunctional family environment may not be directly related to the involvement in youth gangs, since not all siblings from the same family necessarily join gangs. Friedman et al. (1975) further discovered that gang and non-gang delinquents varied very little when characteristics such as parents with criminal histories and broken homes were compared. Spergel (1995, p. 115) also concluded that "distinctive cultural or race/ethnic factors in particular communities may be more important than the contributions of the family structure to the ganging phenomena." Family relationships, albeit important, should therefore be recognized as one factor among many that contributes to youth gang and group involvement.

Other factors at the social institutional level—poor education and lack of positive role models—were also cited by respondents as contributing factors. Poor educational performance or achievement, even though cited by only 15.2 percent of all respondents, are considered high predictors of later criminal patterns and involvement in collective youth criminal activities (Klein, 1968b; Hagedorn, 1988; Clements, 1988; Spergel, 1990; Conly, 1991; Kodluboy and Evenrud, 1993). Gold and Mattick (1974) discovered that school variables, academic achievement, attendance record, and the general educational climate were predictive of delinquency and youth involvement in delinquent gangs and groups. According to Spergel (1995, p. 119-120), "[d]eliquency and antisocial gang behavior may be responses to school failure and the alienation of youths...alienation from school and association with gang peers, along with antisocial behavior, appear to be mutually reinforcing...." However, as Short and Strodtbeck (1965) observed in their research, poor educational performance, and subsequent involvement in youth gangs, may be a result of and compounded by family problems. Once again there needs to be a clear understanding of the interrelationship between several social institutions in order to understand better the dynamics of the problem.

Respondents (63.8 percent) identified four individual-level factors that they perceived contributed to the collective youth crime problem, all of which have received considerable support in the research literature. The most frequently cited factor—need for acceptance (18.7 percent)—supports the research findings that youth collectives provide a social psychological support structure that is not available to individual youths. Social psychological factors have received considerable attention in the research literature on youth gang and group delinquency. The central argument is that social inadequacies contribute to the status dilemmas of youth, and consequently, the search for status and acceptance encourages involvement in youth gang and group delinquency (e.g. Cloward and Ohlin, 1960; Short and Strodtbeck, 1965; Cartwright at al., 1975; Moore, 1978; Horowitz, 1983). The process of achieving status and recognition is often interpreted as a way of resolving a variety of personal and social problems, particularly low self-esteem and the desire for acceptance (Spergel, 1990). What may distinguish the gang youth from others is a deficiency in the organization of his motivational system, whereby the gang or group not only represents an available structure of social attachment during a period of identity crisis, but provides a status-providing system that emphasizes criminal activity as a means to resolve uncertainty, ambiguity, and the lack of attachment

(Spergel, 1995). According to conclusions by Ianni (1989), criminal youth collectives emerged in environments where social institutions failed to provide a social structure that fulfilled the psychological needs of affiliation or where membership in conventional structures were missing, incongruent, or unavailable. Once individuals join a youth gang or group, group processes reinforce mutual associations and also facilitate certain forms of behavior (e.g. drug and alcohol abuse, deviance) that may not have been demonstrated prior to membership (see Thornberry et al., 1993, 1994).

This analysis suggests that there are three causal levels that must be considered when developing appropriate intervention and prevention strategies. The scope and seriousness of collective youth crime in any given community will depend on the presence and combination of social conditions favorable to the formation and persistence of youth gangs and groups. As previously mentioned, the extent to which a community is socially disorganized—e.g. lack of opportunities, poverty, and weak social institutions—most likely has an indirect but significant effect on social and economic opportunities, conventional bonding to accepted norms, exposure to delinquent peers, and the type of youth collectives that form within the community context. If long-term prevention and intervention strategies focus only on one or two causal factors or levels, they may fail to take into account many of the complex and interdependent relationships that exist between these conditions.

D. Conclusion

A number of theories have been developed to specifically explain the gang phenomenon—the leading theories were addressed here—but the trend has been to incorporate specific components and concepts from each level of theoretical explanation (social-psychological, social institutional, and social structural) into a larger integrated/interrelated theoretical framework. Driving this integrated theory movement is the notion that gangs are not "the problem," but merely indicate serious underlying socioeconomic problems (e.g. structural unemployment, poverty, social disorder) that have micro- and meso-level implications (Huff, 1993). Miller (1990, p. 280) concludes that "if youth gangs are a product of the circumstances of the lower class, eliminating or substantially changing these circumstances will eliminate or substantially reduce gang problems." However, theories that focus on poverty, the lower class, opportunity structures, and the underclass (e.g. Miller, 1958; Cloward and Ohlin, 1960; Wilson, 1987) do not fully capture the importance of social-institutional influences on the development of youth gang and group problems, nor on the crime problem in general.

Collective youth crime problems are most often found in poverty-stricken communities, where families concentrated in these areas have higher rates of social and personal problems. It may be more helpful to understand how and why a community, its social agencies, and its families fail to mesh resources and relationships with the motivations of youths. Without a strong social support and control system developed within the context of the family and other social institutions in the community, youth may experience isolation and personal strain that force them to seek other ways to resolve problems of status, uncertainty, and ambiguity. The lack of an adequate social structure within the community adversely affects the development of the youths' social, as well as, personal identities (Spergel, 1995). Addressing the inadequacies of a community's underlying social institutions — families, schools, and civic organizations — may therefore provide some of the answers as to why some youth are more vulnerable to youth gang and group involvement than others.

The effectiveness of prevention and intervention strategies largely depends on whether the design of particular approaches can effectively and adequately address the perceived cause of the problem. Respondents identified twelve causal factors that contributed to the problem, all of which were classified under social structural, social institutional, or social psychological rubrics. Social structural problems or conditions, particularly the lack of opportunities and poverty, were perceived as primary causes of collective youth crime problems, followed closely by social institutional and psychological factors. However, respondents (38.9 percent) most frequently cited the social institutional factor of dysfunctional family relationships as the primary condition that encouraged involvement in gang and group activities. Three causal factors — lack of opportunities, poverty, and dysfunctional family relationships — were cited by 90.1 percent of all respondents as one of the five primary conditions that contributed to the problem.

The findings in this chapter have a particular significance in the examination of prevention and intervention strategies in the following chapter. Implementing effective approaches, whether they involve social intervention, suppression, or the mobilization of the community, requires some understanding of the predictors of youth gang and group membership and the likely impact of prevention efforts. Because the causes of membership in youth collectives are interdependent, interconnected, and generally hard to isolate or treat independently, there has been very little success in mitigating the problem. Collective youth crime problems manifest at the aggregate level — through poverty, inadequate educational processes, population shifts, racism, and segregation (Klein, 1995) — which in turn affects

community social institutional processes and individual social-psychological development. Prevention and intervention strategies are based on different assumptions and goals, and the success of these programs largely
depends on whether they have adequately considered the perceived causes of the problem.

7

Prevention and Intervention Strategies

A. Introduction

An area that needs further exploration in youth gang and group research is the response to the crime problem by state and local organizations, including both criminal justice and community-oriented agencies. Spergel et al. (1990, p. 53) concluded that "we have less information probably on the nature of the response to the gang problem, and its effectiveness, than we have on gang characteristics or the scope and seriousness of the problem." Organizational responses to youth gang and group problems have been labeled as atheoretical or "blandly eclectic," which often results in inconsistent, random, or uncoordinated programming that makes it very difficult to determine the approach that has been implemented. The lack of a well-coordinated and clearly defined response also makes program evaluation highly problematic (Klein, 1971; Spergel, 1990). Prevention and intervention programs and the evaluation of organized responses to collective youth crime were at their zenith in the 1960s, but few research projects have focused on the effectiveness of contemporary strategies (Spergel et al., 1990). This chapter, which represents the final phase of this research endeavor, provides information on some of the prevention and intervention strategies, programs and their structures, and the organizational policies that have been established to address the growing collective youth crime problem in North Carolina.

Contemporary gang intervention and prevention approaches have evolved with the changing assumptions about gang formation and perpetuation. Intervention strategies generally focus on identifying and redirecting gang members and at-risk youths into alternative and positive support structures and activities, while prevention strategies have attempted to divert or deter at-risk youths from initial gang involvement. Recently, the strategy focus in many jurisdictions around the country has shifted away from social and community structural interventions, where priority was placed on understanding gangs, to a strategy that primarily concentrates on crime control (Spergel, 1990; Conly, 1993). According to Spergel (1990, 1991a), many prevention and intervention approaches are often integrated into an array of evolving policies and program arrangements, but can all generally be classified under four strategies. The four primary strategies, typically integrated through organizational and program arrangements, are: 1) neighborhood or community mobilization; 2) social intervention; 3) provision for social and economic opportunities; and 4) suppression and incarceration. A fifth approach, termed organizational development, is less a strategy and more a general organizational-structural response. These four primary strategies, which are closely related to and largely dependent upon organizational development, are often incorporated into either a unidimensional professional approach — often planned and executed by state and local governments — or a community-centered approach, where grassroots organizations and social institutions combine efforts into a singular, integrated strategy.

A discussion of the concepts involved in these strategies, programs, and policies is useful as a frame of reference for understanding what organizations in this study presently do in their efforts to more effectively address the collective youth crime problem. The strategies that have emerged over recent decades are not only related to different assumptions regarding cause and effect, but also to the best methods for controlling and containing the problem (Spergel, 1990). Therefore, by reexamining some of the findings in the previous chapter on perceived causes, it may become possible to understand better some of the rationales for implementing certain prevention and intervention programs. Recent research on youth gangs conducted by the National Youth Gang Suppression and Intervention Research and Development Program (e.g. Spergel et al., 1990; Spergel, 1991a; Spergel and Chance, 1990, 1991; Spergel and Curry, 1990a, 1990b) provided the empirical and theoretical constructs to evaluate the organizational responses to both youth gang and group problems in North Carolina.

The primary focus up to this point has been on the scope and nature of the youth gang and group problem, the characteristics that distinguish youth gangs from youth groups, and the structural characteristics that define an organization's commitment to the problem. Herein lies not only the opportunity to examine prevention and intervention strategies and their perceived effectiveness, but also the opportunity to offer a course of action for future evaluative studies and an opportunity to make research recommendations based on the collective findings from this and all previous chapters. The chapter begins by first summarizing the programs that have been developed through the years, identifying the theoretical constructs that have influenced the particular emphasis of each approach; it then examines the strategies used by respondents in North Carolina, primarily to see if the strategy distribution is related to organizational orientation and if there are differences in regard to the nature of the problem; then, there is an analysis on the patterns of organizational responses (e.g. organizational development) and their relationship to the collective youth crime problem; following this discussion, the perceived effectiveness of strategies in ameliorating youth gang and group problems and their characteristics is addressed; and lastly, an analysis is provided to identify those organizations that demonstrated the most promising approaches.

B. Prevention and Intervention Strategies

1. Community Organization

The community organization strategy, which evolved out of the need to "bring about adjustment, development, or change among groups and organizations in regard to community problems or social needs" (Spergel, 1990, p. 72), has today become a coalition of organizations—e.g. community agencies, schools, criminal justice organizations, community groups, and even former gang members—with the particular goal of collectively solving the gang problem. The primary focus is on the immediate conditions of the neighborhood that give rise to youth gang and group delinquency. The idea of mobilizing the community against youth gang and group delinquency is largely based on Shaw and McKay's (1942) thesis that gangs manifested in communities that were socially disorganized, where there were insufficient social controls, poor supervision, and weak social institutions—such as the family, school, and church. Klein (1995, p. 139) recently observed that "[b]ecause gangs arose in disorganized and transitional inner-city areas, it stood to reason that renewing the social organization would lessen the functional need for gang structures...[t]ying informal community structures to formal agencies—schools, enforcement, welfare—would provide the social structure for healthy socialization and vitiate the need for gangs and other forms of deviance."

The first effort to address the concept of social disorganization and gang delinquency was the Chicago Area Project in the 1930s, which emphasized not only the idea of mobilizing the local community through the coordination of available resources, but also the need to restore a sense of local community through citizen involvement that would hopefully result in youth leading more conventional, law-abiding lifestyles (Kobrin, 1959; Schlossman et al., 1984). The assumptions were that much delinquency was group-related, that delinquency and gang activity was a result of residential patterns and community structures, and that reducing delinquency and gang-related activities would result from residents defining their local problem and determining the appropriate solutions (Klein, 1995). There is no strong empirical evidence as to whether this project was effective at reducing gang delinquency, but the general ideas and strategic framework have remained important.

Over the past twenty years, a number of programs have established broad frameworks for designing and implementing comprehensive community-based strategies. These programs, which involve several phases or components, have recognized the importance of integrating strategies that address the community's structural weaknesses as well as social institutional problems (e.g. failing schools and dysfunctional families). For example, the Community Youth Gangs Services Program (Los Angeles) includes a crisis intervention team, target area coordinators for community mobilization, prevention programs, job development training, and graffiti removal; the Community Reclamation Project (Los Angeles) assists communities in developing creative and safe ways to reclaim neighborhoods from gangs, provides opportunities for youths to build self-esteem, and supports parents who have gang youth; and the Crisis Intervention Network (Los Angeles) coordinates its services with law enforcement and probation agencies within the local community (Conly, 1993). Contemporary community programs now include job development programs, neighborhood watches, community mobilization coordinators, crisis intervention networks, prevention seminars, organized community leadership, and procedures for identifying at-risk youth within schools and the community. But as Spergel (1995, p 174) emphasizes:

> In its most recent evolution in the late 1980s and early 1990s, the community organization and mobilization approach incorporates the development of coalitions of *justice agencies* [emphasis added] with schools, community groups, and even former gang members (as workers or mentors) with local, state, and federal agencies and the resources to deal collectively with the problem of gangs, especially gang violence and drug trafficking...Emphasis is now on community or problem-oriented policing, with law enforcement in key coordinating positions.

Even though many community-based programs lack definitive empirical data on their general effectiveness, community organization—where there is improved communication and joint policy and program development among criminal justice, community-based and grassroots organizations—was perceived as an effective strategy in cities where gang problems were emerging (Spergel, 1990; Spergel and Chance, 1990; Howell, 1994). The critical factor, therefore, involves community responsiveness to what is characterized as an emerging gang problem. A principal goal in any community organization effort should be to first raise the community's awareness of the local gang situation by determining whether gangs have already established their presence in particular neighborhoods or if there is evidence that they are just emerging. Community organization may be most effective where gang problems are emerging, since residents may be more optimistic about their ability to take preventive action (Conly, 1993). As discussed earlier, the presence of gangs may indicate serious social structural and social institutional problems. Community organization strategies may be less effective in changing or mediating social and structural conditions in communities where gang problems have been chronic for long periods of time. This strategy may be unable to, at the point of gang entrenchment, "provide for the needs of youths... [or affect] the broad array of reward structures within the community that makes gang membership attractive to adolescents" (Covey et al., 1992, pp. 239 -240).

2. Social Intervention

Group-level intervention, often termed youth outreach or detached worker programs, flourished in the 1950s and 1960s,[1] but has essentially lost support today. These programs, with a primary goal of value transformation, attempted to re-channel youths' attitudes into more prosocial directions (Klein, 1971; Goldstein, 1991). A key assumption was that youth gangs could be redirected to fit the expectations of larger society and that youth gang member norms and values could be altered through outreach supportive services. Manipulating the gang structure through group counseling, recreation and referral services was central in the efforts to re-orient gang values and behaviors (Spergel, 1995). Covey et al.(1992) suggest that these programs may have been counter-productive in the gang setting and were prone to failure because the efforts and strategies employed

---

1. Four detached worker programs were prominent during this timeframe: the New York City Youth Board Project, the Roxbury Project, the Chicago Youth Development Project, and the Group Guidance Project. The latter three programs received formal evaluations and were noted as unsuccessful in achieving the desired outcomes—reducing delinquent gang involvement (Goldstein, 1991).

The *New York City Youth Board Project* (1950s and 1960s), which was never formally evaluated, used detached workers to ensure youth had connections to legitimate opportunities in the neighborhood. The *Roxbury Project* (late 1950s to early 1960s) incorporated a number of intervention components—e.g. family casework, detached worker, recreation, and job placement; the program evaluation (Miller, 1962), using comparison groups and other data sources (e.g. court appearances), indicated no reduction in criminal behavior and only negligible results in general. The *Chicago Youth Development Project* (1960-1966) emphasized street work with groups; there was no significant reduction in criminal activities in the targeted communities; the detached worker strategy failed to demonstrate any positive effects on school drop-out, unemployment, and arrests rates (Gold and Mattlick, 1974). The *Group Guidance Project* (1961-1965) was a four-year detached worker project that emphasized group programming and value transformation; the evaluation (Klein, 1968b) concluded that efforts to change gang member attitudes, values, and perception through counseling inadvertently increased gang cohesion and delinquency patterns (see also Goldstein, 1991, 1993a; Spergel, 1990; Covey et al., 1992).

were incapable of addressing the "magnitude of the forces that operate on the individual in the neighborhood and community setting" (p. 240). Common program defects included the confusion over program goals and priorities—whether intervention strategies should focus on individual or group-level treatment, provide access to recreational opportunities, include value transformation, or prevent gang violence and related delinquency (Klein, 1971; Spergel, 1990).

Intervention programs were essentially abandoned for a couple of decades, primarily because gang conflict problems became more complex and serious in nature, requiring a stronger mix of suppression and social control in the intervention framework, and because of the general belief that the more criminal and violent youth gang members were less amenable to the approaches inherent in street-work and recreational strategies (Spergel, 1995). There was also reason to believe that programs that attempt to alter values, attitudes, and perceptions through counseling and group activity may inadvertently increase gang cohesion and elevate the commitment to the gang (Klein and Crawford, 1967). This problem was discovered in Short and Strodtbeck's (1965) YMCA detached worker project where gangs accrued status "by virtue of their having a [street] worker" (p. 197) assigned to them, and in Yablonsky's (1962) New York City recreational program, where team sports provided the opportunity for gang member recruitment.

The fundamental problem, and one that consistently appears in all the projects and programs reviewed for this discussion, was the failure to implement adequately and properly the techniques relevant to program prescription. Goldstein (1991) found that numerous projects suffered from a failure in program integrity, where high staff turnover, worker role confusion, bureaucratization, disproportionate and heavy caseloads, and component inflexibility contributed to implementation failure. The vast majority of delinquency intervention programming in detached worker projects failed to address or tailor programs to individual gang members, and thus lacked the program intensity and comprehensiveness necessary for success. Since many members within the gang vary in age, participate at different levels (core versus peripheral or marginal members), and vary in criminal propensity, intervention must not only address group-level dynamics, but must address individual (social-psychological) factors as well.

Contemporary programs—which have been reinvigorated by federal and state initiatives and resources, as well as increasing community concerns—have taken a more integrative approach to gangs and at-risk individuals, incorporating group and individual level approaches. Program support and implementation can be attributed to the diversity of sponsorship: federal, state and local government agencies, community and grassroots organizations, and private groups. The House of Umoja (Philadelphia), The Boys' and Girls' Club of El Monte (California), Project Positive (Miami), and the ACYF (Administration for Children, Youth and Families) Youth Gang Drug Prevention Programs are excellent examples of innovative and integrated approaches that have received mixed sponsorship. There are variations in specific program goals, but they all attempt to provide positive experiences for at-risk youths—such as recreational activities, mentor programs, skill training, field trips, counseling, and community service—by directing them away from negative behavior. However, the dependence on federal, state, and private financial support has placed many programs in precarious positions, whereby the level of service delivery and the scope of the available services are largely dependent upon year to year funding priorities of government agencies.

Social intervention strategies and approaches have evolved into a wide array of services today, implemented by a wide range of community organizations and agencies. Since the 1950s, when youth service agencies were predominantly responsible for designing and implementing intervention programs, intervention programming has slowly become the responsibility of all organizations within the community—criminal justice organizations, schools, grassroots groups, churches, treatment agencies, and youth services organizations. Programs now range from presentence and post-sentence services provided by probation departments to religious counseling provided by local churches, and include a wide variety of other programs and approaches such as crisis intervention, outreach, diversion, counseling, role modeling, mentoring, drug prevention and treatment, tattoo removal, intergang mediation, leadership development, and referral for services (Spergel, 1995). Because contemporary programs, such as those mentioned here, have begun to provide more comprehensive and integrated intervention strategies, these programs may produce more positive results than previous conventional, unidimensional programs. Even in the absence of definitive evaluations on program effectiveness, research (Spergel et al., 1990b; Spergel and Chance, 1990; Spergel, 1991b; Spergel et al., 1994a) has found that social intervention strategies should still be utilized as part of a larger comprehensive approach, especially in communities where gang problems are severe.

3. Opportunity Provisions

Common throughout contemporary delinquency research, including youth gang and group studies, is the emphasis on improving educational services —both school-based and employment training—within crime afflicted communities. School and job opportunity strategies, which are the core of most opportunity programs, incorporate many of the other intervention strategies discussed thus far. The central contention is that the lack of legitimate opportunities, or access to necessary resources (e.g. job training and educational services), leads to structural strain and delinquency, including youth gang criminal activities (Cloward and Ohlin, 1960). The idea of opportunities provision has become more complex and difficult to implement in recent years, since social services and intervention are no longer viewed as the direct avenue for providing the necessary access to opportunities; the issue is one of basic social and economic opportunities such as jobs, job preparation, job placement, job training, and various remedial training and apprenticeships, all of which require more than provisions of social services, organizational changes, and local community mobilization (Spergel, 1995). According to Spergel (1991a), it is important to distinguish strategy emphasis for policy purposes: social intervention programs, for example, are critically linked to the enabling function of basic institutional opportunities; improving the opportunity structure, in following the logic of this argument, facilitates the implementation of more specific intervention measures. This section specifically addresses the two most important programming concerns that are necessary to improve the overall opportunity structure within the community: school-based programming and job programming.

a. School-Based Programming

The National Youth Gang Survey [2] found that gangs were present in every major school district sampled (Spergel and Curry, 1990b). The effect on youths (gang and nongang alike) is direct and indirect: Youths must adapt not only to an environment of fear and intimidation, but also to the direct effects of victimization and coercion into gang membership. This activity impacts students' academic performance, social behavior, and bonds to their school (Spergel, 1990; Kodluboy and Evenrud, 1993). The more threatening and intimidating the school environment, the greater the likelihood that youths will perform poorly, skip class, or drop out altogether. Creating a safe school climate is therefore necessary before more specific intervention approaches can be implemented. This may be accomplished through an array of prevention programming, particularly by increasing the presence and activity of security personnel, removal of graffiti, imple-

---

2. This 1987 survey was part of the National Youth Gang Intervention and Suppression Research and Development Program, sponsored by the U.S. Department of Justice and conducted at the University of Chicago. This survey (see also Spergel et al., 1990; Spergel and Curry, 1990a, 1990b) identified respondent populations from 45 cities and 6 correctional sites who could provide valuable information on the scope of the gang problem and potentially effective prevention and intervention programs.

menting strict behavioral and dress codes, and providing strict sanctions for disciplinary and behavioral infractions (OJJDP, 1989).

Kodluboy and Evenrud (1993) assert that, once a safe environment has been established, academic intervention should be a primary gang intervention focus, since it may have the greatest impact on changing behavior. The need for and importance of school-based intervention programming for at-risk youths has been documented in previous research (Rubel and Ames, 1986; Jenson et al., 1991; Goldstein, 1991). However, academic success — often cited as the primary goal — may only have an indirect effect on gang membership. Therefore, improving instructional strategies and the general learning environment must be complimented by efforts to counteract gang influences, such as implementing prevention education programs focusing on gang and drug involvement.

Programs that attempt to prevent gang involvement within the school and community include California's Paramount School, "10-Schools" Program, "Cities in School" Program, ASPIRA of Florida, and the San Diego Youth and Community Services Neighborhood Outreach Program. The Paramount School, which has served as a model for many gang diversion programs, consists of a tri-level (2nd, 5th, and 7th grades) gang prevention program aimed at raising awareness of gangs and presenting youths with positive role models. The program also consists of a parent-awareness component which increases parental knowledge of the gang problem and provides strategies to discourage their children from becoming involved in gangs. The "10-Schools" and "Cities in School" programs focus on dropout prevention and improving academic performance through specially trained social service workers. ASPIRA of Florida, which has a three-pronged intervention approach within middle and high schools, consists of: conducting gang-awareness training and dropout prevention programs; establishing youth clubs within schools in order to develop leadership skills and expand on career awareness; and providing case management and family intervention. Lastly, the San Diego outreach program, in focusing on middle-school at-risk youths, provides positive role models and recreational activities, in addition to assisting with educational goals, job development, and career placement (Conly, 1992; Spergel, 1991).

Common among the above programs — which may improve the likelihood of success — is community cooperation and collaboration. Programs that demonstrate cooperative and interactive learning may have favorable effects on delinquency if properly implemented. The central strategy in all school-based gang and at-risk youth intervention programming is to negate any condition that will increase the probability of dropping out. To accomplish this task, programming must be innovative and flexible enough to address the particular influence at the various educational grade levels.

Complicating this task is the need to implement programs in communities where gangs are present, while simultaneously making an effort to avoid solely focusing on gangs for fear of labeling youths.

b. Job Programming

The second important component within the opportunities provision rubric is the need to improve employment opportunities within the community. The lack of good jobs, ones that provide growth opportunities and meaningful employment, is "clearly the major factor that has transformed the gang problem in the past few decades" (Hagedorn, 1988, p. 166). Klein (1971) and Spergel (1991a) also found that job opportunities for older youths are critical to reduce gang involvement, since youths with jobs will most likely leave the gang. Hagedorn (1988, 1991) asserts that a lack of job opportunities strongly correlates with an extended involvement in the gang — often into adulthood — and a greater propensity to remain active in the lucrative drug dealing business. Corsica (1993) proposes a comprehensive, holistic approach to solving employment problems — one that affords the flexibility to address individual needs, involves the local community and government, is limited in geographic scope, and involves participants in program design and operation. Support for a comprehensive employment strategy was also found in other studies, particularly those that address the "underclass" argument (Moore, 1985; Duster, 1987; Vigil, 1988; Hagedorn, 1988; Taylor, 1990; Spergel, 1991a; Short, 1989).

Recently, the U.S. Department of Labor's Job Training Partnership Act funded a comprehensive, community-based job placement program entitled Youth Opportunities Unlimited (YOU). The guiding assumption of this program is that gangs, drug addiction, and juvenile delinquency manifest through two sources: poverty and the lack of economic and educational opportunities. By saturating a targeted community with positive programs, the community should experience significant improvement (Conly, 1993). Spergel (1991, p. 146) also reports that the program "must generate an integrated series of initiatives — including school-based and second-chance services — which are designed to address the various needs of each and every young person in a target area." YOU, which will be formally evaluated in a few years, provides employment and job training strategies as well as provisions for improving the delivery system for health care, housing, recreation, and family services (Conly, 1993). The Job Corps, another federally sponsored and funded program, has a similar multi-dimensional focus as YOU, but removes at-risk [3] individuals from their

---

3. According to the Job Corps' program guide, at-risk youths come from dysfunctional families in economically disadvantaged communities. Common individual characteristics

neighborhood and places them in residential facilities where they can acquire necessary job skills training and experience.

A number of local-level programs, which operationalize integrated employment approaches include the YouthBuild/Action Program (YAP), GANG PEACE/FIRST, the Bay Area Youth Employment Project Consortium/Youth Opportunity Program, Project Match, and the planned Dane County (Wisconsin) Juvenile Court Prevention Program. These community-based organizations aim to provide a differential opportunity structure that will encourage legitimate employment. All of these programs focus on at-risk youths from socially disadvantaged neighborhoods and utilize a number of similar approaches: job development and skills training, career awareness and counseling, and job placement. However, YAP incorporates cognitive skill development and places an emphasis on leadership training, while the GANG PEACE/FIRST program stresses the importance of neighborhood outreach and recreational activities (Spergel, 1991; Corsica, 1993). Most of these programs were designed to address problems associated with general youth delinquency and have only recently begun to focus on youth gangs. Miller (1990) emphasizes the importance of designing youth gang prevention and intervention programs based on sound theoretical formulations, yet to what extent the above programs have taken into account the specific theoretical issues relevant to gang formation and perpetuation is not altogether clear.

Even though there is no guarantee that employed gang members and at-risk youth will desist from criminal activity, the programs discussed appear at least to provide a better support network for legitimate opportunities. But as Duster (1987, p. 309) warns, "no longer will short-term job training or job creation programs suffice...what is needed are new approaches that will produce a new mix of skills, experience, and qualifications that can provide entry into viable work careers." This can best be accomplished by concomitantly addressing the special educational needs of younger at-risk youths in schools and through remedial education and vocational training for older youths and young adults.

4. Suppression

The last of the four basic gang intervention and prevention strategies involves the direct involvement of criminal justice organizations. An increase in the use of suppression—emphasizing arrest, prosecution, incarceration, and intensive surveillance and monitoring—has become a dominant pre-

---

include high school drop-out, minority membership, low educational attainment, and a lack of vocational skills.

vention approach in many cities facing both established and emerging gang problems (Spergel et al., 1990). Klein (1995) found that the emphasis on suppression has evolved because of four recent developments: first, the general acceptance that rehabilitation and treatment approaches have failed; second, the improvement in law enforcement capabilities (e.g. intelligence collection and dissemination); third, the emergence of gangs in many cities throughout the country, coupled with an increase in gang violence; and finally, the purported involvement of gangs in drug trafficking. In general, the shift towards suppression approaches can also be attributed to the growing conservatism since the 1980s.

The actual and perceived fear of gang-related activities—especially the accompanying violence—and potential for victimization has increased public pressure on local and state officials (e.g. mayors, governors, district attorneys, and law enforcement chiefs) to remedy the problem. Greater public concern, asserts Jackson and Rudman (1993, p. 259), has been "fueled by the death of innocent bystanders, the intimidation of potential witnesses to gang-related activities, [and] reports of increasing gang violence in schools." Furthermore, the heightened media coverage of gang violence, particularly drive-by shootings in more affluent neighborhoods, may also contribute to and potentially exacerbate the public's perception of the seriousness of the gang problem. The demand for action most often results in heightened activity by law enforcement. According to Spergel (1991a, p. 106) the conventional or traditional police suppression strategy is to "quickly and effectively arrest, investigate, track, and assist in the prosecution and sentencing of gang members, especially hard-core members or leaders, and keep them in jail as long as possible." Although traditional crime control approaches are still the norm in communities experiencing gang problems, community-based and problem-oriented policing techniques have emerged and demonstrated considerable promise in many localities. These new models, which promote proactive rather than reactive policing in gang neighborhoods "are consistent with the current thinking that solutions to gang problems lie in making fundamental changes in the community structure" (Conly, 1993, p. 48). The need to build better rapport with gang members and community residents is necessary to improve or develop prevention activities.[4]

---

4. These activities may include: participating in community awareness campaigns; contacting parents of peripheral gang members to alert them of gang involvement; sponsoring gang hotlines to gather information; organizing athletic events with teams of law enforcement officers; establishing working relationships with local social service organizations; making presentations on gangs to schools and community groups; sponsoring school-based gang and drug prevention programs (e.g. Drug Abuse Resistance Education); serving as a referral for jobs and community service; expanding block clubs and neighbor-

Needle and Stapleton (1983) found that police departments in the majority of cities surveyed did not have special programs directed exclusively at gang control or prevention, even though all of the cities had a gang presence. Most cities employed general crime prevention and control approaches — which essentially subject youth gangs to the same prevention programming that targets all juvenile offenders — rather than gang-specific strategies. However, the study did discover that the majority of cities surveyed participated in extra-departmental alliances — involving information sharing, cooperation, and coordination and planning — but once again, cooperative efforts focused on the general juvenile crime problem. The few programs and projects classified as gang-specific include: Operation Safe Streets (California), Los Angeles County Inter-Agency Task Force on Gang Violence (California), Probation and Police Suppression of Youth Gang Activity Project (California), Juvenile Gang Reduction Specialist Project (Arizona), and the Crisis Intervention Network (Pennsylvania).

The most innovative and comprehensive suppression approach has been the Los Angeles County Inter-Agency Task Force on Gang Violence, which involves criminal justice agencies as well as community grassroots organizations.[5] According to Needle and Stapleton (1983), the systematic planning and coordination, and high-level visibility of participating organizations has contributed to a reduction in gang-related homicides. A number of other state and local-level task forces have formed to address the specific needs of law enforcement, prosecutors, corrections, probation and parole, community-based agencies and local government. As a result, special legal approaches, such as California's Street Terrorism Enforcement Program and Operation Hardcore (vertical prosecution program), have been implemented; unique gang supervision programs have been established; specialized law enforcement sections (e.g. youth services program, gang detail, and gang unit) and new tactics have evolved; new information and tracking systems have been developed; and a plethora of agencies and grassroots organizations has emerged to coordinate prevention efforts with law enforcement organizations.

Strategies that have focused on eliminating or harassing gang members — such as police sweeps, intense monitoring, and unique laws — have had

---

hood watches; and using mobile gang prevention and intervention units (Conly, 1993, p. 47-49).

5. The task force includes the Los Angeles County Sheriff's Operation Safe Streets, the District Attorney's Operation Hardcore (vertical prosecution), the Probation Department's Specialized Gang Supervision Program, the Community Youth Gang Services Project, the California Youth Authority Parole Service, the Los Angeles City Schools Security Unit, Los Angeles County Schools, and the Los Angeles Police Department's CRASH (Community Resources Against Street Hoodlums) program.

mixed results. Klein (1995) questions the effect of the guiding deterrence principles (celerity, severity, and certainty of punishment) in numerous gang suppression programs in California. The programs, Klein argues, may actually produce a negative effect: focusing on gangs and gang members not only provides the status and identity desired, but may inadvertently increase the internal cohesion of the gang. Exacerbating this problem is the fact that within many neighborhoods there already exists tension between residents and law enforcement; this makes it much more difficult to gain the initial cooperation necessary for effective prevention (Conly, 1993).

The primary focus of suppression programs is undoubtedly to reduce the criminal activities of gangs and gang members through deterrence threats. However, the trend in suppression programming has begun to involve the integration of different organization, agency, and police strategies. Integrating community-based organizations with criminal justice agencies possibly signifies that suppression alone may not be effective. There is a growing consensus, according to Conly (1993, p. 53), "that the way to control gangs is to focus considerable attention on the problems of the communities ... community and problem-oriented policing models offer much promise for improving the relationship between communities and their police forces and thereby addressing the problem of gangs." But because there is little evaluative data on the effectiveness of community policing in cities experiencing gang problems, there is a need to first determine if multidimensional, community and gang-targeted approaches work, and this can only be accomplished with systematic evaluation research involving comparative research designs.

5. Organizational Development

The effective and systematic implementation of prevention and intervention strategies requires an organized and appropriately integrated effort from organizations within the community. Organizational development pertains to the methods, techniques, programs, and policies that organizations adopt and utilize in order to effectively deal with particular crime problems, such as those created by youth gangs and groups. In essence, the extent to which an organization develops and effectively uses available or potential resources, both within and across agencies in the community or jurisdiction, has a significant impact on how efficiently and effectively prevention and intervention programs are integrated and coordinated. Those features that best indicate the level of organizational development within organizations include the development of special policies, the implementation of special units, the use of special training programs, and the existence of interagency coordination and advisory structures (Spergel et al., 1990; Spergel, 1995; see also Spergel, 1994b and Spergel and Chance, 1990).

One of the most significant indicators of an organized response to collective youth criminal activities is the existence of special guidelines and policies within the organizational structure. Special policies may exist in a variety of forms, but they are generally either formally documented in writing or expressed orally. Spergel et al. (1990) assert that the production of written policies is evidence of a greater commitment and effort by an organization to address the problem. A second indicator that is demonstrative of a strong commitment to reducing collective youth crime is the establishment of special organizational units — e.g. youth gang unit, threat group detail — that are designed to react specifically to youth gangs and groups. Special units are most prevalent among criminal justice agencies, particularly police and sheriff's departments in large urban areas. Needle and Stapleton (1983) discovered three specialized forms of youth gang control in their survey of police departments. The most common approach, however, involved traditional police unit personnel who were assigned gang control responsibilities, though these personnel were not assigned principally nor exclusively to gang control duties. The two more specialized units — gang detail and gang unit — involved officers who were assigned exclusively to gang control work. The study further discovered that specialization was most characteristic of larger police departments and in jurisdictions where the perception of the gang problem was considered most serious. Thus, most police department units (e.g. patrol, investigations, youth division, and crime prevention) typically share gang control responsibilities or support the individuals who are assigned these duties. Other special organizational units, such as gang prosecution and gang probation, were not discovered in the present research, but they can be found in other cities throughout the country, particularly cities suffering from the most serious forms of youth gang activity (e.g. Needle and Stapleton, 1983; Spergel et al., 1990; Spergel, 1991b; Reiner, 1992; Spergel et al., 1994b).

A third indicator of commitment involves special structures or procedures that enhance the coordination of community-wide efforts. Evidence of community coordination mechanisms, such as external advisory structures and task forces consisting of multiple community and government agencies, may be viewed as an effort to reduce organizational fragmentation or disorganization; it may also indicate an effort to improve the delivery of prevention and intervention programming. The absence of an advisory or interagency coordination structure could possible impede community-wide efforts and increase organizational isolation (Spergel et al., 1990). The last indicator that demonstrates a commitment to addressing the collective youth crime problem — albeit at a much lower level than the previous indicators—is the provision of special training programs that increase the general awareness of the problem or provide more advanced training for staff personnel. Training programs may indicate a recognition of a potential or established crime problem. However, special training programs alone do not necessarily demonstrate a significant level of commitment, since many agencies and organizations, especially criminal justice agencies, often have some type of general awareness training on youth gang and other high threat criminal groups.

These four strategies, and the organizational development component, are to varying degrees interdependent and interrelated. It is very difficult to implement effective prevention and intervention strategies without the internal and external organizational coordination of goals, objectives, procedures, and services. Strategies need to be organized and integrated on the basis of the specific mission and responsibilities of the organizations, as well as the scope and nature of the problem within the community (Spergel, 1995). For the most part, the extent to which organizations develop specific programs and policies aimed at ameliorating youth gang and group problems largely depends on the perceptions of the problem. Where the collective youth crime problem is perceived as more serious, there may be some evidence that organizations adopt particular programs and policies, but where the problem is perceived as less serious, there appears to be a much lower likelihood that organizations will do anything to address specifically the activities of youth gangs and groups. Therefore, an examination of the prevention and intervention strategies organizations employ should not only be linked closely to the perceptions of the problem (see previous chapter), but should also be related to organizational development—e.g. special policies, programs, units, and training.

C. Organizational Strategies and Their Perceived Effectiveness

The evaluation of strategies is once again based on the perceptions of professionals who had to deal with a variety of criminal problems, of which youth gang and group activities were but one aspect. The analysis and findings must not be treated as an evaluative study, since reliable quantitative and qualitative data based on longitudinal or historical methods were not available. However, based on the information provided by respondents, a measure of general organizational effectiveness (e.g. the effectiveness of adopted strategies) could be determined in terms of three variables: perceived improvement or worsening of the youth gang or group problem, perceived effectiveness of organizational efforts, and perceived effectiveness of interagency task forces and community-wide coordination structures (e.g. Spergel et al., 1990; Spergel and Curry, 1990a). This discussion also provided the opportunity to compare any differences that may exist between the response to youth gangs versus youth groups. Respondents were first asked the following question (Appendix, Section VI) in order to determine the distribution of organizational strategies; this particular question further enabled the subsequent analysis of the three variables mentioned above:

> *What do you think are the five best ways employed by your department or organization for dealing with the youth group or gang problem? Please rank.*

Because the strategies and approaches come in a variety of forms and respondents may or may not use the same precise terms to identify similar programs, respondents were afforded the opportunity to identify in their own words the strategies and approaches employed by their respective organizations. Recent research (Spergel et al., 1990; Spergel and Chance, 1990; Spergel and Curry, 1990b; Spergel et al., 1994b; see also Spergel, 1990, 1991a) similarly noted the wide range of terms used to describe organizational and community level prevention and intervention strategies, including the use of different terms and concepts to describe essentially the same strategy. Therefore, Spergel et al.'s (1990) classification system was adopted to code and categorize the many key words and phrases discovered in the responses.

The classification system afforded an opportunity to categorize important words and phrases that have historically distinguished the four primary prevention and intervention strategies along empirical and theoretical dimensions. This effort was painstaking and laborious, and also required a significant degree of subjectivity. Not all of the responses analyzed fit precisely nor easily into any singular category, therefore the classification of the more ambiguous terms and phrases required an appropriate justification that included closely considering the professional orientation of respondents and the respondents' community context. For example, the term *networking*, when used by school officials or court counselors, was classified as community mobilization, but when the term was used by law enforcement officials, it was classified as suppression, since networking in the law enforcement context typically implies intelligence gathering. References to attending meetings with community leaders were always considered community mobilization strategies (see Spergel et al., 1990). Defined below are the primary prevention and intervention strategies discussed earlier and the definitional indicators or dimensions that guided the classification process. For the benefit of the reader, each strategy is briefly summarized to aid in the understanding of the why certain terms fall within particular approaches.

• *Neighborhood or Community Mobilization*

The idea of neighborhood mobilization can best be described as an effort to collectively (e.g. community groups, agencies, and schools) and consensually reduce problems associated with youth gangs and groups, particularly drug-related and violent activities. Conceptually, neighborhood mobilization involves bringing about adjustment or change among organizations—such as through interagency cooperation, grassroots citizen participation, and youth involvement—in regard to community problems and social needs (Spergel and Curry, 1990a, 1990b; Spergel et al., 1990). References to "prevention" or "intervention" efforts across community agencies and the larger community, community meetings and community planning sessions, and activities such as "intergroup organizing," and "inter-organizational cooperation," were classified as neighborhood or community mobilization. Furthermore, the following goals or activities also served as indicators of this strategy (e.g. Spergel et al., 1990):

cleaning up the community	educating the community
involvement in schools	changing the community
building community trust	improving agency cooperation

• *Social Intervention*

Social intervention has evolved from a detached and street worker concept, focussing on the transformation of deviant values (Klein, 1971; Spergel, 1990; Covey et al., 1992) to a much broader array of programs that now include counseling, diversion, mediation, tattoo removal, sports and recreation, substance abuse treatment, and referrals to social service agencies. Social intervention can generally be classified as any program that emphasizes and reinforces positive behavior at the individual level. As Spergel et al.(1990, p. 73) succinctly states, "Social intervention includes counseling or direct attempts—informational or guidance—to change the values of youth in such a way as to make gang [and group] involvement less likely." The following terms or phrases served as the indicators and guidelines for classifying a response within the social intervention category (e.g. Spergel et al., 1990):

crisis intervention	group counseling
service activities	counseling
diversion	drug prevention/treatment
outreach	psychological approaches

role models   referral for social service
recreational programs

• *Opportunities Provision*

The primary focus of the opportunities provision strategy is to stimulate the development of programs that contribute directly to improving
social status and personal achievement. From a general perspective, this
strategy involves large scale resource infusion and efforts to change both
employment and educational structures within the community. Efforts
typically involve the development and improvement of school, vocational, and job training programs, but also include individual educational
assistance and job placement opportunities (Spergel, 1990; Spergel et al.,
1990; Covey et al., 1992). Thus, providing opportunities involves efforts
and approaches at both the individual and community levels. The key
terms and phrases that best describe this strategy are as follows (e.g. Spergel
et al., 1990):

job preparation   job development
job training   remedial education
job placement   tutoring
improve educational system   improve employment
                                                              opportunities

• *Suppression*

The last of the four primary prevention and intervention strategies
involves the response primarily from agencies and organizations within
the criminal justice system. The guiding philosophy of arrest, prosecution,
and sentencing has stimulated the development of special patrols, task
forces, and special units (Spergel, 1990). Law enforcement agencies have
become the primary organizations tasked to develop and implement the necessary suppression approaches in many communities throughout the State.
Responsibilities not only involve surveillance and tactical patrols, but also
the gathering and dissemination of criminal intelligence. Other key terms
that fall within this rubric include (e.g. Spergel et al., 1990):

enforcement   monitoring
neutralization   arrest
investigation   intelligence
apprehension   identification
eradication   sentence

• *Organizational Development*

According to Spergel (1990), organizational policies and programs may
provide a reliable frame of reference to evaluate what organizations have

done or may do to address collective youth crime more effectively. This approach more typically accompanies one or more of the other strategies, and indicates a modifying or limited development quality that facilitates the implementation and execution of the other strategies. Characteristic of this approach is the creation of special units (e.g. a gang unit) within the larger organization, and an emphasis on programs, training, and needs assessment. Key terms and phrases include (e.g. Spergel et al., 1990):

interagency coordination	special policies
program development	special units
special training	need for resources
interagency cooperation	

The analysis of primary strategies begins by examining their distribution over all respondents who cited youth gang and group problems in their communities and jurisdictions. The variations in primary strategy by respondent category are explored in order to determine the emphasis of particular strategies based on the nature of the problem—e.g. whether it involved youth gangs or youth groups. There is also a brief discussion of the perceived causes of the collective youth crime problem—which was discussed in greater detail in the previous chapter—and their relationship to the strategies that were employed by respondent organizations. It is not very clear whether and to what extent perceived cause precedes agency strategy, but there are assumptions that certain categories of cause should be related to particular strategies (Spergel et al., 1990). For example, social institutional problems, such as poor educational performance and dysfunctional family relationships, are best addressed using social intervention methods (e.g. counseling, outreach); whereas poverty and the lack of opportunities (e.g. recreational and employment) must be addressed at the social-structural level using opportunity provision strategies. Selected measures of the problem and organizational characteristics were also correlated with measures of interagency effectiveness in order to ascertain whether there is a possibility that changes in the problem were due to particular policies, procedures, and strategies.

D. Distribution of Strategies

The distribution of the primary prevention and intervention strategies for respondents who cited youth gang and group strategies (N=104) is illustrated in Table 7.1. The grid shows the ranking of each respective strategy. Respondents were afforded the opportunity to identify and rank the five most effective methods employed by their organization or department for dealing with collective youth crime problems. The ranking scheme—

identified on the horizontal axis by the numbers one through five—indicates where on the grid each strategy was ranked relative to one another. For example, suppression was the strategy most frequently chosen as the primary approach (42.3 percent), since it was ranked as the number one strategy more frequently than the other four; conversely, neighborhood mobilization received the lowest ranking as the number one strategy (5.8 percent). When examining the cells along the vertical axis of the grid, it becomes easier to see how the strategies were ranked. Because there were many strategy ranking combinations, this method was the most practical and coherent way to gain some idea of the importance placed on certain strategies and approaches. In general, suppression and social intervention strategies and approaches were listed by respondents as the two key methods for dealing with the collective youth crime problem in their communities. Not all respondents provided information regarding strategies, in fact most respondents typically identified only two or three strategies that their organizations actively employed. If a respondent cited and ranked the same strategy more than once—such as using different terminology or concepts to describe the same strategy—the duplicates were not counted as two separate strategies and the higher ranking duplicate strategy was the one used for this analysis.

Table 7.1
Strategy Distribution for Youth Gangs and Groups

| | Rankings | | | | | |
	1	2	3	4	5	Totals (%)
Neighborhood Mobilization	5.8 (6)	3.8 (4)	6.7 (7)	5.8 (6)	0 (0)	22.1 (23)
Social Interv.	28.8 (30)	10.6 (11)	9.6 (10)	4.8 (5)	5.8 (6)	59.6 (62)
Opp. Provision	6.7 (7)	6.7 (7)	4.8 (5)	.96 (1)	.96 (1)	20.2 (21)
Suppression	42.3 (44)	14.4 (15)	9.6 (10)	3.8 (4)	1.9 (2)	72.1 (75)
Organizational Development	15.4 (16)	13.5 (14)	9.6 (10)	12.5 (13)	6.7 (7)	57.7 (60)

The aggregated data revealed in general terms that the suppression strategy was the favored approach in both priority ranking (42.3 percent) and cumulatively across all five rankings (72.1 percent) for dealing with youth gang and group problems. Social intervention was the second most frequently cited approach, for both priority ranking (28.8 percent) and across all rankings (59.6 percent). In other words, these two strategies were widely listed by respondents as two of the five primary strategies for dealing with youth gang and group problems. The other two primary strategies—neighborhood mobilization and opportunities provision—were the least cited approaches and also ranked relatively low as one of the five strategies. The fifth approach—organizational development—did not receive very strong representation as the most important strategy, but was cited as one of the five approaches listed by 57.7 percent of the respondents. Even though organizational development is not a strategy per se, organizational policies and programs—such as internal agency coordination, special training, and inter-agency cooperation—appear to be important in the development and implementation of organizational strategies. As Spergel (1995) noted, a general and continuing bureaucratic or modernization process enables organizations to adapt policies and alter organizational programs and arrangements. Organizational development and modernization efforts and activities, in effect, facilitate the delivery of services and improve operational capabilities.

There were differences in priority rankings between those strategies that were developed and implemented for youth gangs and those targeting youth groups. The frequency at which strategies were cited by respondents generally replicated the pattern discovered in the aggregate analysis, but there were notable differences: suppression was more often cited by respondents experiencing youth gangs (93.1 percent) versus youth groups (56.7 percent); next came social intervention (86.4 and 40.0 percent respectively for gangs and groups); and lastly came the two least cited strategies of neighborhood mobilization (36.3 and 11.7 percent respectively for gangs and groups) and opportunities provision (27.3 and 15.0 percent respectively for gangs and groups). Organizational development was chosen as one of the five approaches by 84.1 percent of the gang respondents, but only by 36.7 percent of the group respondents. These data indicate that the four primary strategies and the one approach (organizational development) were more important for addressing youth gang problems. The variations in percentages of cited strategies—when comparing youth gang and group respondents—were statistically significant at the .05 level for all strategies, with the exception of opportunities provision. Moreover, suppression was ranked as the number one strategy for dealing with both gangs and groups, but the differences in the frequency of their citation (54.5 for gangs and 33.3 percent for groups) was statistically significant at the .05 level.

In comparing the cumulative strategy distributions targeting both youth gangs and groups, it becomes more evident that clearly articulated and formally implemented strategies appear to focus on the more serious problems associated with youth gangs. By and large, the vast majority of respondents who were experiencing youth group problems did not identify nor employ strategies that necessarily focussed on these collectives. Conversely, respondents citing youth gang problems were able to designate or at least convey the specific strategies implemented by their agencies and organization. Research has commonly found a more aggressive and organized response against youth gangs, when compared to delinquent youth groups and other forms of crime. However, this finding may be significant in that it signals a certain degree of inaction against potentially nascent gang formations or serious delinquent groups that may not have been viewed as youth gangs.

Table 7.2
Strategy Distribution by Respondent Category
for Youth Gangs and Groups

	Neighborhood Mobilization	Social Interv.	Opportunity Provision	Suppression	Org. Change
Police (N=28)	7.1 (2)	14.3 (4)	0	60.7 (17)	21.7 (5)
Sheriff (N=23)	13.0 (3)	17.4 (4)	0	56.5 (13)	13.0 (3)
Schools (N=22)	13.6 (3)	54.5 (12)	18.2 (4)	4.5 (1)	9.1 (2)
Corrections (N=7)	0	42.8 (3)	28.6 (2)	28.6 (2)	0
Court (N=19) Counselors	15.8 (3)	36.8 (7)	15.8 (3)	21.1 (4)	10.5 (2)

The strategy (emphasis) also varied across respondent categories (Table 7.2). The table demonstrates that some of the prevention and intervention approaches discussed earlier in this chapter were not even cited as strategies by respondents in certain categories. Not surprisingly, law enforcement organizations (police and sheriff's departments) relied more on suppression than any other approach. Though most law enforcement organizations adhered to traditional tactics and strategies that involved deterrence and apprehension, there were quite a few respondents who mentioned involvement in problem-oriented, community policing—activities that were in close collaboration with community residents and local criminal justice agencies, such as court counselor offices—as a key strategy. This may be a positive sign, since "it is critically important that the court workers, police, and probation officers work closely at the front end of the justice system to share information and develop appropriate supervisory and social service approaches... Otherwise the justice system remains fragmented and does not fulfill its potential as the public component of a preventive community control and support system" (Spergel, 1995, p. 201). Schools, court counselor agencies, and correctional institutions relied more on social intervention strategies—predominantly counseling, diversion, recreational, and outreach approaches. The focus of organizational activity was on managing youth in the community, especially after they have entered the criminal justice system.

Even though it is not demonstrated in the table (7.2), a majority of respondents (52.3 percent) stated that their organizations utilized two or three strategies concurrently; however, there was also a modest percentage of respondents (30.7 percent) who claimed that their organizations relied on only one approach (see also Spergel et al., 1990). The two-tier or multidimensional strategy was most prevalent among law enforcement organizations and court counselor agencies, while a unidimensional approach was more typical of schools and correctional institutions. However, because the sample size for correctional institutions was small (N=7), and the institutions were only for youthful offenders, the finding may not be typical of adult facilities that may have experienced gang and group problems. Law enforcement organizations relied heavily on suppression, but were also involved in community or neighborhood mobilization efforts and certain social intervention approaches, such as crisis intervention, mentor or role model programs, and recreational activities. Court counselor agencies offered a variety of strategy combinations, but most multidimensional approaches included social intervention as one of the strategies. This particular analysis did not attempt to examine separately or compare the strategy variations that may exist between youth gang and groups, primarily because the small sample size for each collective would been restrictive and would have limited any conclusions that could have been drawn.

One final analysis was conducted in this section to determine the relationship between the perceived primary cause of the collective youth crime problem and the primary prevention and intervention strategy employed by organizations. Even though this analysis was inferential, because respondents were not asked to provide a rationale for their strategies, and was performed using aggregated data, the statistical correlations (Table 7.3) provided meaningful information on the strength and direction of the relationship between cause and strategy. If you recall from the previous chapter, there were three causal levels that must be considered when developing appropriate intervention and prevention strategies — social structural, social institutional, and social psychological. Respondents considered social structural conditions, particularly the lack of opportunities and poverty, as the key factors that lead to involvement in youth gangs and groups, but they also specified one social institutional condition, dysfunctional families, as the single leading cause of gang and group delinquency.

The general effectiveness of prevention and intervention strategies not only depends on how well they are developed and implemented, but whether the underlying principles of the strategy design adequately address the perceived root cause or causes of the problem. There must be a direct relationship between the strategies and approaches chosen for implementation and the causal level of the problem, otherwise efforts will be futile and resources will be squandered.

Table 7.3
Biserial Correlations Between Perceived Causes and Primary Strategy (N=104)

Perceived Cause	Neighborhood Mobilization	Social Interv.	Opportunities Provision	Suppression	Organizational Development
Social Structural	.011	-.126*	.314*	-.033	.102
Social Institutional	.037	.203*	.071	-.002	.025
Social Psychological	-.022	.218**	-.112	.058	-.108

$p \leq 0.05*$ $p \leq 0.01**$ $p \leq 0.001***$

The scope and seriousness of collective youth crime in any given community will depend on the presence and combination of social conditions favorable to the formation and persistence of youth gangs and groups. The extent to which a community is socially disorganized—e.g. lack of opportunities, poverty, and weak social institutions—most likely has an indirect but significant effect on social and economic opportunities, conventional bonding to accepted norms, exposure to delinquent peers, and the type of youth collectives that form within the community context. If long-term prevention and intervention strategies focus only on one or two causal factors or levels, they may fail to take into account many of the complex and interdependent relationships that exist between these conditions. A series of point biserial statistical correlations were conducted to determine the strength and direction of the relationship between what respondents perceived as the causes of the collective youth crime problem (level) and the strategies they employed to address the problem. There were four statistically significant relationships that emerged from the correlations. Social structural causes were positively related to an opportunities provision strategy and negatively to social intervention. These relationships were logical since opportunity provisions are designed to address issues relating to poverty, unemployment, lack of legitimate opportunities (both economic and social), and similar community-level problems. The other significant positive relationships were between social institutional and social psychological causes and approaches classified under the social intervention rubric.

Organizations appear to employ appropriate strategies based on causal perceptions. Social intervention approaches (e.g. outreach, diversion, counseling, and drug treatment) are most effective at addressing social institutional problems, such as dysfunctional family relationships and poor educational performance; moreover, social intervention strategies most like-ly offer the best approaches for mitigating problems at the individual or social psychological level. These findings indicate that organizations could have been responding to the perceived causes of collective youth crime with appropriate strategies. The discussion in the forthcoming sections will address, in greater detail, the organizational response (e.g. extent of organizational development) to the problem and whether prevention and intervention strategies were having any positive effect at reducing the scope and nature of the problem. Various measures of program effectiveness are examined and correlated with characteristics of the youth gang and group problem and selected organizational-structural characteristics.

E. Patterns of Organizational Development and their Relationship to Youth Gang and Group Problems

1. Special Policies

The formulation of special organizational policies or procedures demon-strates the greatest level of proactive involvement, concern, and commit-ment by organizations. Moreover, whether organizational procedures and policies were formally documented demonstrates an even greater con-cern for the problem, especially if the policies are official guidelines or operational regulations Respondents were asked whether special policies or procedures existed within their respective departments or agencies and if these policies were officially documented. The following questions elicit-ed information necessary to measure these particular interests (Appen-dix, Section IV). Responses to these questions and others noted in the previous, as well as the following sections, were also correlated to deter-mine any relationships that may exist between variables.

> Are there special policies and procedures which guide staff in their activities with youth groups or youth gangs?
> Are such policies and procedures written?

The data in Table 7.4 demonstrates that the vast majority of respondents did not have special policies—neither oral nor written—to direct or guide staff members in their actions pertaining to both youth gangs and groups. Law enforcement organizations (police and sheriff's departments) and cor-rectional institutions, when compared to the respondents in the other orga-nizational categories, were more likely to have formal policies and documents pertaining to the investigation, reporting, and collection of intelligence information pertaining to both youth gangs and groups. The correlations between the type of respondent organization — in this case law enforcement and corrections — and whether these organizations had special policies produced statistically significant positive relationships (.223 and .192 respectively) at the .05 level. The correlations between having special policies and the other two types of organizations (court counselors, schools) did not produce statistically significant relationships.

Table 7.4
Frequency of Respondents Citing Special Policies

	Youth Gangs (N)		Youth Groups (N)		Totals
Yes	21.6	11	14.5	8	19
No	78.4	40	85.5	47	87
Totals	100.0	51	100.0	55	106

There were statistically significant relationships between specialized policies and the four organizational features that demonstrate a commitment to collective youth crime problems (Table 7.5). The data reveals that, where youth gang problems were present, there were significant relationships between special policies and the two structural features identified as external advisory structure and specialized training. This relationship demonstrates that where there exists an external advisory or community coordination structure (e.g. action committee) to coordinate community-wide prevention and intervention efforts, there was a strong probability that various organizations and agencies within the community also had implemented special policies and guidelines designating duties and responsibilities. There was also a statistically significant correlation between special policies and special training programs where gang problems were present. A potential interpretation of this relationship may be that where there was a need for special policies, there was also a need for specialized training to execute and enforce established policies. The only significant statistical relationship discovered for the youth group category was between special policies and training. Again, the most plausible interpretation of this relationship would be similar to that discussed for youth gangs.

Table 7.5
Biserial Correlations Between Special Policies
and Structural Features

	Written	External Advisory Structure	Special Training	Task Force
Youth Gangs (N=51)				
Special Policies	-.123	.274*	.296**	-.141
Written Guidelines	—	.281*	.105	.251*
Youth Groups (N=55)				
Special Policies	-.097	.037	.228*	-.001
Written Guidelines	—	.117	.134	.080

$p \leq 0.05$* $p \leq 0.01$** $p \leq 0.001$***

It is logical to conclude that, because of the more serious nature of youth gangs, there may have been greater need for agencies to establish specialized policies and training programs that focused on gang-related activities; furthermore, there was likely to be an influence from external or interagency advisory structures to establish procedures and guidelines for coordinating community-wide prevention and intervention efforts. Table 7.5 further examines the relationship between formal written guidelines and the same structural features. Once again, the most significant relationships were discovered for youth gangs. The data, which indicate strong statistical correlations between formal written guidelines and an external advisory structure and task force, support the argument that youth gangs may require or instigate a more organized response than youth groups, potentially because of the more serious scope and nature of their activities.

Table 7.6
Point Biserial Correlations Between Special Policies
and Selected Characteristics

	Est. Number of Members	Ave. Size of Collectives	%White	%Black	%Hisp.	%Asian
Youth Gangs (N=51)						
Special Policies	.278*	.304**	.013	-.008	-.039	-.124
Youth Groups (N=55)						
Special Policies	.214*	.046	.153	.015	-.074	-.102

$p \leq 0.05$* $p \leq 0.01$** $p \leq 0.001$***

The remaining analysis in this section pertains to the relationship between the establishment of special policies (oral and written) and selected characteristics of the problem. Special policies strongly correlated with the estimated number of members in both youth gangs and groups, and with the average size of youth gangs (Table 7.6). The positive correlations possibly indicate that as the number of members increased in particular jurisdictions, there was a strong probability that agencies and organizations also had special policies to address the problem. Furthermore, as the average size of youth gangs increased in particular jurisdictions, there was also a strong likelihood that organizations developed and implemented special policies to counter the potential problem that may accompany larger gang formations. However, an alternative interpretation may be that these special policies had little effect on reducing gang and group member populations, and in particular, on the average size of youth gang collectives. The racial makeup of youth gangs and groups had little to no effect on whether an organization or agency established special policies.

Table 7.7
Point Biserial Correlations Between Special Policies and Measures of Criminality

	Affil. w/Adult Groups	Drug Dist.	Drug Import	% Index Offenses
Youth Gangs (N=51)				
Special Policies	.335*	.277*	.210*	.189*
Youth Groups (N=55)				
Special Policies	.178*	.122	.102	.069

p≤0.05* p≤0.01** p≤0.001***

The data in Table 7.7 illustrate the relationships between special policies and key measures that define the seriousness of the youth gang and group problem. All four measures—affiliation with adult criminal organizations, drug distribution as a primary activity, involvement in drug importation activities, and the percentage of index offenses attributed to collectives—had significant positive statistical correlations with the establishment of special youth gang policies. However, for youth groups, the only significant correlation that emerged was between special policies and affiliation with adult groups. Again, these relationships demonstrate that youth gangs affiliated with adult criminal groups may have engaged in activity that required a more formal and defined response from organizations and agencies involved in prevention efforts.

Where there was a greater involvement of youth gangs in illicit activities, particularly drug distribution and generally for index offenses, there was a higher probability that agencies had established more formal policies and guidelines. Youth group affiliation with adult criminal groups was the only activity that had any significant relationship to the establishment of special policies. Since youth groups typically are not as serious as youth gangs, as evidenced by the data and analysis presented in previous chapters, many agencies and organizations had not identified the need to establish special policies, perhaps because current policies had been judged sufficiently effective. But as the previous analysis similarly suggested, the establishment of special policies may also have had very little effect in reducing the key measures associated with the scope and seriousness of both youth gang and group activities.

The last set of data (Table 7.8) presents the correlations between special policies and the estimated percentage of members who were adults, and the presence of collectives whose members reside outside the community. For both youth gang and groups, there was a significant negative statistical relationship between special policies and the percentage of members who were adults. This finding may indicate that special policies were developed and implemented independent of the demographic characteristics of members. The only other significant finding was the relationship between special policies and the presence of youth gangs and groups from surrounding communities. The highly significant correlation at the 0.01 level for youth gangs demonstrates a particular concern or perception that these collectives actively migrate from other nearby communities, towns, or cities, most likely to import and distribute illicit substances. The data also revealed a similar, albeit less significant, relationship for youth groups.

Table 7.8
Point Biserial Correlations Between Special Policies and Selected Characteristics

	% Incidents Adults	Same Neighborhood	Different Neighborhood
Youth Gangs (N=51)			
Special Policies	-.293*	.112.	321**
Youth Groups (N=55)			
Special Policies	-.256*	.024	.243*

p≤0.05* p≤0.01** p≤0.001***

The analysis of the characteristics that influence the establishment of policies, procedures, and guidelines identified two very different patterns for youth gangs and youth groups. Where youth gang problems were present, the establishment of policies was most dependent on the seriousness of the activities, particularly if the activity was drug-related or involved general index offenses; moreover, the policies were most likely articulated in writing when a systematic response was necessary. In communities experiencing youth groups, organizations were more inclined to utilize less formal responses, and when policies were established, they were likely to be dependent upon the size of the groups and the member population, and not necessarily the seriousness of activities. Determining the scope of the problem based on member populations and the size of collectives is problematic and may ultimately be ineffective for prevention and intervention programming, since not all youth who belong to youth gangs and groups are actively involved in criminal activities.

2. Special Organizational Units

Spergel et al. (1990) noted that the establishment of special units within larger agencies and organizations should have an impact on and be related to the development and implementation of specialized training and policy. The following analysis examines the strength of this relationship and the relationship of special units to these selected characteristics of the problem: average size of collectives, estimated number of members, drug distribution and importation activities, percentage of index offenses attributed to collectives, and the percentage of incidents attributed to juveniles and adults. Information derived from the question below (Appendix, Section IV) was central to the analysis in this section. The correlations that were conducted were based on responses to the above characteristics, which were examined earlier, and the responses to other questions addressed in future sections of this chapter. For simplicity purposes, key questions were listed in the sections where they are specifically addressed.

> Does your department have a special unit that investigates and monitors youth groups or youth gangs within your jurisdiction?

Within the sample of respondents who addressed the above question, 21.7 percent confirmed that their organization had such specialized units, while 78.3 percent stated that their organization did not. Table 7.9 illustrates the frequency of responses based on the nature of the collective youth crime problem. There was a more frequent reporting of specialized units by respondents who were experiencing youth gang problems compared to those respondents who cited youth group problems. All the respondents who cited having special units were from the law enforcement category, which consisted of police agencies and sheriff's departments; for youth groups, all except four respondents were from law enforcement organizations, with the other four respondents coming from correctional institutions.

The specialized units within law enforcement organizations consisted mostly of youth divisions that had specially trained individuals who were responsible for youth gang and youth group investigations and intelligence collection, rather than a formalized unit that works exclusively on youth gang and group control (e.g. Needle and Stapleton, 1983). Specialized units within correctional institutions were designated as either threat advisory groups or threat group committees and were designed to address the criminal and hostile activities associated with all group formations, not principally youth gangs. No such units were reported by respondents within the school systems nor court counselor agencies.

Table 7.9
Frequency of Respondents Citing Special Units

	Youth Gangs (N)		Youth Groups (N)		Totals
Yes	29.4	15	14.5	8	23
No	70.6	36	85.5	47	83
Totals	100.0	51	100.0	55	106

The correlations between special units and other organizational structural features (Table 7.10) only revealed three significant statistical relationships for both youth gangs and groups. Whether an organization had a special unit did not have a particularly strong effect on the establishment of special policies (or vice-versa). However, for both types of collectives, there was a strong correlation between organizations having special units and the availability of special training programs. It is reasonable to conclude that, because most of the special units located in organizations had a multitude of functions, and did not exclusively target youth gang and group activities per se, general or standard policies and procedures may have sufficed. But where organizations had established units or at least had delegated responsibilities to certain personnel or divisions, organizations most likely addressed the need for specialized training.

The only other significant correlation involved the relationship between special units and community or statewide task forces that target youth gang activities. The increasing sophistication of youth gang activities (typically drug-related) and the violent offenses that often accompany these activities, have required the formation of task forces in many jurisdictions throughout the State. The strong positive correlation between special units and task forces that targeted gangs possibly indicates that organizations relied on special structures to coordinate and participate in multi-level and multi-agency prevention and intervention initiatives. A more detailed analysis of the relationship between task forces and other organizational structures and group characteristics is discussed later in this chapter.

Table 7.10
Biserial Correlations Between Special Units and Organizational Features

	Task Force	Special Policies	Written Policies	Special Training
Youth Gangs (N=51)				
Special Unit	.267*	-.049	.112	.244*
Youth Groups (N=55)				
Special Unit	.166	-.102	.075	.227*

p≤ 0.05* p≤ 0.01** p≤0.001***

Table 7.11
Point Biserial Correlations Between Special Unit and Selected Characteristics

	Est. # Members	Ave. Size	%Adult	Drug Dist.	Drug Import
Youth Gangs (N=51)					
Special Unit	.248*	-.128	.338**	-.077	.237*
Youth Groups (N=55)					
Special Unit	.050	-.106	.219*	.222*	.036

p≤ 0.05* p≤0.01** p≤0.001***

The final analysis in this section examines the relationship between special units and characteristics or measures of the youth gang and group problem (Table 7.11). There were a number of significant statistical correlations that illustrated an interesting contrast between the two different types of collectives. For youth gangs, special units were strongly related to the number of gang members in a particular community or jurisdiction, the percentage of members classified as adults, and drug importation activities. All three relationships were statistically significant, with the relationship between special units and adult membership achieving a 0.01 significance level. In contrast, the data for youth groups indicate significant positive correlations between special units and the percentage of members who were adults (but at the 0.05 level), but drug distribution activities received the more significant statistical correlation, rather than involvement in drug importation.

No other significant relationships emerged, which indicates that the other features had very little influence on the formation of special units.

In interpreting these findings, the establishment of special units that target youth gangs was most likely related to the seriousness and sophistication of activities. Drug importation is generally perpetrated by older youth and young adults and probably demands more ingenuity, networking, and cunning, than typical street-level drug dealing; in general, as the number of gang members increased, there was probably an exponential increase in network size and the quantity and pace of drug importation activities. Therefore, special units, adept at investigating and collecting intelligence pertaining to drug importation activities, were most likely created to counter this problem. Special units that focus on youth group activities form more in response to less sophisticated, though equally problematic, street-level drug dealing activities conducted predominantly by younger individuals. Even though the significant correlations may indicate the activities or characteristics that effect whether organizations create special units, it was not altogether clear if these special units were effective at performing their functions.

3. Special Coordination Structures and Task Forces

The conceptualization of community coordination occurs at two distinct, but interconnected levels: government, which consists of federal, state, county, and city agencies; and grassroots, which involves citizen groups and nonprofit sectarian agencies at the local-community or neighborhood levels (Spergel, 1990). Special coordination structures involving organizations at both the government and grassroots levels, and the use of more organized and proactive task forces, are often formed to coordinate and establish more unified prevention and intervention strategies. Interagency communication and coordination is critically important for addressing a serious problem such as youth gang and group crime. But as the following analysis demonstrates, the use of task forces—dominated by criminal justice organizations, particularly law enforcement—may not produce the desired and expected outcome of reducing the scope and seriousness of the crime problem.

Generally, task forces are designed to achieve results within a relatively short timeframe, such as reducing drug trafficking activities within two years, or are established to research a problem and offer recommendations or a course of action. Most typically, task forces are established to achieve specific short-term goals, and once the goals have been achieved, the task forces are often discontinued. Community coordination structures, conversely, are designed to establish and coordinate long-term, as well as short-term, prevention and intervention strategies; these structures often have a wider representation of professionals from grassroots and local agencies and remain active in communities for many years. The frequencies at which respondents cited whether their organizations were actively involved in task forces (local and State-wide) and whether a community structure assisted in the coordination and implementation of prevention and intervention programs are illustrated in Table 7.12. The findings are based on responses to the following questions (Appendix, Section V):

> *Are there any interagency task forces or community-wide organizations which attempted to coordinate efforts to deal with the youth gang or youth group problem in recent years?*
>
> *Is there a community group your organization works with that assists you in the coordination and implementation of youth group or youth gang intervention and prevention programs?*

The data demonstrate that the large majority of respondents had neither been involved in task forces nor participated in community coordination structures, even though there were youth gang or group problems in their communities and jurisdictions. There was a slightly higher percentage of respondents from the youth gang category who participated in task forces and community coordination structures; however, based on chi square test results, there were no significant variations at the .05 level between the nature of the problem — youth gang versus youth group — and the likelihood that organizations were involved in task forces.

Table 7.12
Frequency of Respondents Citing Participation in Task Forces and Community Coordination Structures

	Youth Gangs	(N)	Youth Groups	(N)	Totals
Task Force					
Yes	35.3	18	23.6	13	31
No	64.7	33	76.4	42	75
Totals	100.0	51	100.0	55	106
Community Coordination Structure					
Yes	37.3	19	29.1	16	35
No	62.7	32	70.9	39	71
Totals	100.0	51	100.0	55	106

Table 7.13
Point Biserial Correlations Between Task Force and Selected Characteristics

	Est. Number of Members	Ave. Size	%White	%Black	%Hisp.	%Asian
Youth Gangs (N=51)						
Task Force	.242*	.245*	.102	.302**	-.094	-.045
Youth Groups (N=55)						
Task Force	.029	.141	.126	.198*	-.076	-.050

p≤0.05* p≤0.01** p≤0.001***

In order to gain a greater understanding of the relationship between select-ed youth gang and group characteristics and task forces and community coor-dination structures, additional correlations were performed. The correlation results in Table 7.13 indicate that task forces had a statistically significant relationship to the estimated number of members belonging to youth gangs, the average size of gangs, and the percentage of members who were black. Sim-ilarly, there were also positive correlations for the same characteristics in the youth group category, but only the percentage of members who were black revealed a relationship that was statistically significant. Table 7.14 further highlights the relationships between task forces and the key measures that define the level of youth gang and group criminality. For youth gangs, there were statistically significant positive correlations between task forces and the percentage of members with prior criminal records, drug importation activ-ities, and youth gang affiliation with adult criminal enterprises. The only sig-nificant relationship produced in the youth group correlations was between task forces and the percentage of members with prior criminal records.

Table 7.14
Point Biserial Correlations Between Task Force and Measures of Criminality

	%Index Offenses	%Prior Criminal Records	Drug Dist.	Drug Import	Affil. w/Adult Group
Youth Gangs (N=51)					
Task Force	.035	.274*	.087	.173*	.394*
Youth Groups (N=55)					
Task Force	.126	.228*	.125	-.044	.131

p≤0.05* p≤0.01** p≤0.001***

The data from the tables in this section reveal relationship patterns that appear to contravene the basic strategies of task forces: reduce membership levels and participation in criminal activities. The strong positive associations that emerged not only indicate the factors that may influence organizational participation in task forces, but quite possibly that task forces actually increase the levels of participation, particularly of black youth gang members; however, it was difficult to ascertain, based on the correlations, the causal effect if any. Previous research by Klein and Crawford (1967), and recent work by Klein (1995), assert that an external stimulus —such as a strong response from law enforcement—potentially has an undesirable effect on youth gangs, causing them to become more cohesive and delinquent. Thornberry (1993) similarly concluded that the dimensions of solidarity and gang cohesion, regardless of how they manifest, most likely increase the criminality level of members. It is possible that task forces inadvertently provide the stimulus that leads to greater cohesion; greater cohesion, in turn, may attract other youth into joining gangs, thereby increasing the size of these collectives. Once youth join gangs, group processes begin to have a significant influence on the scope and nature of activities.

Table 7.15
Point Biserial Correlations Between Coordination Structure and
Selected Characteristics

	Est. Number of Members	Ave. Size	%White	%Black	%Hisp.	%Asian
Youth Gangs (N=51)						
Coordination Structure	-.172*	-.214*	.114	-.194*	.057	-.011
Youth Groups (N=55)						
Coordination Structure	-.238*	-.127	.067	.058	.054	-.021

p≤0.05* p≤0.01** p≤0.001***

Table 7.16
Point Biserial Correlations Between Coordination Structure and
Measures of Criminality

	%Index Offenses	%Prior Crim. Record	Drug. Dist.	DrugAffil. Import	w/Adult Criminal Groups
Youth Gangs (N=51)					
Coordination Structure	.217	-.228*	-.208	-.290*	.102
Youth Groups (N=55)					
Coordination Structure	.085	-.231*	-.125*	.068	.093

p≤0.05* p≤0.01** p≤0.001***

Tables 7.15 and 7.16 present data on the relationship between community coordination structure (abbreviated *coordination structure*) and the same characteristics and measures utilized in the two previous tables. The correlations reveal a significant and important difference in the relationship patterns. The statistically significant negative relationship between community coordination structure and the number of individuals belonging to youth gangs and groups, the average size of youth gangs, and the percentage of gang members who are black suggests that community coordination structures, rather than task forces, have an effect on reducing gang and group membership. Furthermore, the relationships in Table 7.16 also indicate a possible impact on two measures of criminality: community coordination structures may effectively reduce recidivism rates among the gang and group member populations, particularly for youth gang members; and these coordinating structures appear to have some effect on reducing drug-related activities by both types of collectives.

These preliminary findings clearly demonstrate the need to reevaluate existing prevention and intervention coordinating structures. Ideally, community and state task forces should focus on the immediate threats to public safety, but it is also vitally important to establish well-coordinated and clearly articulated long-term approaches that involve multiple community groups and government agencies, not only those from the criminal justice system. Community coordination structures potentially have an appreciable effect on some of the key characteristics and measures of criminality that define the scope and nature of the problem. Conversely, task forces, with all their good intentions, may provide some positive short-term results or have an impact on certain aspects of the youth gang and group problem, but the data indicate that activities and strategies may be less effective and, quite possibly, more adverse than previously thought.

4. Special Training Programs

This final section examines the relationship between organizations that have special training programs for staff personnel and selected characteristics of the problem. Similar to the previous discussions, it also explores the interrelationship between special training programs and the measures of criminality that best define the seriousness of the collective youth crime problem. In the previous sections of this chapter, it was discovered that there were statistically significant positive correlations between an organization having a special training program and the establishment of special policies and units. The following analysis attempts to determine what factors influence the development and implementation of special training programs and if training provisions have a desired or undesired effect on the selected measures of the problem.

The data in Table 7.17 illustrate that most respondents experiencing youth gang and group problems did not have special training programs within their organizations and agencies. The data were derived from responses to the following question (Appendix, Section IV):

> Is special training available to personnel for dealing with youth groups or youth gangs?

However, after examining the response rate for each professional category, it was discovered that respondents from correctional institutions most frequently cited having established programs, followed by law enforcement organizations, court counselor agencies, and schools. Furthermore, respondents belonging to organizations that were experiencing youth gang problems, rather than youth group problems, more frequently cited special training programs. But according to chi square test results, there were no significant statistical findings (e.g. $p < 0.05$) that would indicate the existence of a relationship between special training programs and the nature of the problem. The establishment of programs may therefore depend largely on the seriousness of the criminal activities associated with the youth collectives, and not necessarily on whether the problem involves gangs or groups.

Table 7.17
Frequency of Respondents Citing Special Training Programs

	Youth Gangs (N)		Youth Groups (N)		Totals
Yes	37.3	19	29.1	16	35
No	62.7	32	70.9	39	71
Totals	100.0	51	100.0	55	106

The correlations between special training programs and selected characteristics of the problem demonstrate a number of strong statistical relationships (Table 7.18). Special training was strongly associated with the estimated number of individual youth gang and group members within an organization's jurisdiction, as well as with the average size of youth gangs, in particular. These statistically significant positive correlations may indicate that special training became important and was more likely established in jurisdictions where there was a relatively large population of gang and group members, or perhaps where there was a growth in populations. The data also illustrate that demographic characteristics had very little effect on the establishment of special training programs: none of the correlations produced statistically significant relationships.

Table 7.18
Point Biserial Correlations Between Special Training and Selected Characteristics

	Est. Number of Members	Ave. Size	%White	%Black	%Hisp.	%Asian
Youth Gangs (N=51)						
Special Training	.249*	.209*	-.016	-.050	.012	-.032
Youth Groups (N=55)						
Special Training	.237*	.053	.044	-.101	-.113	.097

p≤0.05* p≤0.01** p≤0.001***

Table 7.19
Point Biserial Correlations Between Special Training and Measures of Criminality

	%Index Offenses	%Prior Crim. Record	Drug. Dist.	Drug Import	Affil. w/Adult Criminal Groups
Youth Gangs (N=51)					
Special Training	-.126*	.133	.121	-.271*	-.104
Youth Groups (N=55)					
Special Training	-.065	.148	-.243*	-.107	-.081

p≤0.05* p≤0.01** p≤0.001***

According to the correlations in Table 7.19, special training programs appear to have an effect on index offenses attributed to youth gangs and their involvement in drug importation activities. A similar pattern emerged for youth groups, yet the only significant finding involved the negative relationship between special training and drug distribution activities. A better trained staff may contribute to a reduction in particular offenses and activities. For both youth gangs and groups, the number of youth gang members within a jurisdiction had a significant influence on whether an organization developed and implemented a special training curriculum; and for organizations experiencing youth gang problems, the average size of gangs produced the strongest correlation. Special training programs focussing on gangs may have been effective at reducing drug importation activities *and* the percent of index offenses that were gang-related, while special training may have only been effective at reducing drug distribution activities by youth groups. This pattern possibly indicates that special training programs targeting youth gangs were better developed and implemented, with goals clearly articulated and responsibilities of staff well-defined.

F. Effectiveness of Prevention and Intervention Strategies

1. Changes in the Level of the Problem

One of the primary purposes of this study, in addition to gaining a better understanding of the scope and nature of collective youth crime problems, was to determine if the seriousness of the crime problem had changed in the past three years and if certain policies, procedures, and strategies had in any way contributed to these changes (e.g. Spergel et al., 1990). Evaluative research on different strategies and practices was not available, therefore, the perceptions of respondents were the only practical means for obtaining information on organizational responses to the problem and, in particular, the effectiveness of prevention and intervention strategies. Many of the variables used in earlier discussions were again useful in the present analysis. Even though the results of the various statistical tests employed can only be considered tentative, they do provide a basis for future field testing of the most promising strategies.

The first objective was to determine whether the youth gang or group problem had changed in recent years, becoming more or less serious, or for that matter remained stable. The content analysis of responses, based on answers to the following question (Appendix, Section III), indicated that the problem for both types of collectives had generally become more serious in the past few years (Table 7.20):

Has the youth group or youth gang situation changed in recent years? If yes, how?

Respondents who were experiencing youth gang problems (N=51) indicated a worsening of the problem at a slightly lower frequency than those experiencing youth groups (N=55). By and large, there was a widely held perception among respondents that youth gang and group problems had either remained the same or worsened in the past three years, with few respondents citing an improvement in the situation in their respective jurisdictions. Law enforcement and court counselor respondents, with the exception of a few, all indicated that the youth gang and group problem had worsened in recent years. Officials in correctional institutions were more likely to report that the problem had remained relatively stable, while school officials were most apt to report an improvement in the situation. In general terms, respondents who reported a worsening in youth gang and group problems were from cities and counties with relatively large populations in the State (i.e. cities with populations in excess of 30,000 and counties with populations in excess of 70,000).

Table 7.20
Perception of Situation Change (Frequencies Based on Respondent Totals)

	Worsened	Same	Improved	Totals
Youth Gangs	68.6 (35)	21.6 (11)	9.8 (5)	51
Youth Groups	69.1 (38)	21.8 (12)	9.5 (5)	55
Totals	68.9 (73)	21.7 (23)	9.4 (10)	106

What factors or characteristics could have influenced these perceptions? The perceptions of an improvement or worsening of the problem may be attributable to a number of factors, but are there one or two factors that may be more influential than the others? To find out, the means of seven measures, those that may have influenced the perceptions of respondents, were derived for further analysis (Table 7.21). For each of the measures, a t-test for significance was conducted to ascertain the most significant mean differences between respondents who had perceived an improvement and worsening of the situation in recent years; the more significant mean differences indicate the criteria that most likely had the greatest influence on the perceptions of the problem (Spergel et al., 1990). The three most significant characteristics that may have influenced the perceptions of whether the problem had improved/stabilized or worsened included: the number of youth gang and group members within the community, the average size of youth gang collectives, and the percentage of both youth gang and group members who had prior criminal records. However, the data do not provide a clear picture as to causal order. Quite possibly an increase or decrease in the number of members, the average size of collectives, and the estimated percentage of members who had prior criminal records did in fact directly influence each respondent's perception of the problem; but it is also plausible that a perceived worsening or improvement of the problem may actually lead to increases or decreases in the estimations of these same factors. In other words, if an individual thinks the problem has worsened, he or she may give a higher estimate of the number of members, the size of collectives, and so forth.

Table 7.21
Means for Selected Characteristics of the Problem and Perceived Change
in Recent Years

Characteristics	Youth Gangs (N=51)			Youth Groups (N=55)		
	Same/ Improved	Worsened	(t)	Same/ Improved	Worsened	(t)
Number of Members	10.5	49.9	**	51.8	86.4	*
Ave. Size of Collectives	11.4	22.7	**	10.6	16.9	ns
Percent Black Members	61.9	66.4	ns	73.5	63.9	ns
Percent White Members	23.3	26.2	ns	20.3	26.7	ns
Percent Incident Adults	41.5	47.5	ns	43.2	43.1	ns
Percent Index Offenses	7.5	9.5	ns	7.3	7.8	ns
Percent Members w/Records	30.0	58.4	*	36.9	50.4	*

$p \leq 0.05$* $p \leq 0.01$** $p \leq 0.001$*** ns=not significant

The two most significant factors that may have affected the perceptions of the problem pertained to youth gangs: an improvement or worsening of the problem was strongly associated with the perceived size of collectives and the member population. The number of youth group members was also a significant factor in the perceived worsening of the problem, albeit at a less significant level than gangs; however, the average size of groups did not prove highly significant. For both youth gangs and groups, the percentage of members with prior criminal records was the other key factor that affected perceptions. The remaining measures—the percent of black and white members, the percent of incidents involving adults, and the percentage of index offenses attributed to these collectives—did not attain any level of significance. There were very few respondents who reported an improvement in youth gang or group problems, therefore it was beneficial to examine four additional measures and their relationship to a worsening in the problem. The four measures—presence of nonindigenous collectives in the community, affiliation with adult criminal organizations, drug distribution as a primary purpose, and the involvement in drug importation activities — represent the conditions that best define the seriousness and nature of the problem and most likely have the most significant influence on the perceptions of the problem (Spergel et al., 1990). The data in Table 7.22 indicate the frequency at which respondents reported the four aforementioned measures and the correlations of these measures with a worsening of the problem. The perceptions that the youth gang problem had worsened was strongly associated with the presence of nonindigenous gangs within the community and the involvement of gangs in drug-related activities; for respondents who were experiencing youth group crime problems, the most significant influence on perceptions was group involvement in drug distribution activities. Interestingly, for respondents who reported a worsening of the problem, a majority indicated the presence of each measure within their respective jurisdictions. Law enforcement and court counselor respondents were most likely to report the presence of all four measures, while school officials typically reported only two. With the exception of the nonindigenous measure, all correctional respondents reported the presence of the other three measures in their systems. It is therefore reasonable to assert that each of the four measures, collectively or individually, contributed to the overall perceptions of the problem, and that any perceived improvement should be closely associated with a reduction of some or all of these measures.

Table 7.22
Frequency and Biserial Correlations of Selected Measures of Criminality
(Respondents Reporting a Worsening of the Problem)

Measures	Youth Gangs (N=35)			Youth Groups (N=38)		
	No	Yes	Corr.	No	Yes	Corr.
Nonindigenous	28.6 (10)	71.4 (25)	.221*	42.1 (16)	57.9 (22)	.125
Affil. w/Adults	42.9 (15)	57.1 (20)	.030	60.5 (23)	39.5 (15)	.079
Drug Distribution	37.1 (13)	62.9 (22)	.215*	28.9 (11)	71.0 (27)	.291*
Drug Importation	25.7 (9)	74.3 (26)	.261*	44.7 (17)	55.3 (21)	.116

$p \leq 0.05^*$ $p \leq 0.01^{**}$ $p \leq 0.001^{***}$

Lastly, the analysis turns to the relationship between policy and organizational characteristics — e.g. community coordination structure, interagency task force, special policies, and written policies — and the *perceived worsening* of the youth gang or group problem. The data pertaining to both types of collectives were again aggregated to facilitate this analysis. The results of the correlations (Table 7.23) indicate only two statistically significant relationships that may potentially have policy implications. It appears that the perception of the problem did not depend to any great extent on how organizations responded. However, the positive statistical correlation suggests that task forces may actually contribute to a worsening of the problem; conversely, community advisory structures, which produced the only negative statistical correlation, may be causally related to a perceived improvement or reduction in the problem (e.g. Spergel et al., 1990).

Table 7.23
Biserial Correlations Between Selected Organizational Aspects and
a Perceived Worsening in the Problem (N=73)

	Community Coord. Structure	Task Force	Special Training	Special Policies	Special Unit
Situation Worsened	-.142*	.187*	.044	.112	.037

$p \le 0.05*$ $p \le 0.01**$ $p \le 0.001***$

The data from the last four tables (7.20 to 7.23) demonstrate that respondents thought that the collective youth crime problem had become perceptively worse in recent years, especially regarding youth gang activities. These perceptions were strongly associated with the perceived number of youth gang members within the community, the average size of collectives, and the percentage of members with prior criminal records; more specifically, the level of drug-related activities conducted by both gangs and groups who reside outside the community appears to strongly influence the perceived improvement or worsening of the problem. Quite possibly, organizations that were involved in community coordination structures contributed to the perceived or actual improvement in the problem, but task forces appear to have the opposite effect.

2. Organization and Interagency Effectiveness

The analysis in this section is concerned with the perceived effectiveness of organizational and interagency efforts in addressing youth gang and group crime. Since problems have worsened in recent years, positive correlations between the effectiveness rating and selected characteristics may not necessarily translate into a reduction in the problem, but may possibly indicate the areas where agency efforts were having some success. Moreover, positive correlations between ratings and organizational characteristics (e.g. special policies, special training) may have had more to do with evaluating the amount and quality of agency and community efforts than having experienced a reduction in the problem due to the implementation of particular policies and programs (Spergel et al., 1990). The first part of this discussion examines the features that influenced organizational and agency effectiveness ratings, and then it proceeds to a similar discussion of interagency or community-level effectiveness.

Table 7.24
Evaluation of Agency and Organization Effectiveness (N=106)

	Very Effective	Mod. Effective	Not Effective	Unsure	Totals
Youth Gangs	11.8 (6)	33.3 (17)	15.7 (8)	39.2 (20)	51
Youth Groups	20.0 (11)	43.6 (24)	21.8 (12)	14.5 (8)	55
Totals	16.0 (17)	38.7 (41)	18.9 (20)	26.4 (28)	106

In order to obtain a general idea of the effectiveness of agency efforts, respondents were asked to evaluate their agency's general success at reducing collective youth crime problems. Responses to the following question supported this analysis (Appendix, Section VI):

> How effective do you think your organization was in 1993 in dealing with the youth gang or group problem? (a rating option of not sure, not effective, moderately effective, and very effective was provided for coding purposes)

The data in Table 7.24 suggest that agency efforts were considered to be moderately or very effective (54.7 percent) at reducing youth gang and group problems, with only 18.9 percent indicating efforts had been ineffective; a relatively large proportion (26.4 percent) were unsure if their agencies' efforts were producing positive results. Respondents' ratings were almost equally proportionate when comparing youth gangs and groups. Law enforcement respondents were most likely to rate their agencies' efforts as moderate or very effective, while court counselors were less optimistic, typically reporting moderate effectiveness or uncertainty. School officials, more often than not, were unsure or unable to evaluate the effectiveness of their organizations' efforts. And assessments made by correctional officials were almost evenly divided across each of the possible ratings. Interestingly, the high proportion of effectiveness ratings (moderately and very effective) and the low proportion of ineffectiveness ratings, did not logically correspond to the earlier perceptions (see Table 7.20) that both youth gang and group problems had worsened in recent years; it is therefore likely that respondents perceived that a worsening of the problem was caused by factors outside the agency.

Table 7.25
Pearson Correlations Between Agency Effectiveness Rating and Selected Features

	Number of Members	Ave. Size Collective	%Index Offenses	%Prior Record	Drug Dist.	Drug Import
Youth Gangs (N=51) Effectiveness Rating	.164	.137	.079	.332*	-.122	-.103
Youth Groups (N=55) Effectiveness Rating	.112	.082	.058	.218*	-.131	-.018

p≤ 0.05* p≤ 0.01** p ≤0.001***

To further examine the factors that may have influenced the assessment of agency and organizational efforts, the effectiveness ratings were coded (i.e. a rating of very effective received a score of one, moderately effective received a score of two, least effective received a score of three) and correlated with six selected features that serve as the best measures of the collective youth crime problem (Table 7.25). The disproportionately strong effectiveness ratings were not significantly related to five of the six selected measures. Only one variable—percent of members with prior criminal records—was statistically significant for both types of collectives, and this correlation was only significant at the 0.05 level. This relationship suggests that the perception of agency effectiveness depends largely on whether the agency had an impact on reducing recidivism rates among gang and group members; the higher the agency effectiveness rating, the greater the likelihood that the agency was able to reduce the rate of re-offending in its jurisdictions. Since only one of the six measures proved significant in the evaluation of agency efforts, could there be other factors that were more influential? As Table 7.26 clearly demonstrates, the perception of agency effectiveness was strongly associated with a number of selected *organizational-structural* features. However, these structural features may have had a more significant influence on effectiveness ratings for organizations that had experienced youth gang problems. For organizations that had experienced youth gang problems, the development and implementation of special training programs may have had a significant effect on perceived agency and organization effectiveness, followed by special policies, and the participation in community advisory structures and task forces. Special training programs and policies were the only two statistically significant features that may have influenced the perceived effectiveness of organizations that had experienced youth group problems.

Table 7.26
Point Biserial Correlations Between Agency Effectiveness Rating and
Organizational Features

	Special Policies	Written Policies	Special Trng.	Special Unit	Coord. Structure	Task Force
Youth Gangs (N=51)						
Effectiveness Rating	.215*	-.108	.224**	-.100	.166*	.158*
Youth Groups (N=55)						
Effectiveness Rating	.134*	-.098	.171*	.088	.024-	.039

p≤0.05* p≤0.01** p≤0.001***

There appears to be a disjuncture between the relatively strong organizational effectiveness rating — the criteria that most likely influenced these ratings — and the overwhelming perception that collective youth crime problems had worsened. Respondents more than likely based their perceptions of effectiveness on the degree to which programs and policies were developed within their respective organizations and agencies, rather than on the more salient measures associated with the actual problem, such as reductions in index offenses and drug-related activities attributed to gangs and groups. Perhaps, as Spergel et al. (1990, p. 90) concluded, "the agencies may simply be addressing and trying hard to deal with the gang [and group] problem," but whether these efforts effectively reduced key measures of the problem was of little consequence.

The effectiveness of community coordination structures reveals a markedly different pattern of relationships compared to the previous discussion on agency effectiveness. Because of the small sample size (N=35) of respondents who reported involvement in community-wide or interagency coordination structures, the analysis combined all responses, regardless of whether problems involved youth gangs or groups. The following question was posed to respondents (Appendix, Section V):

> *Are there any interagency task forces or community-wide organizations which attempted to coordinate efforts to deal with the youth group or youth gang problem in recent years?* (respondents were asked to classify these efforts as not effective, somewhat effective, or very effective)

The data in Table 7.27 indicate that the large majority of respondents considered coordination structures to be very effective (42.9 percent) at generally reducing collective youth crime problems; however, almost one-third of the respondents (31.4 percent) were either unsure or considered community coordination structures to be ineffective at mitigating collective youth crime problems in their jurisdictions. There were only minor differences in the effectiveness ratings based on the nature of the problem. Law enforcement organizations were most likely to participate in community coordination structures, often leading the efforts within communities. However, the jurisdictions where coordination structures could be found were in relatively large urban areas and municipalities, such as Charlotte, Raleigh, Durham, Greensboro, Lumberton, and Asheville. Only six court counselor and seven school respondents reported involvement in coordination structures (again, these respondents were located in the larger jurisdictions), and only two corrections officials indicated that their administrations made efforts to work with other community agencies and organizations (both from minimum security training schools).

Table 7.27
Evaluation of Community Coordination Structures (N=35)

	Very Effective	Somewhat Effective	Not Effective	Unsure	Totals
Youth Gangs	47.4 (9)	21.1 (4)	15.8 (3)	15.8 (3)	19
Youth Groups	37.5 (6)	31.3 (5)	18.8 (3)	12.5 (2)	16
Totals	42.9 (15)	25.7 (9)	17.1 (6)	14.3 (5)	35

Similar to a previous analysis, effectiveness rating scores (this time for community coordination structures) were correlated with selected measures of the problem, as well as with organizational-structural features. The correlations in Table 7.28 provide substantially more credence to the effectiveness ratings of community coordination structures when compared to the ratings of agencies. The relationships suggest that youth gang and group characteristics, rather than organizational-structural features, provided the basis for the ratings. Four out of six youth gang and group characteristics revealed statistically significant associations to coordination structures. These correlations indicate that coordination structures may have been particularly effective at reducing the number of members within the community, the average size of youth collectives, the percentage of index offenses attributed to youth collectives, and drug distribution activities. Only one organizational characteristic — task forces — was significantly related to the perceived effectiveness of community coordination structures.

Table 7.28
Pearson Correlations Between Coordination Structure Effectiveness Rating
and Selected Features (N=35)

	Number Members	Ave. Size Collective	%Index Offenses	%Prior Record	Drug Dist.	Drug Import
Effectiveness Rating	-.189**	-.160*	-.142*	.086	-.157*	.118

	Special Policies	Written Policies	Special Trng.	Special Unit	Task Force
Effectiveness Rating	.106	.098	.052	.113	.264**

$p \leq 0.05*$ $p \leq 0.01**$ $p \leq 0.001***$

It can be deduced that two significantly different sets of criteria were used to ascertain agency effectiveness and community or interagency coordination structure effectiveness. Within particular agencies and organizations, perceptions of effectiveness were closely related to program and policy developments, and not to the characteristics of the actual youth gang and group problem; the perceived effectiveness of coordination structures, conversely, was more likely shaped by reductions in key measures of the problem. The perceptions were not significantly influenced by the area or location of the respondents, though most of the respondents who reported involvement in community coordination structures were from the more populated jurisdictions. The findings in this section become considerably important when efforts are made to identify agencies and organizations that have promising approaches, whether for possible replication or future evaluation.

3. Selecting Promising Approaches

The final objective of this chapter involved selecting the organizations that potentially employed the most promising prevention and intervention strategies. This action not only affords other organizations and agencies the opportunity to replicate or adopt effective approaches used by other agencies, but also provides a basis for examining these strategies more scrupulously and systematically in future research. The general effectiveness of strategies could best be determined by using three key dimensions: perceived improvement in the problem, perceived agency and organization effectiveness, and perceived effectiveness of community coordination structures. Using respondents who addressed these three measures, a systematic examination of organizations and their strategies was conducted. Since the large majority of respondents reported a worsening of the problem—35 (68.6 percent) of those experiencing youth gangs and 38 (69.1 percent) experiencing youth groups—it was necessary to combine respondents (N=23) reporting no change in their collective youth crime situation with the small number of respondents (N=10) who had experienced improvements. In communities where youth gang and group problems did not change (neither worsened nor improved), it was also plausible that agency prevention and intervention efforts may have been effective. By combining these two sets of respondents, the number of organizations and agencies eligible for this analysis increased from 10 to 33.

A content analysis was then conducted to determine how respondents rated their own organizations' effectiveness and the effectiveness of community coordination structures. Only respondents who provided positive ratings—i.e. moderate and very effective for agency effectiveness and somewhat or very effective for coordination structure effectiveness—were retained. One additional discriminating factor—seriousness rating (see previous chapter)—was also utilized to ensure organizations that demonstrated promising approaches had at least moderately serious youth gang and group problems. Using the four criteria discussed above (perceived improvement, positive effectiveness rating for agency efforts, positive effectiveness rating for community coordination structure, and moderately serious collective youth crime problem), a model was developed to identify the organizations that may have promising approaches. The model identified sixteen agencies or organizations in twelve localities (four cities, three counties, two judicial districts, and three correctional facilities) that exhibited promising prevention and intervention strategies where youth gang problems were present. For youth groups, the analysis produced fewer organizations and localities—eight organizations in seven localities (Table 7.29).

Because the program assessment methods relied upon respondent perceptions and not verifiable statistical data using more rigorous procedures (e.g. trend analysis, quantitative evaluations), the results must remain tentative until more reliable data become available for analysis. Since the model for determining strategy effectiveness was not elaborate, an external validity check was performed; this action involved recontacting by telephone the respondents from all of the organizations and agencies listed in the table and reexamining the available information on the four empirical indicators (perceived number of members, average size of collectives, percent of index offenses attributed to collectives, and drug-related activities). This procedural safeguard revealed that the four empirical indicators had either improved or stabilized, based on the information provided by respondents. Spergel et al.'s (1990) discovery of a strong correlation between "perceived improvement" and essentially the same empirical indicators is further evidence that perceptual assessments serve as valid measures for determining the general effectiveness of prevention and intervention efforts.

Table 7.29
Localities Exhibiting Promising Approaches

		Youth Gangs		
Location	*Organization*	*Problem Rating*	*Primary Strategy*	*Effectiveness*
Charlotte	Police, School Sys.	Very Serious	Community Mob.	Very Effective
Havelock	Police	Serious	Suppression	Mod. Effective
Morganton	Police	Mod. Serious	Suppression	Mod. Effective
So. Pines	Police	Serious	Suppression	Mod. Effective
Caldwell Co.	Sheriff, School Sys.	Very Serious	Social Intervention	Very Effective
Guilford Co.	Sheriff, School Sys.	Mod. Serious	Suppression/ Interv.	Mod. Effective
Mecklen. Co.	Police, School Sys.	Very Serious	Suppression/ Opportunities Prov.	Mod. Effective
Jud. Dist. 6B	Court Counselor	Very Serious	Intervention	Mod. Effective
Jud. Dist. 21	Court Counselor	Very Serious	Community Mob.	Very Effective
Morrison	Corrections	Very Serious	Suppression	Very Effective
Blanch	Corrections	Very Serious	Intervention	Mod. Effective
Sandhills	Corrections	Serious	Suppression	Very Effective

		Youth Gangs		
Location	*Organization*	*Problem Rating*	*Primary Strategy*	*Effectiveness*
Goldsboro	Police	Mod. Serious	Suppression	Mod. Effective
Henderson	Police	Very Serious	Suppression	Mod. Effective
Moorehead City	Police	Mod. Serious	Intervention	Mod. Effective
Winston-Salem	Police	Mod. Serious	Opportunities Prov.	Mod. Effective
Pitt Co.	Sheriff	Serious	Intervention	Mod. Serious
Yadkin Co.	Sheriff, School Sys.	Mod. Serious	Intervention	Mod. Effective
Jud. Dist. 24	Court Counselor	Serious	Intervention	Mod. Effective

An earlier discussion of strategies indicated that suppression was the primary approach used by organizations experiencing both youth gang and group problems. This finding was not surprising given the fact that

45.2 percent of the respondents reporting youth gang and group problems represented police agencies and sheriff's departments. The analysis indicated that suppression was the primary strategy for nine organizations, of which seven organizations rated this strategy moderately effective and two rated it very effective. Suppression represented the most promising approach where youth gangs were the primary problem; however, social intervention strategies appeared most promising in communities where youth groups were present. Organizations in two localities (Charlotte and the 21st Judicial District) which reported very serious youth gang problems, also indicated that community mobilization efforts within their jurisdictions were very effective at reducing or stabilizing the problem.

There were five localities — four within the youth gang and one within the youth group categories — where two organizations identified effective approaches. Two counties localities (Caldwell County and Yadkin County) had organizations that utilized the same primary strategy, two others (Guilford County and Mecklenburg County) used a combination of suppression and one other strategy, and one (Charlotte) relied primarily on community mobilization. Most important, all organizations and agencies fulfilled the model criteria discussed earlier. It was interesting to note that, in the two localities (Charlotte and Caldwell County) where two organizations adopted the same primary strategies for dealing with youth gang problems, the respondents perceived the problem as very serious and also rated their organization's efforts as very effective; moreover, the primary strategies did not emphasize suppression approaches.

These findings, albeit suggestive in nature, provide some framework from which to assess primary strategies with greater scrutiny in future research. One must keep in mind that the collective youth crime problem most likely differed markedly in scope and nature across the State; some localities undoubtedly experienced more serious drug-related and general criminal problems than others, and perhaps the variations in demographic characteristics also contributed to the differences in criminal patterns and the seriousness of the problems. The complexity and seriousness of the problem, the variations in organizational and community resources, and the differences in prevention and intervention philosophies across communities, dictate the particular strategies and approaches that are ultimately supported and implemented. What strategy may work in one community, may not necessarily work or even get adopted by organizations in others. Nevertheless, this analysis at least provided some starting point at which more thorough and rigorous research on effective approaches can commence.

G. Conclusion

The central purpose of this chapter was to identify the primary prevention and intervention strategies employed by the organizations and agencies that were experiencing youth gang and group problems. A summary
of the four primary strategies — neighborhood mobilization, social intervention, opportunities provision, and suppression — and the one organizational approach (organizational development) was presented to place
this study's findings in perspective. The strategies identified by respondents
were then analyzed to determine their distribution across organizations
and whether the nature of the problem (gang versus groups) had any effect
on the type of strategy employed. The primary strategy used by organizations, regardless of the nature of the collective youth crime problem, was
suppression. This strategy, which stresses enforcement and apprehension,
was cited as the primary strategy by 42.3 percent of all respondents; social
intervention (28.8 percent) was the second most frequently cited strategy;
opportunities provision (6.7 percent) and neighborhood mobilization (5.8
percent) were the least cited strategies. Organizational development was cited
as one of the five possible responses by 57.7 percent of all respondents;
however, this response was more indicative of structural activities within
the organization, rather than a general strategy (e.g. Spergel et al., 1990;
Spergel, 1990). All four strategies and the one structural response were
more frequently cited by respondents experiencing youth gang problems,
which suggests that the scope and nature of gang activities draw forth a
more formal and organized response. The majority of respondents (52.3
percent) used a multidimensional approach (two to three strategies) within a larger intervention framework. However, almost one-third of all respondents relied on a singular, unidimensional strategy. Law enforcement and
court counselor agencies most often demonstrated multiple strategies, typically comprised of suppression and social intervention approaches.

The organizational response patterns were also analyzed to determine
the level of commitment to reducing collective youth crime problems. The
patterns — special policies, special units, special coordination structure
and task forces, and special training programs — were correlated with
selected youth gang and group features and measures of criminality to
determine the strength of the relationships and to highlight the differences
between how organizations responded to youth gangs and groups. The
presence of youth gangs in the community generated the most statistically significant and highly interrelated patterns. The more serious nature of
youth gangs most likely necessitates the establishment of clearly articulated programs and policies. The implementation of special policies was significantly associated with the percent of index offenses that were attributed

to these collectives, the level of drug distribution and importation activities, and the degree to which gang members affiliated with adult criminal organizations; special policies were also positively correlated with the size of youth gangs and the member population within the community. In communities experiencing youth group problems, the two factors that affected the development and implementation of special policies were the group member populations and whether these groups affiliated with adult criminal groups. These statistically significant correlations, however, may also indicate that special policies in their present form had not necessarily contributed to a reduction in these particular measures.

Special units were more frequently cited by organizations experiencing youth gang problems. The correlation patterns between special units and selected features and measures again revealed that the most significant relationships came from organizations experiencing youth gangs. Special units and task forces were highly related, which possibly indicates that organizations respond to task force involvement by creating special units or assigning personnel support responsibilities. There was a very strong relationship between special units and the percentage of youth gang members who were adults, the estimated gang member population within the community, and gang involvement in drug importation activities. For youth groups, conversely, there were strong associations between special units and the percentage of group members who were juveniles and drug distribution activities. The correlations, however, did not clearly indicate whether special units were effective at reducing drug-related activities or other characteristics of the problem.

The positive correlations between community coordination structure and selected measures of the youth gang and group problem appear very promising for prevention and intervention. The statistically significant associations indicated that community coordination structures may have contributed to a reduction in key measures and characteristics of the collective youth crime problem. In contrast, task forces, which typically employ suppression tactics, may potentially exacerbate and have a minimal long-term effect on reducing youth gang and group criminal activities. In comparing the data on task forces and community coordination structures (Tables 7.13 through 7.16), the remarkably different correlations should invite a reexamination of current programs and strategies. The analysis of special training programs indicated a potentially beneficial effect at reducing drug-related activities for both youth gangs and groups and the general criminal activities of youth gangs. In general terms, the correlations indicated that special training programs may have had a broader effect on the problems and characteristics associated with youth gangs, perhaps this was due to the quality and attention given to the development and implementation of such programs.

The relationship between the four primary strategies and perceived causes of the problem was relatively strong. In a previous chapter, respondents identified twelve causal factors that contributed to the problem, all of which were classified under social structural, social institutional, or social psychological rubrics. Social structural problems or conditions, particularly the lack of opportunities and poverty, were perceived as primary causes of collective youth crime problems, followed closely by social institutional and social psychological factors. A correlation analysis demonstrated that organizations and agencies had generally addressed the perceived causes with the most appropriate strategies. For instance, social intervention, one of the most widely employed strategies, appears to be utilized where the perceived causes involved social institutional and social psychological problems. However, even though social structural problems in general were perceived as the primary cause, the most appropriate strategies, community mobilization and opportunities provision, were not selected as key strategies. This finding is not surprising since the large majority of organizations came from the criminal justice field, where the mission focus does not involve addressing community-structural problems.

There was an overwhelming perception that youth gang and group problems had become progressively worse in the past few years. These perceptions were closely associated with the number of youth gang and group members in the community, the average size of collectives, and the percentage of members with prior criminal histories. In particular, the perceived worsening of the youth gang problem was strongly related to gang involvement in drug-related activities, as well as the presence of nonlocal gangs within the community; for youth groups, a perceived worsening of the problem was strongly associated with the level of involvement in drug-distribution activities. Organizations and agencies reported general success in dealing with youth gang and group problems; these perceptions, however, were not significantly related to key measures of the problem, but were more closely associated with the development and implementation of organizational policies and programs. Conversely, in jurisdictions that had community-level coordination structures, the organizational ratings were strongly associated with reductions in key measures of the problem.

Finally, using four interrelated dimensions, a model was developed to identify the organizations that exhibited the most promising prevention and intervention strategies for future evaluation. There were sixteen organizations — including police agencies, sheriff's departments, school systems, and correctional institutions — from twelve jurisdictions that exhibited promising approaches targeting youth gangs; there were also eight organizations in seven jurisdictions that exhibited potentially promising approaches that focus on youth groups. Respondents from these organizations, with the exception of correctional institutions, rated their organizations' and community coordination efforts as relatively effective at reducing or maintaining youth gang and group problems within their respective communities, and generally confirmed that the problems within their respective jurisdictions had at least stabilized in recent years.

The analysis throughout this chapter utilized a variety of statistical procedures to determine the interrelationship of organizational features, as well as the relationship between organizational features and the perception of the crime problem. By interrelating organizational policies, structures, and programs to youth gang and group problem characteristics, it became possible to determine, to some extent, the relationship between the level of problem severity and organizational response (e.g. Spergel et al., 1990). However, because of the limitations in the methodologies used in this study, the assessment of organizational effectiveness cannot in any way be considered definitive. Further research involving systematic data collection methods is necessary before conclusive assessment can be made with any degree of confidence. Nevertheless, the information does provide some direction from which more detailed exploratory and evaluative research can be conducted.

8

Summary
and Recommendations

A. Introduction

This research endeavor represents the first attempt to gather information on the collective youth crime problem in North Carolina. The study not only attempted to ascertain the prevalence and locations of youth gangs and groups across a state that has relatively small metropolitan areas, it also provided important insights, from the youth practitioners perspective, on the scope and nature of criminal activities. These insights were particularly important for a couple of reasons: first, because there was a lack of statistical data or other, relevant reports on collective youth crime in the State, the only viable alternative was to seek information from the individuals who were in the best positions to address key faucets of the problem; and secondly, from a public policy perspective, there was a practical need to gather information pertaining to how organizations responded to the problem and the perceived effectiveness of the responses. From a general research perspective, the findings are valuable because they address a growing criminal justice problem in North Carolina, a state that has received relatively little attention in the research literature on youth gangs and other criminal youth groups.

Youth gang and group criminal activities reported across North Carolina were much more widespread and serious than previously indicated in the available national-level and State-level assessments (see Curry et al., 1993; Curry, 1994; North Carolina Governor's Crime Commission, 1992). Even though the seriousness (e.g. lethality) of criminal activities may not compare to that discovered in may other states—especially states whose cities have a strong history of youth gang problems (see Spergel, 1984; Spergel et al., 1990; Jankowski, 1991; Morales, 1992; Curry et al., 1993) —there is a tremendous need for focused evaluative and exploratory field research. The most challenging aspect of this study involved gathering data and information that would provide some basis for assessing the scope and nature of the problem. Even though descriptive and analytical stud-

239

ies on gang and group problems in the State were not available, the lack of available resources did not impede the general research goals that were established at the onset of this study. The broad goals involved addressing three key questions, all of which continuously guided this research: What was the perceived scope and nature of the phenomenon? Could it be explained? and, What actions were implemented to eliminate, reduce, or mitigate the problem? These important issues, Miller (1982) asserts, should be kept at the heart of any research project that endeavors to understand the crime problem. Moreover, four fundamental concerns that pertained specifically to the study of youth gangs also received considerable attention. The concerns included gang-related definitions, youth gang proliferation and migration across the State, the connection between gangs and drug-related activities, and the central organizational concepts that differentiate youth gangs from other criminal youth groups. This research, in particular, involved comparing and contrasting the differences that may exist between youth gangs and youth groups, such as how respondents defined the problem, the perceived scope and nature of criminal activities, and the organizational responses to the problem. Since it is likely that youth gang and group activities involve different dimensions of criminality and group processes, and should be approached from different etiological points on the group-to-gang continuum (Cohen, 1969; see also Thornberry et al., 1993, 1994), clearly understanding the characteristics of the problem became paramount when it came time to analyze organizational responses.

In order to gain the necessary knowledge to the aforementioned issues and concerns, a survey instrument was forwarded to a universe of respondents who belonged to organizations that were most capable of addressing questions pertaining to collective youth crime problems across the State. The survey instrument, developed and modified from two national-level projects (Spergel et al., 1990; Needle and Stapleton, 1983), elicited information on the nature of the problem, definitional criteria and the scope of activities, organizational responses to the problem, community responses to the problem, and an evaluation of organizational and community effectiveness at reducing the problem. The ultimate sample for the analysis included 257 respondents (62.7 percent response rate) from three distinct organizational categories: Law Enforcement, which included city police agencies and county sheriff's departments, constituted 47.6 percent of the entire sample; Youth Services, the second largest respondent category representing 33.8 percent of the sample, was composed of juvenile court counselor agencies and youth correctional institutions; and Education, representing only 16.5 percent of the sample, comprised officials from county and city school districts and selected urban high schools. The respondents from these three organizational categories collectively represented organizations and agencies in 58 (64.4 percent) cities with populations of 5,000 or more, 95 (95.0 percent) counties throughout the State, 32 (84.2 percent) judicial districts, and 11 (61.1 percent) youth correctional institutions.

The study relied heavily on law enforcement perceptions, not only because these organizations provided the keenest insight into the seriousness and magnitude of the problem, but also because they achieved the greatest consensus in defining key characteristics that distinguish gangs from groups. Furthermore, police agencies and sheriff's departments quite often provided the only reasonable estimates of youth gang and group involvement in index offenses and drug-related activities. However, information provided by juvenile court counselors, correctional officials, and school officials was also considered valuable, since these respondents provided unique perspectives on the scope and nature of activities in very diverse environments. Recent trends in evaluative research have recognized the importance of relying on the perceptions of community professionals from a variety of fields (e.g. Miller, 1982; Needle and Stapleton, 1983; Spergel et al., 1990; Spergel and Chance, 1990; Maxson and Klein, 1993) and official reports (Maxson et al., 1985; Klein and Maxson, 1989; Curry and Spergel, 1988; Curry et al., 1993, 1994) for assessing the scope and nature of collective youth crime. Data gathered using official sources, though generally lacking significant cultural and sociological insight, often provides the most accurate and accessible information for measuring trends in youth gang and group criminal patterns — a critical objective for developing sound criminal justice policy.

Even though the information and data provided by respondents was very important and critical for understanding the collective youth crime problem in the State, there were a number of data limitations and reliability concerns that affected the research findings. First, the lack of statistical data on collective youth crime and related activities was the most serious drawback, making it difficult to validate respondent estimates of index offenses and the relative seriousness of criminal activities. The only practical method available involved extrapolation — e.g. cross-referencing respondent estimates with official crime statistics provided by the State Bureau of Investigation. Second, the lack of uniform gang definitions also made it very difficult to comparably assess the scope and nature of the problem across jurisdictions throughout the State; what is perceived as a gang problem in one jurisdiction may not be considered a problem in another, even though the characteristics and activities may be similar. Third, because this research involved multiple sites and multiple organizations, there were most likely many interdepartmental differences in how organizations collected and maintained relevant data pertaining to both youth gangs and groups (Maxson, 1995). Respondent organizations, whether they were schools, police departments, or correctional institutions, most likely employed different policies (e.g. data recording and reporting practices) and programs to address gang or group problems, all of which affected the ability to make truly accurate assessments. And fourth, the question of data reliability was further complicated because of the fact that organizations with multidisciplinary responsibilities and missions were the sources of information on a very complex social phenomenon. The variations in the professional backgrounds of respondents, as well as their level of experience, personal biases, and prejudices, probably had a significant effect on their perceptions of the problem and the manner in which they may have responded to certain survey questions.

Furthermore, despite the respectable response rate (62.7 percent), the findings may have been substantially different if more respondents from a wider variety of fields had participated. Quite possibly gang and group definitions, as well as perceptions of the problem, would have been even more diverse if judges, prosecutors, defense attorneys, grassroots organizations, political leaders, and other youth agencies had been involved. If there had been a greater number of multiple respondents from each locality, it would have been possible to better test the validity and reliability of survey data from each locality as well as make cross-jurisdiction comparisons. Since the data collection was conducted over a relatively short period of time, it was not possible to determine whether there had been any historical variation in the scope and nature of the collective youth crime problem. It was particularly difficult to confidently assert whether the problem had actually worsened, improved, or remained the same. The statistical correlations only provided some indication of the relationship between two variables, and in many cases the causal directions — which variable influenced the other — were difficult to discern.

The remaining sections in this chapter summarize the most significant findings discovered in this research. In particular, the first section attempts to place the research findings within the broader empirical and theoretical body of research on collective youth crime, in essence by touching on the four themes discussed in the introduction and throughout this study. These themes include gang-related definitions, the issue of gang proliferation and growth, the connection between gangs, drugs, and violence, and the characteristics that differentiate gangs from other criminal groups. The second and third sections provide highlights of the policies, procedures, and strategies employed by organizations and agencies and whether these responses had any perceived effect at reducing the problem. The last section provides policy and research recommendations, along with intervention models that address the problem in terms of the community context and the distinct organizational missions of law enforcement, probation, corrections, and schools (e.g. Spergel et al., 1994a).

B. Scope and Nature of Collective Youth Crime Problems in North Carolina

The most critical step in ascertaining the scope and nature of the problem involved establishing a conceptual framework that would effectively serve as the unit of analysis. Using Miller's (1982) characterization of youth gangs (e.g. self-formed association of peers, identifiable leadership, internal organization, specific purpose, established identity, territorial, and involvement in illegal activities) and groups (e.g. loosely organized, lacking structure and identity, involvement in illegal activities) afforded the opportunity to distinguish respondent definitions based more on model characteristics than strict definitional criteria. According to Klein (1995), the adoption of model characteristics for distinguishing youth gangs from youth groups and the consistent use of accepted definitions have a number of important implications. The inconsistent use of definitions—what constitutes a youth gang or group, their members, and incidents that are gang and group-related—could lead to the appearance of changes in the scope and nature of the problem. Furthermore, any altered perception of what constitutes a gang or group could also lead to the impression that collective youth crime problems have either improved or worsened. It therefore becomes very important to clarify what should be included and excluded in the concepts of youth gang and youth group if any attempt is taken to measure the trends and cycles of activities.

Even though gang definitions and the perceptions of the scope and nature of the collective youth crime problem across North Carolina came in many variations, there was nevertheless a common theme underlying the information that was provided. Based on the general consensus of respondents, youth gangs were considered somewhat structured collectives that displayed unique identifiers (e.g. personal symbols or colors), were territorial, and often engaged in serious criminal activities, especially drug trafficking. Research has indicated that youth gangs can be loosely-knit or tightly organized, depending on particular points in time, the types of activities in which collectives are involved, the cities where the gangs are located, and the racial and ethnic characteristics of the gang (Taylor, 1990; Moore, 1990; Spergel and Curry, 1990; Jankowski, 1991; Skolnick, 1993; Skolnick et al., 1993). The distinction between youth gangs and other criminally oriented youth groups was far from simplistic, but as Klein (1995, p. 218) explains, "street gangs are delinquent groups that have passed a 'tipping point' in their confrontational stance as a group. They have set themselves apart from their neighborhoods in their own perceptions, and many members of the local community have come to see them as a group apart." Generally, as the research literature has similarly indi-

cated, youth gang members tended to be older than their nongang counterparts, typically but not always territorial, highly versatile in criminal
offenses, and were perceived to be involved in a disproportionate number
of violent offenses when compared members in youth groups (see Cohen,
1965, 1969; Klein and Myerhoff, 1967; Friedman et al., 1975; Rand,
1987; Reiner, 1992; Klein, 1995).

Most youth collectives (both gang and group) ranged in size from three
to twenty members, with the average size youth gang reportedly having a significantly higher number of members when compared to youth groups (18
versus seven). This finding may possibly indicate that youth gangs attract
and maintain more cohesive assemblages of individuals. Cohesiveness,
whether manifesting internally or generated by external factors, has been
shown to have a particularly strong effect on the nature of gang activities,
member interaction and gang attraction, and membership size (Short and
Strodtbeck, 1965; Klein and Crawford, 1967; Cartwright et al., 1975;
Horowitz, 1983; see also Thornberry et al., 1994). Demographically, respondents reported that the vast majority of youth gang and group members
who came to their attention were male and from black (approximately 64.0
percent) and white (approximately 25.0 percent) racial and ethnic groups;
based on the available estimates, youth gang and group members appeared
to be disproportionately represented by individuals who were between the
ages of 16 and 19. According to research findings, the typical age range of
youth gang members is between eight and twenty-two years. A small number of studies on youth gangs reported membership starting at very early
ages (e.g. 8 to 9 years of age) and continuing well into adulthood, yet the median age of gang membership was generally reported to be between 17 and
19 years of age (Collins, 1979; Miller, 1982; Horowitz, 1983; Spergel, 1986;
Bobrowski, 1988). The age estimates were similar to those reported for
youth group members. Though the findings for age are consistent with those
found in the research literature, the findings for gang member race and ethnicity were quite different. For instance, Miller's (1982) survey findings discovered that Hispanics (44.4 percent) and blacks (42.9 percent) constituted
the majority of gangs in nine of the largest American cities, while white and
Asian gangs together made up only 13 percent. In another study, Spergel et
al. (1990) found that black gang members most often came to the attention
of survey respondents in the 45 cities they surveyed. And in a more recent
study, Curry et al. (1994) noted that the reported ethnic composition was
largely Hispanic (42.7 percent) and African-American (47.8 percent), with
whites (4.4 percent) and Asians (5.2 percent) making up only a small minority.
Thus, the differences between the race findings in the national-level research
projects and those reported here are quite substantial.

There may be a couple of explanations for these racial discrepancies:
first, the national-level projects have generally focused on problems in

larger cities, especially those with modest sized minority populations (both black and Hispanic) and cities with established or emerging youth gang problems; and second, North Carolina's less populated, rural communities may somehow facilitate the growth of white youth gangs and groups, while factors in urban areas contribute more to minority involvement in gangs and groups. Moreover, because North Carolina has a relatively small Hispanic, as well as Asian, population, it is not that surprising to discover low estimates of gang and group members in these racial categories. The above finding may demonstrate a need to focus gang-related research on smaller cities and rural communities, since there may be different factors and circumstances that give rise to gang and group involvement in rural areas, particularly those areas where minority populations are relatively small. Studies have consistently indicated that youth gangs and groups are disproportionately located in lower-class, minority communities (Moore, 1978; Hagedorn, 1988; Spergel, 1990). However, characteristics that influence gang involvement in minority communities — e.g. social instability, poverty, unemployment, and social isolation — may not necessarily contribute to white gang development in the same ways. Because race and ethnicity may influence the types of crimes perpetrated by members and their collectives (see Curry and Spergel, 1988; Skolnick et al., 1988, 1993; Spergel et al., 1990; Chin, 1990), in essence defining the scope and nature of activities, it becomes very important to know the racial characteristics of the problem.

The proliferation and growth of collective youth crime problems in North Carolina, especially youth gang, appear to be growing at a relatively brisk pace. There were an estimated 2,772 youth gang members and 1,450 youth group members reported by respondents across a number of different localities throughout North Carolina — cities, counties, judicial districts, and correctional institutions. Youth gangs were reported in 39 of these localities and youth groups were reported in 42; however, many of the respondents who reported youth gangs in their communities or institutions also reported youth groups, which provides support for the theory that gangs may evolve from other loosely-knit group formations (see Thrasher, 1936). These figures, however, may be on the conservative side because of the potential effect of nonresponse. Recent survey research (Spergel et al., 1990) failed to identify any North Carolina cities that could be classified as having chronic or emerging youth gang problems. Another project (Curry et al., 1994) identified only the largest city in North Carolina (Charlotte) as having youth gang problems, and classified the problems in the Raleigh-Durham metropolitan region as "gang-like." The contemporary gang situation, according to Klein's (1995) recent work, identifies 13 North Carolina cities with youth gang problems, albeit the data was from 1992; all of the cities designated in Klein's study were also classified as having youth gang problems in the present research, so apparently the problems in these cities may not have improved over the past few years. The key point is that the data presented in this study may reflect a relatively modest growth in the number of new cities in the State that reportedly have youth gang problems. It may be appropriate to conclude that, even if some of the cities were mislabeled due to definitional or methodological problems, they may be on the "cusp" of becoming cities with true gang problems; furthermore, it is also necessary to note those cities classified as having youth group problems, since these cities may also be on the verge of experiencing more serious problems in the future.

According to the self-reports of respondents, the youth gang and group problem across the State also appears to be worsening, with respect to the scope and nature of activities. The majority of respondents (69.4 percent) perceived that the collective youth crime problem, both gang and group, had become more serious in the past three years in their communities. In 28 localities experiencing youth gangs, the problems were rated as serious or very serious, based largely on respondent estimations of criminal activities; for youth groups, 15 localities were given the same ratings. The perceptions among a large proportion of respondents were based on two factors that may be interrelated: an increased presence of gangs and groups in communities that had not experienced problems in the past few years, or a growth in membership in communities that had only minor problems; and an increase in drug-related activities, primarily drug distribution rather than drug-use, and violence perpetrated by members in both gangs and groups. These perceptions, insofar as youth gangs were concerned, were very similar to those found in research conducted by Spergel et al. (1990).

Research findings on the migratory patterns of youth gangs are very mixed, while similar research on criminal youth groups is all but nonexistent. The two issues at the heart of the migration/proliferation debate revolve around whether gangs systematically move into communities for enterprising purposes, such as for drug distribution (e.g. Taylor, 1990), or whether other factors — such as increases in law enforcement activities or family movement — are the primary causes (Hanson, 1990; Reiner, 1992; Maxson, 1993). There was a wide perception that drug-related activities were responsible for the growing problem in most cities and jurisdictions, especially small towns and rural communities. But without corroborative offense or intelligence data, these assertions can only will remain tentative. However, conclusions in a recent report (NNICC, 1995, p.8) may lend support to these perceptions: "A combination of factors — saturated markets, low prices [for drugs], violent competition, and/or effective police pressures in major urban areas — has forced some crack distribution groups, in conjunction with local gangs, to develop new markets in smaller towns and rural areas." Information provided by the State Bureau of Investigation and the Federal Bureau of Investigation indicate that North Carolina does in fact have a prominent problem with Jamaican drug trafficking organizations, often referred to as "posses," in the cities of Charlotte, Greensboro, and Winston-Salem. It may be reasonable to surmise that these organizations may recruit youth gangs and other criminal groups for street-level drug distribution, but there was insufficient evidence to conclude that youth gangs and groups were exhibiting features commonly used to characterize drug organizations—e.g. centralized leadership, sales market territory, competition controlled (see Klein, 1995, p. 132). But as other researchers have made clear, gang involvement in the drug business —whether as look-outs, mules, or for protecting territory—may be indicative of an important transformation, one that has made distinguishing between street gangs and drug gangs quite difficult (Ianni, 1974; Fagan, 1990; Jankowski, 1991; Skolnick, 1992). Moreover, "[t]he employees of these drug organizations represents a symbiosis between youth gangs and drug dealers that has grown stronger, more pervasive, and may not be confined simply to inner-city or ghetto area low-income residents" (Spergel, 1995, p. 135). The findings in the present study do largely support what Maxson and Klein (1993) concluded about gang migration: migration was widespread, but the proportion of cities with large gang influxes was relatively small. The most serious problems, both in membership expansion and characteristics of criminal activities, were reported in the largest metropolitan areas in the State—Charlotte, Raleigh, Durham, and Fayetteville. Yet, youth gang member growth and the seriousness of activities in smaller cities and communities, particularly Lumberton, Elizabeth City, and Southern Pines, must also be underscored.

There may be reason to suspect that there is a strong relationship between the seriousness of criminal activities, age, race, and whether the problem involved gangs or groups. Gangs with older, black members in numerous jurisdictions were closely linked to drug importation activities and more violent offenses, while street-level dealing, and less serious offenses were strongly associated with younger, white youth group members. Research indicates that black youth gangs were more heavily involved in turf-related violence and vice activities when compared to gangs in other racial groups (Bobrowski, 1988; Block et. al, 1993), while white gangs were more involved in property crime (Spergel, 1990). There is also evidence that the choice of drugs for trafficking and dealing purposes is also related to the racial composition of gangs, with crack cocaine the drug of choice for black gangs, and methamphetamines and marijuana the favored drug among white gangs and groups (Skolnick, 1988). Reports by officials in the present research project support these findings. However, many respondents were also quick to assume there was a nexus between drug-related

gang activities and violence, in the sense that the violence was functionally related to the drug activities. The available studies generally conclude
that gang violence is most often independent of drug activities, with gang
involvement in drug dealing no more likely to include higher levels of violence than in situations where gangs were not involved (Maxson et al.,
1985, 1993; Fagan, 1989; Klein and Maxson, 1989; Klein, 1991; Reiner,
1992; see also Spergel, 1990).

The present research findings were particularly consistent with Spergel
and Curry's (1990) conclusions regarding the relationships among the variables of race, gang organization, and criminal activities: "The greater the
percent of black gang members in an area, the greater the likelihood that
drugs are being sold by gangs . . . [and] When drug distribution is a primary purpose of the gang, there is a significantly higher percent of the
total of all index crime attributed to gangs" (p. 88). These findings were
based on the perceptions of law enforcement officials in forty-five cities.
However, the empirical data on the connection between gang *violence* and
drug trafficking do not support the general perceptions of officials surveyed in various studies, including the present one (see e.g. Spergel et al.,
1990; Virginia State Crime Commission, 1991). Five key studies (Fagan,
1988; Klein et al., 1988; Bobrowski, 1988; Reiner, 1992; Institute of Law
and Justice, 1994) concluded that gang violence was rarely instigated by
drug-related motives. Even though drug-trafficking and violence often in-
tersect in many street situations, the problem may be more common in
nongang situations.

Locations that were experiencing what could be characterized as youth
gang problems were generally more serious in scope and nature. Respondents reporting youth gang problems also reported higher estimates of serious offenses attributed to these collectives. Of all Index offenses (Part I
crimes of the UCR) known to the respondents, it was estimated that 8.8
percent of the offenses were attributable to youth gangs, compared to 5.0
percent for youth groups; according to respondents' best estimates, youth
gangs were more frequently involved in violent offenses, particularly the
crimes of robbery and aggravated assault, while youth groups, on the other
hand, were disproportionately involved in offenses against property. The
criminal patterns and group processes of youth gangs and their members
appear to be distinctly different from those demonstrated by nongang
groups, thus partially explaining the variations in certain offenses. This
research finding is strongly supported by the theoretical and empirical
studies that make similar distinctions and conclusions (Thrasher, 1936;
Sellin and Wolfgang, 1964; Cohen, 1965, 1969; Kornhauser, 1978; Spergel,
1984; see also Thornberry et al., 1994). Conversely, the finding is in sharp
contrast to other classical theoretical studies (Miller, 1958; Cohen and
Short, 1958; Cloward and Ohlin, 1960; and Short and Strodtbeck, 1965)

that did not differentiate nongang criminal behavior with that of youth gangs. Group processes that revolve around status, solidarity, and cohesion —all of which are typical dimensions found in youth gangs—are likely to result in higher levels of criminality (Thornberry et. al., 1993; see also Cohen, 1955; Klein and Crawford, 1964 and Horowitz and Schwartz, 1974). But even though research has consistently indicated that gang members are more prone to criminal activities, including those that are drug-related, than nongang members, there is still an air of uncertainty as to whether gangs attract criminally-oriented individuals or create them (Thornberry et al., 1994).

Why some locations were experiencing youth gang and group problems elicited a number of opinions from respondents. Twelve causal factors—classified under social structural, social institutional, or social psychological categories—were thought to have contributed significantly to the conditions that lead to collective youth crime problems. Social structural problems or conditions, particularly the lack of opportunities and poverty, were perceived as primary causes of collective youth crime problems. This perspective is supported by the theories that view criminal activities as the only viable option where legitimate opportunities, particularly in impoverished communities, are not available (Durkheim, 1933; Merton, 1938; Cloward and Ohlin, 1960; Wilson, 1987). In essence, the lack of legitimate opportunities encourage youth to enter gangs and groups so that normative rules can be redefined, deviant behavior can be legitimized, and economic needs can be fulfilled. The strain theories developed by Durkheim, Merton, and Cloward and Ohlin, however, do not easily explain the presence of gangs and groups in communities that are not suffering from economic or legitimate opportunity problems. Therefore, it may be necessary to examine other perceived causes, as well as theoretical offerings, in order to gain greater insights.

Of all the possible causes that encourage involvement in youth gangs and groups, respondents (38.9 percent) most frequently cited the social institutional factor of dysfunctional family relationships. There is no singular method for defining a dysfunctional family, but the concept can be broadly characterized as any familial situation where the family is insufficiently organized and ineffective in providing the needs of support, social control, and socialization of its youth. Insufficient support in the family institutional setting often results in youth selecting and associating with peer groups that can better provide for their social, and even economic, needs. Dysfunctional family relationships, and how this condition may lead to involvement in youth gangs and groups, is best explained by social control theory (Reckless, 1961; Hirschi, 1969) and the theory of differential association (Sutherland and Cressey, 1974; see also Burgess and Akers, 1966). Social control theory posits that individuals who are inadequately socialized or controlled, because of weak social bonds to parents and other legitimate social institutions, will be more inclined to become involved in criminal activities and to establish relations with delinquent peer groups. Proper and adequate social control regulates normative behavior by directing individuals away from deviant influences and towards legitimate societal expectations (Reckless, 1961). Where parental supervision and control is weak, peer influences take on an important dimension, influencing the scope of activities and quality of group interaction (Vigil, 1988; Horowitz, 1983; Goldstein, 1991). Peer influences that are criminal or antisocial in nature, further increase the probability that individuals will adopt more criminogenic behavioral traits, depending on how often the association occurs and the importance placed on the associations (Sutherland and Cressey, 1974; see also Gottfredson and Hirschi, 1990).

It is important to note that the lack of opportunities, poverty, and dysfunctional family relationships were cited by the vast majority of respondents as the primary conditions that contributed to youth gang and group problems, in fact a large number of respondents cited all three factors. Though these three conditions have been quite often cited in previous research as key contributors to youth gang and other group problems, it is likely that social and economic problems, unemployment and poverty, and the failure of parents and social institutions to adequately socialize and supervise youth, are interactive in creating the structural and social conditions that lead to variations in the collective youth crime problem across communities. The seriousness of a gang or group problem in a specific community will most likely be dependent upon the extent to which some or all of these conditions are present. However, the importance of social institutions was underscored by Spergel (1995, p. 153): "The youth gang arises under circumstances in which the social relatedness...needs of its members have not been adequately satisfied by local community institutional capacities and arrangements. Vulnerable youth find each other and create, or join already established, peer groups to meet these needs." Understanding the inadequacies of a community's social institutions may therefore provide the clues needed to discern why some youth are more vulnerable to gang and group involvement than others.

C. Current Organizational Policies and Procedures

Organizations and agencies responded to collective youth crime problems in a variety of ways. The most formalized and structured responses came from law enforcement organizations; these organizations demonstrated the greatest propensity for developing and implementing special policies and training programs and also for participating in task forces and community coordination structures. The other two criminal justice organizations —juvenile court counselor agencies and youth correctional institutions— were also actively involved in program development and coordinating structures, but at less frequent rates than police agencies and sheriff's departments. For all the criminal justice organizations, the trend in policy and procedures was centered around implementing and executing suppression approaches. This finding, which is not surprising given the primary mission of these organizations, has also been a common conclusion in other research (Needle and Stapleton, 1983; Duran, 1987; Camp and Camp, 1988; McKinney, 1988; National Institute of Corrections, 1991; Reiner, 1992; Duxbury, 1993). County and city school systems and individual high schools were the least active in developing programs that specifically focused on youth gangs or other at-risk youth, though larger school districts across the State had begun developing "gang awareness" programs, albeit as part of other drug and substance abuse prevention programs (see e.g. Rubel and Ames, 1986; Spergel and Alexander, 1991; Goldstein, 1993a).

Youth gangs in the community instigated the most explicit and organized response, regardless of the type of organization or agency. The establishment of special policies and guidelines was strongly related to the perceived level of drug distribution and drug importation activities of both types of collectives, but particularly to the proportion of index offenses attributed to youth gangs. As the youth gang member population and the size of gang collectives increased, organizations were also likely to adopt special policies to address this phenomenon. This finding is contrary to what Spergel et al. (1990) discovered: "The expression of special gang policy in an agency seems not related to any of the several measures of the youth gang nature of the problem. The existence of such gang policy is not significantly related to the number of gangs, number of gang members, size of the larger gangs, gang ethnicity, incidents, involvement of adults, or criminality of gang members" (p. 60). In communities where youth groups were problematic, the development of special policies was significantly dependent on the group member population and whether these collectives affiliated with adult criminal groups.

Special units were most often employed by organizations and agencies that were experiencing youth gang problems, particularly law enforcement agencies (see e.g. Needle and Stapleton, 1983; Spergel, 1991a); and again, special units were strongly associated with estimates of gang member populations in the community and the perceived level of involvement in drug-related activities. Spergel et al. (1990) also found that organizational specialization was strongly associated with the number of gang members in a jurisdiction and drug distribution activities. Where the problem involved youth groups, drug distribution activities by juvenile members were the most significant factors that influenced the creation of special units. Organizational arrangements appear to reflect perceived differences in the scope and nature of the problem (gang versus group), the size of the organization's jurisdiction, and the availability of human and fiscal resources (see Spergel, 1995). In communities where task forces were active in solving collective youth crime problems, local organizations and agencies were also likely to have special units, if only for the duration of task forces.

The presence of special policies and guidelines, special units, task forces, and community coordination structures were strongly related to a perceived worsening in both youth gang and group problems. Organizations and agencies appear to respond to a worsening problem through structural changes and modifications; however, special policies, units, and task forces may not have contributed to mitigating the problem—e.g. reducing member populations, involvement in index offenses, and adult involvement in these collectives. In other research (Spergel et al., 1990; see also Spergel et al., 1994b; Spergel and Curry, 1990b), little association was discovered between a decline in the scope and nature of gang problems and specific organizational policies and characteristics. It is also possible that task forces, which are largely suppressive in nature, may have inadvertently contributed to the worsening of the scope and nature of activities. As Klein (1995) asserts, increased threats of punishment, promulgated by certain law enforcement tactics for instance, may in the gang context function as an incentive to commit crime, since group processes and their pressures not only inhibit the outward expression of any fear of sanction, but also create an opportunity to convert stigmata into symbols of status. The most promising organizational approach—participation in community coordination structures—may have had the most significant influence in reducing key measures of the problem, namely membership populations, the size of collectives, and the percentage of members with prior criminal histories. An external advisory structure, Spergel et al. (1990) suggests, may be the most effective mechanism for reducing gang problems within the community, since it can serve to oversee, guide, and coordinate the development of prevention and intervention programs.

D. Effectiveness of Prevention and Intervention Strategies

There were four primary prevention and intervention strategies and one organizational approach that characterized the responses to the problem.

These strategies—community mobilization, social intervention, opportunity provision, suppression, and organizational development—have been well documented in recent research (Spergel, 1990, 1991a; Spergel and Chance, 1991; Spergel and Curry, 1990a, 1990b, Spergel at al., 1990a, 1994b; Conly, 1993). Gangs strategies over the past few decades, though closely linked to assumptions about cause and effect, have evolved and been modified with the advent of new tactics, technology, policies, and priorities. Strategy implementation—which is dependent upon such factors as organizational arrangements, services, procedures, and the institutional structures for developing these approaches—has been the responsibility of youth agencies, criminal justice organizations, community organizations and schools, and governments (Spergel, 1995). According to Conly (1993), the strategy emphasis in recent years has shifted from social and structural interventions, such as youth outreach programs and creating job opportunities, to crime control and suppression. The emphasis on crime control and suppression was also found in the present research. According to 42.3 percent of all respondents, their organizations placed the greatest emphasis on suppression approaches, which incorporate a number of activities such as intelligence collection, investigations, and monitoring. But the ultimate objective was simply to apprehend, prosecute, and sentence serious and habitual offenders using whatever techniques necessary.

Social intervention, cited by 28.8 percent of all respondents as the second most important strategy, involves programs that emphasize and reinforce positive behavior, such as counseling, diversion, outreach, sports and recreation, and drug prevention. The least cited strategies, opportunities provision (6.7 percent) and neighborhood mobilization (5.8 percent), focus less on individual and social institutional problems and more on social structural or community-level conditions. Opportunity provision involves efforts to improve educational and employment structures through job training and placement, remedial education, and similar programs; neighborhood mobilization is best characterized as mobilizing political and community interests to remedy the problem. Organizational development, though not a strategy per se, was considered an integral component in the broader strategic framework; 57.7 percent of all respondents cited features such as special programs, special units, and interagency coordination. Spergel et al.'s (1990) survey results demonstrated a similar pattern, in that suppression was the primary strategy followed by social intervention; however, organizational development was only cited by 12.5 percent of all respondents in their study.

Research has also found that the four basic strategies are typically incorporated into a larger unidimensional, integrated strategy, whereby the planning and execution of prevention and intervention efforts are jointly conducted by government or community institutions (see e.g. Spergel and

Chance, 1990; Spergel, 1991b; Spergel and Kane, 1991; Spergel and Ehrensaft, 1991; Spergel et al., 1994b). In the present study, the strategies were combined to form more comprehensive, multidimensional approaches by 52.3 percent of the respondents, but 30.7 percent utilized a single, unidimensional strategy to address the problem. A multidimensional approach was most often demonstrated by police agencies, sheriff's departments, and court counselor agencies; these organizations typically cited suppression and social intervention as the two key strategies, with organizations from law enforcement emphasizing suppression as the most important feature in their comprehensive approach. Spergel et al. (1990) also discovered that the most common number of strategies used by organizations was two or three, but also found that law enforcement agencies were more apt to use the two-strategy combination of suppression and community mobilization. Schools and correctional institutions most often adopted a singular approach, but also stressed either suppression or intervention strategies. The four primary strategies were cited most frequently by organizations and agencies experiencing youth gang problems, which provides further evidence that youth gang activities call for a more formalized and organized response.

In order to implement appropriate youth gang and group prevention and intervention strategies, it is important first to have some idea of what conditions contribute to the problem. As previously noted, respondents perceived that the lack of opportunities, poverty, and dysfunctional family relationships were the primary conditions that contribute to both youth gang and group problems in their communities. There was a strong relationship between the primary strategies employed by organizations and what respondents perceived as the causes of the problem. Where the perceptions of the problem were of a social institutional (e.g. dysfunctional family relationships, poor educational achievement) or social psychological (e.g. drug abuse, need for acceptance) nature, social intervention approaches were either the primary strategy or were included in a more comprehensive framework (see e.g. Spergel et al., 1990; Spergel and Chance, 1990; Spergel, 1991b; Goldstein, 1991). It is important to note that, even though respondents cited social structural conditions as a proximal cause of collective youth crime problems, they infrequently cited opportunities provision or community mobilization, the most appropriate approaches, as primary strategies. However, correlations indicated that organizations did not ostensibly address social structural problems using social institutional and social psychological interventions.

There was an unusually strong perception among respondents that their organizations' prevention and intervention strategies were effective in addressing youth gang and group problems. These effectiveness ratings, however, were strongly associated with the implementation of organizational features, such as special policies and programs, rather than actual measures or characteristics of the problem. This finding made it difficult to judge whether an organization's prevention and intervention strategies were particularly promising. However, in communities where there were interagency coordination structures, organizational effectiveness ratings were strongly related to the key measures of the problem (see Spergel et al., 1990). In other words, interagency coordination structures most likely unified and coordinated community-wide strategies, and these efforts produced positive results in reducing the key measures of the problem. The organizations that exhibited the most promising strategies not only rated their respective organizational efforts as moderately or very effective, but also rated community coordination efforts similarly.

E. Recommendations

This study identified the localities that were likely experiencing collective youth crime problems throughout North Carolina and the locations and organizations that may have promising prevention and intervention programs. These findings were suggestive rather than definitive, therefore more detailed and systematic evaluative research is necessary to determine the effectiveness of program designs and the factors that may contribute to the emergence and persistence of youth gangs and groups in particular cities and communities. Hagedorn (1990) emphasizes the need for new studies because of recent research suggesting that contemporary youth gangs have changed fundamentally in the most recent decade. These fundamental changes have included an evolution and variation in gang typologies, structures, and criminal activities. This final section offers a number of suggestions and recommendations that should guide future research and policy endeavors; in particular, how to go about assessing the collective youth crime problem, recommended definitions to use when framing research questions, recommended research methods, and research priorities.

Assessing the Problem. The distinctive characteristics of a particular collective youth crime problem in the community context need to be carefully assessed. According to the present research findings, the cities with the more chronic problems (e.g. youth gangs) most likely contain loose-knit structures of older, minority youth and young adults who frequently engage in serious forms of criminal behavior. Problems may also be confined to specific neighborhoods and schools, or may involve large sections of the city. Some locations may experience a variety of problems that cover a broad spectrum of activities and characteristics. There are also assumptions or claims that necessitate greater scrutiny through research. For instance, there was a strong perception that youth collectives from larger urban communities had begun migrating into smaller towns and rural communities throughout the State, primarily to import and distribute illicit substances; perhaps this phenomenon is most characteristic of smaller, more organized drug gangs, rather than less cohesive, territorial, and traditional street gangs (e.g. Klein, 1995). Focused research on this latter point could potentially enable a more critical understanding of the characteristics of the crime problem in specific terms. In the broadest perspective, the assessment of the scope and nature of the problem must attempt to address the following empirical questions: Where in the community are the problems located? What are the age, race/ethnicity, gender, and criminal history characteristics of participants? How are the collectives structured in terms of core and fringe members? What are the school and job statuses of members? What proportion of index offenses committed by offenders are gang or group-related? What types of crimes are they committing? To what extent are youth collectives involved in drug-related activities? Can youth collectives in different cities be distinguished by age, race, or criminal activities? What are the socioeconomic and socio-demographic characteristics of the communities where youth gangs and groups arise? (see e.g. Howell, 1994; Spergel and Kane, 1991).

Definitions. The definitions of youth gangs and groups, and the incidents attributed to these two types of youth collectives, are important for recognizing the problem where it exists and to preclude excessive labeling (Spergel, 1990). In most cases, definitions are typically determined by law enforcement, but reflect local community values and interests. Broader definitions are most likely to include a wide spectrum of criminal activities committed by members, whether or not the activity is functionally related to gangs and groups; narrow definitions emphasize a delimited set of criminal activities that manifest out of gang and group interests, situations, functions, and age considerations. The adoption of narrow definitional parameters for research purposes is recommended for a number of reasons: it will provide for better targeting of high profile gangs and groups and the more serious offenders, and it will reduce the likelihood of exaggerating the seriousness of the problem. Youth groups should be defined as gangs only if they maintain a high profile (e.g. colors, clothing, name, turf), engage in serious criminal activities, and when their primary purpose for existence is communal. A gang or group-related incident should not only be an illegal act committed by a known or suspected member, but should also arise out of motivation, function, and circumstances related to the collective; membership, per se, is not sufficient reason for designating an incident as gang or group-related (see e.g. Spergel, 1990; Spergel, 1991b; Spergel et al., 1994b).

Research Methods. Focused survey research should provide a fruitful first-step in acquiring more detailed information on youth gangs and groups. Fagan's (1989) random sample survey of inner-city, high crime neighborhoods—which elicited valuable information regarding the relationship between drug use, drug dealing, and delinquency of urban gangs—is one study recommended for replication. The research methods and techniques could be replicated using the highest crime areas of three diverse cities where there are perceived youth gang problems (e.g. Charlotte, Raleigh, Fayetteville). The primary goal of the research should be to elicit general information—such as self-reported delinquency, gang affiliation, drug use and sales, involvement in school and family life—as well as more specific information related to the structure of gangs, particular activities, recruitment, and territory. It is quite plausible that the data generated from the three sample subsets could be examined and compared to determine if gang behaviors and processes vary based on ecological correlates. Moreover, by classifying gang activity into typologies (e.g. general delinquent, drug-oriented) and further comparing the typologies that emerge in different cities and neighborhoods, it would also be possible to determine if behavioral patterns represent natural variations among collectives in different ecological settings.

No single source or research technique is going to provide a truly accurate or complete picture of youth gangs and groups, therefore it becomes paramount to incorporate triangulation strategies to reduce potential research bias. Sanders (1994) designed an *observation schedule*— consisting of an interview schedule, survey, and participant-observation techniques —for his research on youth gang violence. Observations were conducted while accompanying police gang units on routine patrols, but the research also included interviewing and providing questionnaires to police officers and gang members. This promising and innovative technique permitted the opportunity to analyze data quantitatively, using coded data derived from interviews and questionnaires, and qualitatively, by reviewing the narrative portions of fieldnotes. The importance of exploring the collective youth crime problem in local jurisdictions using a variety of techniques, methodologies, and resources cannot be overemphasized, since data reliability and validity are greatly dependent upon the ability to corroborate information. Crime reports, statistical studies, and other official data (e.g. police and census reports) should supplement field-related research.

Most research will also have some inherent perspective from which the project is approached, with particular research objectives and goals. Research sponsorship and funding support also take on a very important role, since granting organizations and agencies have objectives and prescribed timeframes within which the research must be completed. The point is that regardless of what perspective researchers approach the study of collective youth crime (e.g. crime control and public policy, corrections, intervention and prevention, or sociological) the findings will only provide a slice of information or knowledge on the nature of the problem; but if viewed collectively, the findings could potentially provide insightful information leading to a better understanding of why youth join collectives, commit certain crimes, and how to effectively prevent the most serious forms of behavior. There are limitations and advantages to all research methodologies, "but the issue is not a matter of some version of political correctness in [selecting] methods so much as it is the question the researcher asks about gangs. We should look at problems and questions posed by theoretical issues, and then use whatever method that can best deliver valid data to answer those questions" (Sanders, 1994, p. 186).

Research Priorities. Because collective youth crime problems are typically viewed in parochial terms, instead of from the State-level perspective, resources for program development and formal evaluation are rarely available. Prevention and intervention programs are often implemented in the absence of valid theoretical rationales and the resources allocated to the problem are often incommensurate with the severity of the problem. Determining which approaches are most effective at reducing key measures and characteristics of the problem must be based on evaluative research that is carefully conducted. Specific programs available in the community, such as outreach and family counseling services, need to be identified and the quality of these and other programs should be carefully assessed (Spergel and Kane, 1991). Ribisl and Davidson (1993) assert that the first task in evaluating specific programs involves determining if the interventions operate as planned; the outcome criteria depends on the goals of particular programs, but most will include the reduction of criminal behavior as one criteria.

A study utilizing an experimental design will enable the comparisons of project outcomes for participants and nonparticipants in prevention and intervention programs that provide direct services. Consideration must be given to the demographic characteristics (as well as criminal background) of the sample group, since age and race may make some participants more amenable to prevention and intervention effects (e.g. Cohen et al., 1994). The methods used for collecting and analyzing data on prepost behavior could include either self-report surveys or personal interviews with subjects and staff members. The primary research objectives should be to ascertain how effective the programs are at preventing or reducing involvement in youth gangs and groups, criminal activities, drug use, and poor school performance. The research should also examine whether the length of participating in programs had any effect on the outcome objectives mentioned above—i.e. compare the outcome results of individuals who participated for less than a month, three months, and six months. This project would necessarily need to be done at the community-level, and would require the cooperation of numerous agencies and organizations, particularly law enforcement, grassroots, community service, and schools. Spergel and Ehrensaft (1991) noted that a full-scale or valid evaluation of the community organizations' contributions to reducing collective youth crime would also require cross-neighborhood comparisons, whereby the same variables could be carefully controlled and evaluated over a period of time.

Systematic program evaluation, which must be conducted on a regular basis, serves several functions: it informs the organization whether program objectives are being achieved; second, it identifies the successful and unsuccessful program elements, as well as ones that can be modified; and third, evaluations of program effects are critical to advancing knowledge for improving policy and practice (Kane and Regulus, 1990). Based on the available research and theory, the highest research priority should be given to evaluating the intervention and prevention strategies and programs that involve mobilizing the community. Conversely, programs that rely on a unidimensional strategy, especially programs that have not demonstrated successful results in the past (e.g. recreational programs, non-targeted deterrent approaches, short-term crisis intervention), should not receive substantial attention. In communities experiencing serious or chronic youth gang and group problems, the evaluation of social opportunity programs should receive emphasis: for at-risk youth, these may be special prevention services found in elementary and middle schools; for older youth, these may be programs that focus on job training and educational assistance. New and established suppression approaches, such as community policing and special probation monitoring in emerging problem communities, should be systematically evaluated.

Finally, there is a particular need to conduct systematic research on youth gang and group crime problems in the State's prison system. There is a close, interconnected relationship between correctional institutions, the community, and collective youth crime problems (Camp and Camp, 1985). Youth gangs and groups may evolve in the correctional setting or may be outgrowths of community-based collectives, but eventually these youth return to the community and often to their criminal gang and group patterns (Spergel, 1990; Regulus, 1991). It is important to recognize that collective youth crime problems are part of a community-institutional continuum. Assessing the scope and nature of the problem in the institutional setting requires answers to the following questions: Are youth gang or group members present in the institutions? How many gangs and groups are there? How large is the gang and group membership population? What overt and covert problems are related to these collectives? Is the problem recent, chronic, or recurrent? Are there serious, ongoing interactions between different collectives? and, What links exist between institutional and community youth gangs or groups? The last question is particularly important, since research has not been able to clearly establish the links nor significance of contacts between prison gangs or groups with those found on the streets, though there is evidence that contacts take place (Knox, 1991; Regulus, 1991; Reiner, 1992; Hunt et al., 1993).

Programs and Policy. An organized and unified response to the problem leads to the development of more consistent, positive relations among community groups, and more effective targeting of gangs and groups (Spergel, 1991b; Spergel and Kane, 1991). Community organizations, agencies, grassroots groups, and leaders must collectively identify and define the scope of the problem in strategic terms in order to facilitate a systematic discussion of potential community responses. Organizations and groups that do not cooperate in developing an effective community mobilization process will fail to maximize their organization's prevention and intervention program resources. Failures or delayed involvement in mobilization efforts occur when organizations and agencies seek to protect or enhance their unique interests, or where there already exists interagency rivalries and divergent perceptions regarding the nature of the problem and the most effective response. Equally problematic is when departments within the same organization fail to share beneficial information. The lack of interagency and intra-agency cooperation and the delayed involvement in community efforts increases the probability that organizational programs will be insufficiently related to one another and ineffectively coordinated (Spergel, 1991b). The following recommendations provide some guidance in how to promote more effective youth gang and group programming within agencies, as well as coordination between community organizations.

Law enforcement agencies need to expand juvenile or general investigative structures to incorporate intelligence collection and reporting of youth gang and group criminal activities; a mechanism to flag youth gang-related incidents at the local level would provide the necessary data for accurately measuring trends and activities in particular communities over long periods of time. State-level law enforcement (State Bureau of Investigation) must take the initiative to ensure local law enforcement agencies provide the necessary data for annual compilation and analysis. These actions would also facilitate the periodic evaluation of prevention and intervention efforts for law enforcement agencies and the community as a whole. There is also a need to train police agency and sheriff's department personnel, as well as other criminal justice and community-based agency staff, in the recognition of youth gangs, members, and gang-related incidents. Development of social intervention activities, while secondary to suppression efforts, should be incorporated into the broader enforcement framework; interventions could include collaborating with community-based agencies in targeting at-risk youth for special school or job development programs (Spergel, 1990; Ehrensaft and Spergel, 1991; Huff and McBride, 1993; Spergel et al., 1994a).

Juvenile court counselor agencies must also adopt a multi-dimensional strategy for implementing their dual mission of protecting the community and reintegrating youth into normative behavioral patterns. These agencies are particularly important in community mobilization efforts. In communities where youth gang and group problems are serious, activities should include: assisting community-based youth agencies and criminal justice organizations with suppression strategies; collaborating with schools to develop prevention and early intervention programming for youth at different risk levels; coordinating with youth service organizations (e.g. YMCA) in the development of after-school programs; and advising the courts on ways youth gang and at-risk probationers can contribute to community improvement (Chance, 1991). Agencies should also implement reporting mechanisms that identify youth gang members and incidents, since gang intelligence and related information could be shared with law enforcement and other organizations for suppression purposes, trend analysis, and for the assessment of program effectiveness.

In the correctional setting, establishing special policies and intelligence collection procedures are most important. These actions will enhance the institution's proactive capabilities, rather than depending upon defensive and reactive suppression and intervention approaches after problems have become chronic and more serious. Special coordinating structures should also be established to monitor intelligence information and to share this information with other correctional facilities, court counselor agencies, and law enforcement organizations at the local and State levels. Specific policies targeting youth gang and group problems will largely depend on the seriousness of activities; the more serious problems require the formulation and implementation of special guidelines and procedures. Corrections staff must receive adequate training that enables the recognition of youth gang and group criminal patterns, the distinctions between these two types of collectives, and a clear understanding of methods necessary to address youth gang and group crises — e.g. intimidation, assaults, and drug-trafficking (Regulus, 1991; Spergel et al., 1994a; see also Duxbury, 1993).

Lastly, schools are an integral component in any community mobilization effort, since they can provide youth with flexible and meaningful curriculum, positive role models, and access to opportunities within school that may not be available in the wider community. Youth who are involved in youth gang and group criminal and deviant activities in the community, may also demonstrate similar behavior within the school environment. Therefore schools must develop approaches that address at-risk youth and those who are known to be actively involved in group activities. Schools must build an alliance with local community-based youth agencies, citizen groups, parents, and criminal justice agencies in order to support mobilization and opportunity provision efforts. In order to achieve primary academic and social goals, the following objectives are recommended: 1) create a structure for flexible curriculum delivery to at-risk youth; 2) provide vocational education and employment experience; 3) develop a learning support system; 4) coordinate prevention and intervention efforts with community and outreach agencies; 5) formally evaluate intervention programs to determine effectiveness; and 6) develop and implement youth gang and group awareness programs for staff and students (Spergel and Alexander, 1991; Stephens, 1993). Within county and city school systems, a coordinating structure—consisting of security and behavioral specialists, school administrators, and local school program directors—should provide the central leadership for developing, implementing, and coordinating the above objectives. A concerted effort involving school officials, community organizations, and agencies will undoubtedly have a greater effect on reducing youth gang and group activity levels than those efforts of individual schools.

These research and policy recommendations are based, to a great extent, on the deficiencies discovered during this research process. At the time of this writing, organizational responses to the problem seem mostly haphazard and fragmented. A great deal of attention needs to be given to exploring the problem of collective youth crime in North Carolina, from assessing the scope of activities in particular neighborhoods or cities, to implementing and evaluating special programs and intervention approaches. The need for a broader, unified community intervention framework cannot be over emphasized. Collective youth crime involves a significant amount of complexity. Multiple causes and the resource competition between organizations and agencies, necessitates a broad and integrated community response to the problem (Spergel, 1991b). Organizational and other community participants must collaborate in an interrelated and interdependent manner, ensuring organizational and program changes remain consistent with objectives established by coordination structures (Spergel and Kane, 1991). Moreover, an integrated strategy must not only have political and economic support from governmental bodies—city and county councils, crime commissions—within the broader community, but it must also satisfy the developmental and survival needs of local organizations and agencies. In other words, there must be some indirect benefit to the organizations that are willing to cooperate in coordinated and integrated community efforts. The allocation of resources, possibly from state-level grants or local governments, must be carefully integrated into the broader strategic framework to avoid interagency competitiveness for funds, the use of inconsistent or redundant approaches, or extending the scope of strategies that do not include at-risk youth or address collective youth crime (Spergel, 1991b; Spergel and Kane, 1992; see also Spergel, 1990 and Spergel et al., 1994a).

F. Conclusion

The proliferation of youth gangs and group problems throughout North Carolina will most likely continue in the foreseeable future. The patterns of growth are most likely cyclical, depending upon very complex and interrelated conditions such as poverty, unemployment, social and economic opportunities, and access to illicit substances and other criminal opportunities. The waxing and waning of collective youth crime problems may also be a consequence of prevention and intervention programming activities; therefore it becomes critical to identify these periodic cycles to capture and utilize the causative factors for reducing the scope of the problem. Unfortunately, these cycles often end at higher plateaus than the previous levels: there are often increases in violent and other criminal activities, the number of members, the upper age limit of members, and the variety of youth gang and group structures (Miller, 1990; Klein, 1995).

The reaction to the problem, especially youth gang activities, is often determined more by political implications or philosophy, than by knowledge of group dynamics. Denial of a collective youth crime problem by public officials is an intuitive and reflexive reaction to protect the community's image and retain the necessary competitiveness for economic development; and when public officials do react, often as a result of a catalytic event or high-profile victimization, the problem is relegated to law enforcement organizations for action (Huff, 1990; Klein, 1995). Policy developments usually involve either conservative (e.g. suppression and deterrence) or liberal (e.g. social intervention) strategies, with scant attention given to sound theoretical causal factors. Perhaps implementing programs in the absence of theoretical considerations has largely contributed to their ineffectiveness at reducing measures of the problem. The virtual abandonment of program evaluation, in light of increases in collective youth crime problems in recent years, has also inhibited the development of more effective approaches and made the selection of programs speculative and inefficient (see e.g. Miller, 1990).

A comprehensive State-level collective youth crime strategy must be developed and coordinated with organizations and agencies in communities experiencing emerging and chronic youth gang and youth group crime problems. The implementation of strategies must be based on carefully researched causal factors and programs must be systematically evaluated for effectiveness. It is particularly important to confront and recognize the social context from which collective youth crime manifests and mobilize the entire community to solve the problem. However, the specific goals and objectives for preventing or reducing collective youth crime must be realistically related to existing political interests and community concerns, as well as to the actual scope and nature of the problem. Long-term comprehensive strategies (e.g. educational development, job training, and employment opportunities) and short-term strategies (e.g. suppression and outreach services) targeting members and at-risk youth, must be selected and explicitly detailed for the community as a whole and for specific organizations and agencies (Spergel and Kane, 1991).

In cities that are experiencing serious youth gang and group problems, communities should establish a coordinating structure, composed of public and private organizations and agencies, to integrate the efforts of police, prosecutors, judges, corrections officials, probation, parole, schools, businesses, and other key community representatives. A less formal collaborative approach should suffice in cities experiencing less serious or emerging collective youth crime problems. Strategies that focus on crime control and protection, social support, community mobilization, and opportunity provisions should guide program development and activities (Spergel, 1990). Regardless of where and in what context youth gangs and groups emerge, prevention and intervention strategies at the organizational and community levels must recognize the significant influences of community disorganization (e.g. social institutional and structural weaknesses) and the lack of social and economic opportunities (Spergel, 1990). Strategies that emphasize therapeutic efforts, asserts Klein (1995), have little effect on the structure of collectives, particularly youth gangs, and the social surroundings from which youth gangs and groups emerge and persist. An integrated strategic framework that incorporates suppression, intervention, and opportunities should guide community efforts. However, the successful design and integration of diverse approaches is not only dependent upon a community's ability to mobilize and coordinate the many diverging organizational interests and goals, but also to understand clearly the conditions that may be contributing to or causing the problem.

Appendix

Survey Questionnaire:
North Carolina Youth Group
Delinquency Project

North Carolina Justice Academy
Research and Development Division
Youth Group Delinquency Project
P.O. Box 99
Salemburg, NC 28385-0099
Phone: 910-525-4151 (Ext. 268 or 267)

I. Agency Identification   Request Anonymity: Yes ❏   No ❏

1. Name of respondent: _____

2. Title of respondent: _____

3. Name of department/organization: _____

4. Specific unit of department/organization of
   which respondent is a member: _____

II. The Youth Group and Youth Gang Problem

1. Do you have youth group problems in your community or juris-diction?

Yes ❏   No ❏   Not sure ❏

2. Do you have youth gang problems in your community or jurisdiction?

Yes ☐   No ☐   Not sure ☐

3. If yes to either of the above questions, describe the nature of the problem (such as characteristics of members, size of group or gang, scope of illegal activities, etc...) Please specify to which you are referring.

4. If the answer is *no* to questions 1 and 2, have you ever had problems in the past?

Yes ☐   No ☐   Not sure ☐

5. Have you ever had youth group or gang activity originating from outside your community? Please specify to which you are referring.

Yes ☐   No ☐

III. Definitional Criteria

Special Note:

For all questions in the remainder of the survey, please specify, where necessary, whether you are referring to youth groups or youth gangs.

1. Does your organization distinguish between youth groups and youth gangs?

Yes ☐   No ☐

2. What is your definition of a youth gang? Youth group? (Indicate key characteristics such as turf, colors, logo, graffiti, type of behavior, organization, etc...)

3. What key activity or behavior makes youth groups or youth gangs a concern or relevance to your work?

4. Are youth groups or youth gangs distinguished by sex, race, age, or other characteristics?

5. What are your organization's principal ways of identifying a youth group or youth gang member case?

6. How many individuals would you estimate are in youth groups or youth gangs in your community or jurisdiction?

_____

7. Does your organization keep records of youth group or youth gang membership?

Yes ☐   No ☐

8. Does your organization compile records on youth group or youth gang crime?

Yes ☐ (How?)   No ☐

9. Please Estimate the percent of each Part 1 or index offenses in your jurisdiction, or according to your caseload, that was attributed to youth groups or youth gangs in 1993.

Homicide: ____%   Rape: ____%   Robbery: ____%

Aggrav. Assault: ____%   Burglary: ____%

Larceny (non-vehicular): ____%   Vehicle theft: ____%

Arson: ____%

10. What is your organization's definition of a youth group or gang-related incident or case?

11. What percentage of youth group or youth gang-related incidents or cases coming to your organization's attention involved adults and juveniles? (according to N.C. statutes juveniles are individuals who are 15 years and younger).

a. adults: _____ %   b. juveniles: _____ %

12. If possible, please estimate the average age range of:

a. juvenile group or gang offender? from ____ to ____

b. adult group or gang offender? from ____ to ____

13. If relevant, describe the inter-relations of juvenile and adult youth group or gang problems.

14. Are there youth groups or youth gangs present which appear to be affiliated with or used by adult criminal organizations for illicit purposes, or for any other reason that would be of concern to your organization? If yes, please specify.

15. Of the youth group or youth gang members who came to your attention in recent years, what percent were:

    a. White: _____%

    b. Black: _____%
    (includes African American, Jamaican, and others)

    c. Hispanic: _____%

    d. Asian: _____%
    (includes any Asian ancestry)

16. What percent of youth group or youth gang offenders who came to your attention in recent years were female?

_____ %

17. What percentage of youth group or youth gang offenders who came to your organization's attention in 1993 had prior police records?

_____ %

18. What are the general characteristics of the youth groups or youth gangs in your community?

    a. What is the average size? from _____ to _____

    b. What is the average age? from _____ to _____

    c. Are they from the same or different neighborhoods or areas?

        Same   Different

    c. Is drug distribution one of the primary purposes of existence?

        Yes ☐   No ☐

    d. Are members involved in the importation of drugs from outside your jurisdiction?

        Yes ☐   No ☐

19. Has the youth group or youth gang situation changed in recent years? If yes, how?

        Yes ☐   No ☐

20 If there is a serious youth group or gang problem in your community, please estimate the current drop out rate of youth from schools in your area.

                _____ %

IV. Organization and Program Structure

1. What is your organization's goals and objectives in regard to the youth group or youth gang problem?

2. Are there special policies and procedures which guide staff in their activities with youth groups or youth gangs?

Yes ☐   No ☐

3. Are such policies and procedures written?

Yes ☐   No ☐

4. Is special training available to personnel for dealing with youth groups or youth gangs? If yes, please describe.

5. What are the primary objectives or goals of your organization in dealing with the youth group or youth gang problem?

V. Community Relations

1. Is there a community group your organization works with that assists you in the coordination and implementation of youth group or youth gang intervention and prevention programs? If yes, please describe.

Yes ☐   No ☐

2. With which other justice or community agencies is your organization in most contact? Please list up to five based on priority.

a.

b.

c.

d.

e.

3. Are there any interagency task forces or community-wide organizations which attempted to coordinate efforts to deal with the youth group or youth gang problem in recent years? If yes, please describe.

Yes ☐   No ☐

4. Classify these efforts:

Not effective ❏   Somewhat effective ❏   Very effective ❏

5. Please comment on your rating.

VI. Program/Policy Evaluation Comments

1. How effective do you think your organization was in 1993 in dealing with the gang problem?

Not sure ❏   Not effective ❏   Moderately effective ❏
Very effective ❏

2. What has your department or organization done that you feel has been particularly successful in dealing with the youth group or youth gang problem? Please provide statistics, if relevant and available.

3. What do you think are the five most important causes of the youth group or youth gang problem in your community? Please rank.

a.

b.

c.

d.

e.

4. What do you think are the five best ways employed by your department or organization for dealing with the youth group or youth gang problem? Please rank.

a.

b.

c.

d.

e.

5. Please comment on your rankings.

6. What specifically do you think should be done in the future, which has not been done thus far, to address the problem of youth group or youth gang delinquency?

VII. Law Enforcement Organizations
(all other organizations skip to section VIII.)

1. How many people are in your police department?

   Total: _____   Civilian: _____   Sworn: _____

2. Does your department have individuals specially trained to investigate and monitor youth groups or youth gangs within your jurisdiction?

   Yes ☐   No ☐ *(go to question 4)*

3. Do these officers receive special training?

   Yes ☐   No ☐

4. Comment on the nature of the training.

5. Does your department have programs or services specifically aimed at youth groups or youth gangs?

   Yes ☐   No ☐ *(go to question 7)*

6. What are these programs or services?

7. Does your department have a budget for specifically addressing youth group or youth gang delinquency? If yes, how much is allocated annually?

Yes ☐   No ☐

Amount allocated: $ _____

8. Given the opportunity and resources, what would your department do to improve programs or practices aimed at youth groups or youth gangs?

9. Has your department ever been involved in local, statewide, or federal task forces that focus on youth groups and youth gang delinquency? If yes, please describe some of your activities and coordination efforts.

Yes ☐   No ☐

10. Does your department have a written policy concerning youth group and youth gang delinquency?

Yes ☐   No ☐

11. Can you send me any available information with this question-naire?

Yes ☐   No ☐

VIII. Final Remarks

1. Are you interested in receiving the results of this study when it is completed?

Yes ☐   No ☐

2. Who else would you recommend contacting within your jurisdiction or within the State who could provide information on the nature and scope of the youth group or youth gang delinquency problem?

<u>Name</u>   <u>Organization Address</u>   <u>Phone</u>

3. If you have any other comments regarding the scope of this survey or have any information which you feel may be of some value to this study, please comment below and/or enclose relevant documents when you return this questionnaire.

4. Your correct mailing address and phone number:

5. Please return this survey as soon as possible, using the self addressed envelope provided. The North Carolina Justice Academy appreciates your support in this research project.

References

Administrative Office of the Courts (1992). *Annual Report of the Administrative Office of the Courts.* North Carolina Department of Justice, Raleigh.

Arizona Criminal Justice Commission (1991). *Substance Abuse in Arizona, Gang Activity in Arizona: Survey of Public Schools, Institutions of Higher Education and Law Enforcement Authorities.* Phoenix, Arizona.

Avery, P. (1988). L.A. Gangs Reportedly Dealing Crack in Alaska. *San Francisco Examiner* (April).

Ball, R. and Curry, D. (1995). The Logic of Definition in Criminology: Purposes and Methods for Defining 'Gangs.' *Criminology*, 33(2): 225-245.

Bastian, L. and Taylor, B. (1991). *School Crime. A National Crime Victimization Survey Report.* U.S. Department of Justice, Office of Justice Programs, Bureau of Justice Statistics.

Block, C., Block R., and Block, R. (1993). *Street Gangs in Chicago.* Research in Brief. National Institute of Justice, Office of Justice Programs, U.S. Department of Justice. Washington, D.C.

Blumstein, A. (1995). Prisons. In J. Wilson and J. Petersilia (Eds.), *Crime.* San Francisco, CA: ICS Press.

_____, Farrington, D., and Miotra, S. (1985). Delinquency Careers: Innocents, Desisters, and Persisters. In M. Tonry and N. Morris (Eds.), *Crime and Justice: An Annual Review of Research* (Vol. 6). Chicago: University of Chicago Press.

_____, Cohen, J., and Farrington, D. (1988). Career Criminal Research: Its Value in Criminology. *Criminology*, 26: 1-35.

Bobrowski, L. (1988). *Collecting, Organizing, and Reporting Street Gang Crime.* Chicago Police Department, Special Functions Group.

Brooks, K. and Bailey, S. (1992). Teen Pleads Guilty in Fatal Shooting at State Fair. *The News and Observer* (February).

Burgess, E. (1928). The Growth of the City. In R. Park, E. Burgess, and R. McKenzie (Eds.), *The City.* Chicago: University of Chicago Press.

_____, and Akers, R. (1966). A Differential Association-Reinforcement Theory of Criminal Behavior. *Social Problems*, 14: 128-147.

Bursik, R. and Grasmick, G. (1993). *Neighborhoods and Crime*. New York: Lexington Books.

Camp, G. and Camp, C. (1985). *Prison Gangs: Their Extent, Nature, and Impact on Prisons*. Washington, D.C.: U.S. Government Printing Office.

_____, and Camp, G. (1988). *Management Strategies for Combating Prison Gang Violence*. South Salem, NY: Criminal Justice Institute (September).

Campbell, A. (1990). Female Participation in Gangs. In C. Huff (Ed.), *Gangs in America*. Newbury Park, CA: Sage.

Cartwright, D. and Howard, K. (1966). *Multivariate Analysis of Gang Delinquency: Ecological Influences*. Multivariate Behavioral Research, 1: 321-337.

_____,Thomson, B., and Schwartz, H. (1975). *Gang Delinquency*. Monterey, CA: Brooks/Cole.

Chin, K. (1990). Chinese Gangs and Extortion. In C. Huff (Ed.), *Gangs in America*. Newbury Park, CA: Sage.

Chance, R. (1991). *Probation Model* (Draft). National Youth Gang Suppression and Intervention Research and Development Program. School of Social Service Administration, University of Chicago.

Clements, C. (1988). Delinquency Prevention and Treatment: A Community-Centered Perspective. *Criminal Justice and Behavior*, 15: 286-305.

Cloward, R. and Ohlin, L. (1960). *Delinquency and Opportunity: A Theory of Delinquent Gangs*. New York: Free Press.

Cohen, A. (1955). *Delinquent Boys: The Culture of the Gang*. New York: Free Press.

Cohen, B. (1965). Intercine Conflict: The Offender. In T. Sellin and M. Wolfgang (Eds.), *Delinquency: Selected Studies*. New York: Wiley and Sons.

_____.(1969). The Delinquency of Gangs and Spontaneous Groups. In T. Sellin and M. Wolfgang (Eds.), *Delinquency: Selected Studies*. New York: Wiley and Sons.

_____, and Land, K. (1987). Sociological Positivism and the Explanation of Criminality. In F. Gottfredson and T. Hirschi (Eds.), *Positive Criminology*. Newbury Park, CA: Sage.

Cohen, A. and Short, J. (1958). Research in Delinquent Subcultures. *Journal of Social Issues*, 14(3): 20-37.

Cohen, J. (1986). Research on Criminal Careers: Individual Frequency Rates and Offense Seriousness. In A. Blumstein, J. Cohen, J. Roth, and C. Visher (Eds.), *Criminal Careers and 'Career Criminals'* (Vol. 1). Washington, D.C.: National Academy Press.

Cohen, M., Williams, K., and Bekelman, A. (1994). *National Evaluation of the Youth Gang Drug Prevention Program* (Executive Summary of Final Report). Administration on Children, Youth and Families. Administration for Children and Families. U.S. Department of Health and Human Services. Washington, D.C.

Collins, C. (1979). *Street Gangs: Profiles for Police*. New York: New York City Police Department.

Conklin, J. (1992). *Criminology* (4th Edition). New York: MacMillian.

Conly, C. (1993). *Street Gangs: Current Knowledge and Strategies*. National Institute of Justice, Office of Justice Programs, U.S. Department of Justice. Washington, D.

Corsica, J. (1993). Employment Training Interventions. In A. Goldstein and R. Huff (Eds.),*The Gang Intervention Handbook*. Champaign, IL: Research Press.

Covey, H., Menard, S., and Franzese, R. (1992). *Juvenile Gangs*. Springfield, IL: Charles C. Thomas Publisher.

Curry, G. (1994). *Extended National Assessment of Anti-Gang Law Enforcement Information Sources* (Preliminary Results). Paper presented at the American Society of Criminology Conference (November 1994).

_____, and Spergel, I. (1988). Gang Homicide, Delinquency, and Community. *Criminology*, 26: 381-405.

_____, and Spergel, I. (1993). Gang Involvement and Delinquency Among Hispanic and African American Adolescent Males. *Journal of Research in Crime and Delinquency*, 29: 273-291.

_____, Bell, A., and Fox, R. (1993). *Law Enforcement Records and Crime Problems*. Interim report submitted to the National Institute of Justice, Office of Justice Programs, U.S. Department of Justice. Washington, D.C.

_____, Ball, R., and Fox, R. (1994). *Gang Crime and Law Enforcement Recordkeeping*. Research in Brief. National Institute of Justice, U.S. Department of Justice. Washington, D.C.

Defleur, L. (1967). Delinquent Gangs in a Cross-Cultural Perspective: The Case of Cordoba. *Journal of Research in Crime and Delinquency*, 4: 132-141.

Dillon, W. and Goldstein, M. (1984). *Multivariate Analysis: Methods and Applications*. New York: Wiley and Sons.

Dolan, E. and Finney, S. (1984). *Youth Gangs*. New York: Simon and Schuster.

Duran, M. (1987). *Specialized Gang Supervision Program Progress Report*. Los Angeles County Probation Department.

Durkheim, E. (1933). *The Division of Labor in Society* (revised edition). New York: Free Press.

Duster, T. (1987). Crime, Youth Unemployment, and the Underclass. *Journal of Research in Crime and Delinquency*, 33(1): 22-29.

Duxbury, E. (1993). Correctional Interventions. In A. Goldstein and C. Huff (Eds.), *The Gang Intervention Handbook*. Champaign, IL: Research Press.

Ehrensaft, K. and Spergel, I. (1991). *Police Model* (Draft). National Youth Gang Suppression and Intervention Research and Development Program. School of Social Service Administration, University of Chicago.

Eisley, M and Seymore, K. (1993). Millbrook Students Try to Duck Gang Label. *The News and Observer* (May).

Erickson, M. and Jensen, G. (1977). Delinquency is Still Group Behavior! Toward Revitalizing the Group Premise in the Sociology of Deviance. *Journal of Criminal Law and Criminology*, 68: 262-273.

Esbensen, F. and Huizinga, D. (1993). Gangs, Drugs, and Delinquency in a Survey of Urban Youth. *Criminology*, 31: 565-587.

Fagan, J. (1988). *The Social Organization of Drug Use and Drug Dealing Among Urban Gangs*. Criminal Justice Center, John Jay College of Criminal Justice, New York.

_____. (1989). The Social Organization of Drug Use and Drug Dealing Among Urban Gangs. *Criminology*, 24: 439-471.

_____. (1990). Social Process of Delinquency and Drug Use Among Urban Gangs. In C. Huff (Ed.), *Gangs in America*. Newbury Park, CA: Sage.

_____, Piper, E., and Moore, M. (1986). Violent Delinquents and Urban Youths. *Criminology*, 24: 439-471.

Farrington, D. (1986). Age and Crime. In M. Tonry and N. Morris (Eds.), *Crime and Justice: An Annual Review of Research* (Vol. 7). Chicago: University of Chicago Press.

_____. (1990). Implication of Criminal Career Research for the Prevention of Offending. *Journal of Adolescence*, 13: 93-113.

_____. (1992). Criminal Career Research: Lessons for Crime Prevention. *Studies on Crime and Crime Prevention* (Vol. 1, No. 1). National Council for Crime Prevention, England.

Feldman, M. (1977). *Criminal Behavior: A Psychological Analysis*. London: Wiley.

Felson, M. (1987). Routine Activities and Crime Prevention in the Developing Metropolis. *Criminology*, 25: 911-931.

Flannery, J. (1989). Big-City Gangs Open Smaller 'Franchises.' *Omaha World Herold* (July).

Ford, A. and Chavez, S. (1992). Gang Report Scorned as Unjust Stereotype. Los Angeles Times (May).

Friedman, J., Mann, F., and Friedman, A. (1975). A Profile of Juvenile Street Gang Members. *Adolescence*, 10: 563-607.

Gardener, S. (1993). *Street Gangs*. New York: Franklin Watts.

Gilbert, J. (1986). *A Cycle of Outrage: America's Reaction to Juvenile Delinquency in the 1950s*. New York: Oxford University Press.

Gold, M. and Mattick, H. (1974). *Experiment in the Streets: The Chicago Youth Development Project*. Institute for Social Research, University of Michigan.

Goldstein, A. (1991). *Delinquent Gangs: A Psychological Perspective*. Champaign, IL: Research Press.

_____. (1993a). Gang Interventions: A Historical Review. In A. Goldstein and C. Huff (Eds.), *The Gang Intervention Handbook*. Champaign, IL: Research Press.

_____. (1993b). Gang Intervention: Issues and Opportunities. In A. Goldstein and C. Huff (Eds.), *The Gang Intervention Handbook*. Champaign, IL: Research Press.

Gorsuch, R. (1983). *Factor Analysis* (2nd Edition). Hillsdale, NJ: Lawrence Erlbaum Associates.

Gottfredson, M. and Hirschi, T. (1990). *A General Theory of Crime*. California: Stanford University Press.

Governor's Organized Crime Prevention Commission (1991). *New Mexico Street Gangs*. Office of the Governor. Albuquerque, New Mexico.

Hagedorn, J. (1988). *People and Folks: Gangs, Crime, and the Underclass in a Rust Belt City*. Chicago: Lake View Press.

_____. (1991). Gangs, Neighborhoods, and Public Policy. *Social Problems*, 38(4): 529-542.

_____. (1990). Back in the Field Again: Gang Research in the Nineties. In R. Huff (Ed.) *Gangs in America*. Newbury Park, CA: Sage.

Hagan, J. (1985). *Modern Criminology: Crime, Criminal Behavior, and its Control*. New York: McGraw-Hill.

Hagan, R. and Jones, W. (1983). A Role-Theoretical Model of Criminal Conduct. In W. Laufer and J. Day (Eds.), *Personality Theory, Moral Development, and Criminal Behavior*. Lexington, MA: Lexington.

Hansen, M., Hurwitz, W., and Madow, W. (1954). *Sample Survey Methods and Theory*. New York: John Wiley and Sons.

Hanson, E. (1990). Gangs Find Fertile Turf Here. *Houston Chronicle* (February).

Hardman, D. (1969). Small Town Gang. *Journal of Criminal Law, Criminology, and Police Science*, 60: 173-181.

Harney, J. and Moses, P. (1992). L.A. Gang Members Moving to New York. *New York Post* (October).

Healy, T. (1993). Police Say Five in Gang Known, Authorities Seek Victims in Rape. *The News and Observer* (April).

Heimberger, A. (1993). Police Seek Man Shot After Fest. *The News and Observer* (April).

Hirschi, T. (1969). *Causes of Delinquency*. Berkeley, CA: University of California Press.

_____. (1986). On the Compatibility of Rational Choice and Social Control Theories of Crime. In D. Cornish and R. Clarke (Eds.), *The Reasoning Criminal: Rational Choice Perspective on Offending*. New York: Springer-Verlag.

Hood, R. and Sparks, R. (1977). Subcultural and Gang Delinquency. In L. Radzinowicz and M. Wolfgang (Eds.), *Crime and Justice, Volume 1*. New York: Basic Books, Inc.

Horowitz, R. (1983). *Honor and the American Dream*. New Brunswick, NJ: Rutgers University Press.

_____. (1987). Community Tolerance of Gang Violence. *Social Problems*, 30(5): 437-450.

_____. (1990). Sociological Perspective on Gangs. In R. Huff (Ed.), *Gangs in America*. Newbury Park, CA: Sage.

_____, and Schwartz, G. (1974). Honor, Normative Ambiguity, and Gang Violence. *American Sociological Review*, 39: 238-251.

Howell, J. (1994). *Recent Youth Gang Research: Program and Research Implications*. Report by the Director of Research and Program Development. Office of Juvenile Justice and Delinquency Prevention, U.S. Department of Justice. Washington, D.C.

Huck, S., Cormier, W., and Bounds, W. (1974). *Reading Statistics and Research*. New York: Harper and Row.

Huff, R. (1989). Youth Gangs and Public Policy. *Crime and Delinquency*, 35: 524-537.

_____.(1993). Gangs and Public Policy: Macrolevel Interventions. In A. Goldstein and R. Huff (Eds.), *The Gang Intervention Handbook*. Champaign, IL: Research Press.

_____, and McBride, W. (1993). Gangs and the Police. In A. Goldstein and C. Huff (Eds.), *The Gang Intervention Handbook*. Champaign, IL: Research Press.

Hunt, G., Reigel, S., Morales, T., and Waldorf, D. (1993). Changes in Prison Culture: Prison Gangs and the Case of the 'Pepsi' Generation. *Social Problems*, 40(3): 398-409.

Ianni, F. (1974). *Black Mafia*. New York: Simon and Schuster.

_____.(1989). *The Search for Structure. Report on American Youth Today*. New York: Free Press.

Inciardi, J. (1990). A Crack-Violence Connection Within a Population of Hardcore Adolescent Offenders. In M. Rosa, E. Lambert, and B. Gropper (Eds.), *Drugs and Violence: Causes, Correlations, and Consequences*. U.S. Department of Health and Human Services, Public Health Service. National Institute on Drug Abuse.

Institute of Law and Justice (1994). *Gang Prosecution in the U.S.* National Institute of Justice, Office of Justice Programs, U.S. Department of Justice.

Jackson, R. and McBride, W. (1985). *Understanding Street Gangs*. Sacramento: Custom Publishing.

Jackson, P. and Rudman, C. (1993). Moral Panic and the Response to Gangs in California. In S. Cummings and D. Monti (Eds.), *Gangs: The Origin and Impact of Contemporary Youth Gangs in the U.S.* Albany, NY: State University of New York Press.

Jankowski, M. (1991). *Islands in the Street: Gangs and American Urban Society*. Berkeley, CA: University of California Press.

Jenson, W., Clark, E., Walker, H., and Kehle, T. (1991). Behavior Disorders: Training Needs for School Psychologists. In G. Stoner, M. Shinn, and H. Walker (Eds.), *Interventions for Achievement and Behavior Problems*. Kent, OH: National Association for School Psychologists.

Johnstone, J. (1981). Youth Gangs and the Black Suburbs. *Pacific Sociological Review*, 24: 355-375.

Jupp, V. (1989). *Methods of Criminological Research*. London: Unwin Hyman.

Kane, C. and Regulus, T. (1990). *Parole Model*. National Youth Gang Suppression and Intervention Research and Development Program, School of Social Service Administration, University of Chicago.

Kennedy, L. and Baron, S. (1993). Routine Activities and a Subculture of Violence: A Study of Violence on the Streets. *Journal of Research in Crime and Delinquency*, 30(1): 88-112.

Kituse, J. and Dietrick, D. (1959). Delinquent Boys: A Critique. *American Sociological Review*, 24: 208-215.

Klein, M. (1968a). Impressions of Juvenile Gang Members. *Adolescence*, 3: 53-78.

_____. (1968b). *From Association to Guilt: The Group Guidance Project in Juvenile Gang Intervention.* Los Angeles, CA: University of Southern California, Youth Studies Center, and the Los Angeles County Probation Department.

_____. (1971). *Street Gangs and Street Workers.* Englewood Cliffs, NJ: Prentice-Hall.

_____. (1992). *Attempting Gang Control by Suppression: The Misuse of Deterrence Principles.* Social Science Research Institute, University of Southern California, Los Angeles. Draft.

_____. (1995). *The American Street Gang: Its Nature, Prevalence, and Control.* New York: Oxford University Press.

_____. (1995). Street Gang Cycles. In J. Wilson and J. Petersilia (Eds.), *Crime.* San Francisco, CA: ICS Press.

_____, and Crawford, L. (1967). Groups, Gangs, and Cohesiveness. *Journal of Research in Crime and Delinquency,* 4: 63-75.

_____, and Maxson, C. (1987). Street Gang Violence. In M. Wolfgang and N. Weiner (Eds.), *Violent Crime, Violent Criminals.* Beverly Hills, CA: Sage.

_____, and Meyerhoff (Eds.)(1967). *Juvenile Gangs in Conflict: Theory, Research, and Action.* Englewood Hills, NJ: Prentice-Hall.

_____, Maxson, C., and Cunningham, L. (1991). "Crack," Street Gangs, and Violence. *Criminology,* 29: 623-650.

Knox, G. (1991). *An Introduction to Gangs.* Berrien Springs, MI: Vande Vere Publishing, Inc.

Kobrin, S. (1959). The Chicago Area Project: A Twenty-Five Year Assessment. *Annals of the American Academy of Political and Social Science,* 322: 1-29.

Kodluboy, D. and Evenrud, L. (1993). School-based Interventions: Best Practices and Critical Issues. In A. Goldstein and R. Huff (Eds.), *The Gang Intervention Handbook.* Champaign, IL: Research Press.

Kornhauser, R. (1978). *Social Sources of Delinquency.* Chicago: University of Chicago Press.

Lucore, P. (1975). Cohesiveness in the Gang. In D. Cartwright, B. Thomson, and H. Schwartz (Eds.), *Gang Delinquency.* Pacific Grove, CA: Brooks/Cole.

Martin, M. (1992). Act Before Violence Begins, Experts Say. *Medford Mail Tribune* (March).

Maxson, C. (1995). *Street Gangs and Drug Sales in Two Suburban Cities.* Research in Brief. National Institute of Justice, U.S. Department of Justice.

_____. (1993). Investigating Gang Migration: Contextual Issues for Intervention. *The Gang Journal*, 1(2): 1-8.

_____, and Klein, M. (1993). *The Scope of Street Gang Migration in the U.S.: An Interim Report to Survey Participants.* National Institute of Justice, Office of Justice Programs, U.S. Department of Justice. Washington, D.C.

_____, and Klein, M. (1990). Street Gang Violence: Twice as Great or Half as Great? In C. Huff (Ed.), *Gangs in America.* Newbury Park, CA: Sage.

_____, Gordon, M. and Klein, M. (1985). Differences Between Gang and Nongang Homicides. *Criminology*, 23: 209-221.

_____, Klein, M. and Cunningham, L. (1993). *Street Gangs and Drug Sales: A Report to the National Institute of Justice.* Office of Justice Programs, U.S. Department of Justice. Washington, D.C.

McClain, K. (1994). *Gang Members Get Record Sentences.* Charlotte Observer (September).

McKinney, K. (1988). Juvenile Gangs: Crime and Drug Trafficking. *Juvenile Justice Bulletin.* Office of Juvenile Justice and Delinquency Prevention, U.S. Department of Justice (September).

Merton, R. (1938). Social Structure and Anomie. *American Sociological Review*, 3: 672-682.

Mieczkowski, T. (1986). Geeking Up and Throwing Down: Heroin Street Life in Detroit. *Criminology*, 24: 645-666.

Miller, W. (1958). Lower Class Culture as a Generating Milieu of Gang Delinquency. *Journal of Social Issues*, 14: 5-19.

_____. (1962). The Impact of 'Total Community' Delinquency Control Project. *Social Problems*, 10: 168-191.

_____. (1975). *Violence by Youth Gangs and Youth Groups as a Crime Problem in Major American Cities.* Report to the Office of Juvenile Justice and Delinquency Prevention, National Institute for Juvenile

Justice and Delinquency Prevention, U.S. Department of Justice. Washington, D.C.

———. (1977). *Conceptions, Definitions, and Images of Youth Gangs.* Cambridge, MA: Center for Criminal Justice, Harvard University.

———. (1982). *Crime by Youth Gangs and Groups in the United States.* Report to the Office of Juvenile Justice and Delinquency Prevention, National Institute for Juvenile Justice and Delinquency Prevention, U.S. Department of Justice. Washington, D.C.

———. (1990). Why the United States has Failed to Solve its Youth Gang Problem. In R. Huff (Ed.), *Gangs in America.* Newbury Park, CA: Sage.

Moore, J. (1978). *Homeboys.* Philadelphia: Temple University Press.

———. (1985). Isolation and Stigmatization in the Development of the Underclass: The Case of Chicano Gangs in East Los Angeles. *Social Problems,* 33: 1-10.

———. (1989). Is There a Hispanic Underclass? *Social Science Quarterly,* 70: 265-284.

———. (1990). Gangs, Drugs, and Violence. In M. Rosa, E. Lambert, and B. Gropper (Eds.), *Drugs and Violence: Causes, Correlates, and Consequences.* U.S. Department of Health and Human Services, Public Health Service, National Institute on Drug Abuse (NIDA Research Monograph 103).

———. (1993). Gangs, Drugs, and Violence. In S. Cummings and D. Monti (Eds.), *Gangs: The Origins and Impact of Contemporary Youth Gangs in the U.S.* Albany, NY: State University of New York Press.

Morales, D. (1992). *The 1992 Texas Attorney General's Gang Report.* Office of the Attorney General, State of Texas.

Morash, M. (1983). Gangs, Groups, and Delinquency. *British Journal of Criminology,* 23(4): 309-335.

National Institute of Corrections (1991). *Management Strategies in Disturbances and with Gangs/Disruptive Groups.* U.S. Department of Justice (October).

Needle, J. and Stapleton, W. (1983). *Police Handling of Youth Gangs.* National Institute of Juvenile Justice and Delinquency Prevention, Office of Juvenile Justice and Delinquency Prevention, U.S. Department of Justice. Washington, D.C.

NNICC (1995). *The National Narcotics Intelligence Consumers Committee Report 1994: The Supply of Illicit Drugs to the United States.* Drug Enforcement Administration, U.S. Department of Justice.

North Carolina Department of Justice (1992). *Crime in North Carolina.* Raleigh: State Bureau of Investigation.

North Carolina Governor's Crime Commission (1992). *Illicit Drugs in North Carolina.* Report by the Criminal Justice Analysis Center. Raleigh, North Carolina.

O'Brien, C. (1993a). Chapel Hill Police Try to Gauge Extent of Gang Activity. *The News and Observer* (January).

_____. (1993b). Teen Gang Member Sees No Escape. *Asheville Citizen-Times* (January).

Office of Juvenile Justice and Delinquency Prevention (1989). *Using the Law to Improve School Order and Safety.* U.S. Department of Justice. Washington, D.C.

Park, R. (1936). Human Ecology. *American Journal of Sociology*, 42: 1-15.

Patterson, G. and Yoerger, K. (1993). Developmental Models for Delinquent Behavior. In S. Hodgins (Ed.), *Mental Disorder and Crime.* Newbury Park, CA: Sage.

Poole, E. and Regoli, R. (1979). Parental Support, Delinquent Friends, and Delinquency: A Test of Interaction Effects. *Journal of Criminal Law and Criminology*, 70(2): 188-193.

Pritchess, P. (1979). *Street Gangs.* Los Angeles County Sheriff's Department, Los Angeles County, Youth Services Bureau, Street Gang Detail.

Rand, A. (1987). Transitional Life Events and Desistance from Delinquency and Crime. In M. Wolfgang, T. Thornberry, and R. Figlio (Eds.), *From Boy to Man, From Delinquency to Crime.* Chicago: University of Chicago Press.

Reckless, W. (1961). *The Crime Problem* (revised edition). New York: Appleton-Century-Crofts.

Regoli, R. and Hewitt, J. (1994). *Delinquency in Society* (second edition). New York: McGraw-Hill.

Regulus, T. (1991). *Corrections Model* (Draft). National Youth Gang Suppression and Intervention Research and Development Program. School of Social Service Administration, University of Chicago.

Reiner, I. (1992). *Gangs, Crime, and Violence in Los Angeles: Findings and Proposals from the District Attorney's Office.* National Institute of Justice, Office of Justice Programs, U.S. Department of Justice. Washington, D.C.

Reiss, A. (1986). Why are Communities Important for Understanding Crime? In A. Reiss and M. Tonry (Eds.), *Communities and Crime.* Chicago: University of Chicago Press.

————. (1988). Co-Offending and Criminal Careers. In M. Tonry and N. Morris (Eds.), *Crime and Justice: A Review of Research* (Vol. 10). Chicago, IL: University of Chicago Press.

————, and Farrington, D. (1991). Advancing Knowledge About Co-Offending: Results From a Prospective Longitudinal Survey of London Males. *Journal of Criminal Law and Criminology*, 82(20): 360-395.

Ribisl, K., and Davidson, W. (1993). Community Change Interventions. In A. Goldstein and C. Huff (Eds.), *The Gang Intervention Handbook.* Champaign, IL: Research Press.

Rosembaum, D. and Grant, J. (1983). *Gangs and Youth Problems in Evanston: Research Findings and Policy Options.* Center for Urban Affairs and Policy Research, Northwestern University.

Rubel, R. and Ames, N. (1986). *Reducing School Crime and Student Misbehavior: A Problem-Solving Strategy. Issues and Practices.* National Institute of Justice, Office of Communication and Research Utilization, U,S, Department of Justice. Washington, D.C.

Rubin, J. (1992). *Punishment Chart for North Carolina Crimes.* Institute of Government, University of North Carolina.

Rutler, M. and Giller, H. (1983). *Juvenile Delinquency: Trends and Perspectives.* New York: The Guilded Press.

Sanders, W. (1994). *Gangbangs and Drive-bys.* New York: Aldine-Gruyter.

Sampson, R. (1986). The Effects of Urbanization and Neighborhood Characteristics on Criminal Victimization. In R. Faglio, S. Hakim, and G. Rengert (Eds.), *Metropolitan Crime Patterns.* Monsey, NY: Willow Tree Press.

_____, and Laub, J. (1993). *Crime in the Making: Pathways and Turning Points Through Life*. Cambridge: Harvard University Press.

Sarnecki, J. (1986). *Delinquent Networks*. Stockholm: Research Division, National Swedish Council for Crime Prevention, Report Number 1986:1.

Schlossman, S., Zellman, G., and Shavelson, R. (1984). *Delinquency Prevention in South Chicago. A Fifty Year Assessment of the Chicago Area Project*. Santa Monica, CA: Rand.

Sellin, T. and Wolfgang, M. (1964). *The Measurement of Delinquency*. New York: John Wiley and Sons.

_____, and Wolfgang, M. (1969). Measuring Delinquency. In T. Sellin and M. Wolfgang (Eds.), *Delinquency: Selected Studies*. New York: John Wiley and Sons.

Shaw, C. and McKay, H. (1942). *Juvenile Delinquency and Urban Areas*. Chicago: University of Chicago Press.

Short, J. (1968). *Gang Delinquency and Delinquent Subcultures*. New York: Harper & Row.

_____, and Strodtbeck, F. (1965). *Group Process and Gang Delinquency*. Chicago: University of Chicago Press.

_____. (1989). Exploring Integration of Theoretical Levels of Explanation: Notes on Gang Delinquency. In S. Messner, K. Krohn and A. Liska (Eds.), *Theoretical Integration in the Study of Deviance and Crime: Problems and Prospects*. Albany, NY: State University of New York Press.

Simons, R., Wu, C., Conger, R., and Lorenz, F. (1994). Two Routes to Delinquency: Difference Between Early and Late Starters in the Impact of Parenting and Deviant Peers. *Criminology*, 32(2): 247-275.

Skolnick, J. (1992). Gangs in the Post-Industrial Ghetto. *The American Prospect*, 8: 109-120.

_____. (1993). *Gang Organization and Migration*. Report to the Department of Justice, State of California.

_____, Bluthenthal, R., and Correl, T. (1993). Gang Organization and Migration. In S. Cummings and D. Monti (Eds.), *Gangs: The Origins and Impact of Contemporary Youth Gangs in the U.S.* Albany, NY: State University of New York.

————, Correl, T., Narrio, E., and Rabb, R. (1988). *The Social Structure of Street Gang Drug Dealing.* Center for the Study of Law and Society, University of California, Berkeley.

Spergel, I. (1964). *Slumtown, Racketville, Haulburg.* Chicago: University of Chicago Press.

————. (1983). *Violent Gangs in Chicago: Segmentation and Integration.* School of Social Service Administration, University of Chicago.

————. (1984). Violent Gangs in Chicago: In Search of Social Policy. *Social Service Review,* 58: 199-226.

————. (1986). The Violent Gang in Chicago: A Local Community Approach. *Social Service Review,* 60: 94-131.

————. (1990). Youth Gangs: Continuity and Change. In N. Morris (Ed.), *Crime and Delinquency: An Annual Review of Research, Vol. 12.* Chicago: University of Chicago Press.

————. (1991a). *Youth Gangs: Problem and Response.* National Youth Gang Suppression and Intervention Program. School of Social Science Administration, University of Chicago.

————. (1991b). *General Community Design Model* (Draft). National Youth Gang Suppression and Intervention Research and Development Program. School of Social Service Administration, University of Chicago.

————. (1995). *The Youth Gang Problem: A Community Approach.* New York: Oxford University Press.

————, and Alexander, A. (1991). *A School-Based Model* (Draft). National Youth Gang Suppression and Intervention Research and Development Program. School of Social Service Administration, University of Chicago.

————, and Chance, R. (1990). *Community and Institutional Responses to the Youth Gang Problem.* National Youth Gang Suppression and Intervention Program. School of Social Science Administration, University of Chicago.

————, and Chance, R. (1991). National Youth Gang Suppression and Intervention Program. *National Institute of Justice Reports,* 224: 21-24.

————, Chance R., Ehrensaft, K., Regulus, T., Kane, C., Laseter, R., Alexander, A., and Oh, S. (1994a). *Gang Suppression and Interven-*

tion: Community Models (Research Summary). National Youth Gang Suppression and Intervention Research and Development Program. School of Social Service Administration, University of Chicago.

_____, and Curry, D. (1990a). Strategies and Perceived Effectiveness in Dealing with the Youth Gang Problem. In C. Huff (Ed.), *Gangs in America*. Newbury Park, CA: Sage.

_____, and Curry, D. (1990b). The National Youth Gang Survey: A Research and Development Process. In A. Goldstein and C. Huff (Eds.), *The Gang Intervention Handbook*. Champaign, IL: Research Press.

_____, Curry, D., Chance R., and Ross, R. (1990). *Survey of Youth Gang Problems and Programs in 45 Cities and 6 Sites*. National Youth Gang Suppression and Intervention Research and Development Program. School of Social Science Administration, University of Chicago.

_____, Curry, D., Chance R., Kane, C., Ross, R., Alexander, A., Simmons, E., and Oh, S. (1994b). *Gang Suppression and Intervention: Problem and Response* (Research Summary). National Youth Gang Suppression and Intervention Research and Development Program. School of Social Service Administration, University of Chicago.

_____, and Ehrensaft, K. (1991). *Grassroots Organization Model* (Draft). National Youth Gang Suppression and Intervention Research and Development Program. School of Social Service Administration, University of Chicago.

_____, and Kane, C. (1991). *Community Mobilization Model* (Draft). National Youth Gang Suppression and Intervention Research and Development Program. School of Social Service Administration, University of Chicago.

Spiller, B. (1965). Delinquency and Middle Class Goals. *Journal of Criminal Law, Criminology, and Police Science*, 56: 463-478.

Stark, R. (1987). Deviant Places: A Theory of the Ecology of Crime. *Criminology*, 25: 893-909.

Stephens, R. (1993). School-Based Interventions: Safety and Security. In A. Goldstein and C. Huff (Eds.), *The Gang Intervention Handbook*. Champaign, IL: Research Press.

Stevens, J. (1986). *Applied Multivariate Statistics for the Social Sciences*. Hillsdale, NJ: Lawrence Erlbaum Associates.

Sutherland, E. and Cressey, D. (1978). *Criminology* (10th edition). Philadelphia: Lippincott.

Sykes, G. and Matza, D. (1957). Techniques of Neutralization: A Theory of Delinquency. *American Sociological Review*, 22: 664-670.

Taylor, C. (1988). Youth Gang Organization for Power, Money. *School Safety*, Spring: 26-27.

————. (1990). Gang Imperialism. In C. Huff (Ed.), *Gangs in America*. Newbury Park, CA: Sage.

Thornberry, T., Lizotte, A., Krohn, M., Farnsworth, M. and Jang, S. (1994). Delinquent Peers, Beliefs, and Delinquent Behavior: A Longitudinal Test of Interactional Theory. *Criminology*, 31(1): 47-83.

————, Krohn, M., Lizotte, A., and Chard-Wierschem, D. (1993). The Role of Juvenile Gangs in Facilitating Delinquent Behavior. *Journal of Research in Crime and Delinquency*, 30(1): 56-87.

Thrasher, F. (1936). *The Gang* (second edition). Chicago: University of Chicago Press.

Torres, D. (1980). *Gang Violence Reduction Project Evaluation Report*. Sacramento: California Youth Authority.

Tracy, P. (1982). *Gang Membership and Violent Offenders: Preliminary Results from the 1958 Cohort Study*. Center for Studies in Criminology and Criminal Law, University of Pennsylvania.

————. (1987). Race and Class Differences in Official and Self-Reported Delinquency. In M. Wolfgang, T. Thornberry, and R. Figlio (Eds.), *From Boy to Man, From Delinquency to Crime*. Chicago: University of Chicago Press.

————, Wolfgang, M., and Figlio, M. (1990). *Delinquency Careers in Two Birth Cohorts*. New York: Plenum.

U.S. Department of Justice (1992). *Crime in the United States*. Washington, D.C.: Federal Bureau of Investigation.

Vigil, J. (1988). *Barrio Gangs*. Austin, TX: University of Texas Press.

————. (1990). Cholos and Gangs: Culture and Change in Street Youths in Los Angeles. In C. Huff (Ed.), *Gangs in America*. Newbury Park, CA: Sage.

————, and Yun, S. (1990). *Vietnamese Youth Gangs in Southern California*. In C. Huff (Ed.), Gangs in America. Newbury Park, CA: Sage.

Virginia State Crime Commission (1991). *Task Force Study of Drug Trafficking, Abuse, and Related Crime.* Report to the Governor. Richmond, Virginia.

Warren, M. (1983). Applications of Interpersonal-Maturity Theory to Offender Populations. In W. Laufer and J. Day (Eds.), *Personality Theory, Moral Development, and Criminal Behavior.* Lexington, MA: Lexington.

Williams, F. and McShane, M. (Eds.) (1993). *Criminology Theory: Selected Classic Readings.* Cincinnati, OH: Anderson.

Whyte, W. (1943). *Street Corner Society.* Chicago: University of Chicago Press.

Wilson, J. and Hernnstein, R. (1985). *Crime and Human Nature.* New York: Simon and Schuster.

Wilson, W. (1987). *The Truly Disadvantaged: The Inner City, the Underclass, and Public Policy.* Chicago: University of Chicago Press.

Winfree, L., Mays, G., and Vigil-Backstrom, T. (1994). Youth Gangs and Incarcerated Delinquents: Exploring the Ties Between Gang Membership, Delinquency, and Social Learning Theory. *Justice Quarterly,* 11(2): 229-255.

Yablonsky, L. (1962). *The Violent Gang.* New York: MacMillan.

Zevitz, R. (1993). Youth Gangs in a Small Midwestern City: Insiders' Perspective. *Journal of Crime and Justice,* 16(1): 149-165.

_____, and Takata, S. (1992). Metropolitan Gang Influence and the Emergence of Group Delinquency in a Regional Community. *Journal of Criminal Justice,* 20: 93-106.

Zimring, F. (1981). Kids, Groups, and Crime: Some Implications of a Well Known Secret. *Journal of Criminal Law and Criminology,* 72: 867-885.

Index